WORTH DYING FOR

ALSO BY TERRY GOULD

How the Blind Make Love (fiction)
The Lifestyle
Paper Fan
Murder Without Borders

WORTH
DYING
FOR

CANADA'S MISSION TO TRAIN POLICE
IN THE WORLD'S FAILING STATES

TERRY GOULD

RANDOM HOUSE CANADA

PUBLISHED BY RANDOM HOUSE CANADA

Copyright © 2014 Terry Gould

www.penguinrandomhouse.ca

Library and Archives Canada Cataloguing in Publication

Gould, Terry, 1949–, author
    Worth dying for : Canada's mission to train police in the world's failing states / Terry Gould.

Includes bibliographical references and index.
Issued in print and electronic formats.

ISBN 978-0-307-36062-5
eBook ISBN 978-0-307-36064-9

    1. Royal Canadian Mounted Police. International Peace Operations Branch. 2. Police training. 3. Failed states. 4. Canada—Foreign relations. I. Title.

HV7909.G69 2014   363.2'2   C2014-901532-1

Cover and text design by Leah Springate; cover image, courtesy of Joe McAllister

Image credits: unless otherwise noted, all interior photographs © Terry Gould

Printed and bound in the United States of America

10 9 8 7 6 5 4 3 2 1

To Leslie, my wife of forty-four years

But his life, as he looked at it, had no meaning as a separate life.
It had meaning only as part of the whole, which he constantly sensed.

LEO TOLSTOY, *War and Peace*

CONTENTS

INTRODUCTION

WE ARE ALL ON A MISSION

Nothing can bring you peace but the triumph of principles.
Ralph Waldo Emerson, "Self-Reliance"

THE ABILITY OF HUMANITARIAN IDEALISTS to retain their courage in the face of impossible odds is a quality that fascinates me. Humanitarians never consider themselves as fighting for a lost cause. They believe, as Martin Luther King said, that "the arc of the moral universe is long but it bends toward justice." The courage of humanitarian idealists is always expressed in action, and as a journalist I am drawn to actions that demonstrate ideals.

I began this book after a decade of reporting from countries where humanitarian idealists were being beaten and jailed by the thousands. The nations I covered in Latin America, the Pacific Rim, South Asia and the Middle East were run like criminal enterprises. The rulers employed the police to enforce their own lawlessness and routinely got away with embezzling the national treasury. Any public resistance to their organized theft was met with organized violence.

Midway through that saddening decade I began documenting the careers of idealistic journalists murdered in their hometowns. The journalists had believed in the principle that the powerful should be prevented from oppressing the weak and were outraged that the rulers believed in the opposite principle: that the weak offered opportunities for the enrichment of the powerful. Standing up for their neighbours, defying an ethic of impunity that guaranteed retribution, the journalists exposed the corruption of their governments and, in almost all the cases I studied, their murders were arranged by the police who served those governments.

As I moved from country to country it became apparent to me that corruption, an ad hoc arrangement in some places, was a formal structure in the most murderous nations, and that the police were crucial to the reign of predatory rulers. Presidents and prime ministers behaved like gang bosses, appointing their closest cronies to top police posts with the understanding that while their salaries would be low, their incomes would be high. In return for support and the sharing of spoils, police chiefs were granted impunity. The chiefs then sold subordinate commands to cronies with the same understanding, until a pyramid of corruption was locked in from the top down. The police channelled the benefits of the economy to the rulers, extorted kickbacks and bribes from the civilian population, enabled fraudulent elections and used torture and murder to crush any possibility of reform.

The police chiefs I interviewed in these countries showed no sign of conscience as they justified a system that left most citizens poor, desperate and futureless. Not every cop I met was corrupt, of course, but I found the clean ones concentrated in the junior ranks. They were only recently separated from their communities by their uniforms and had not yet developed the carapace of cynicism necessary to commit crimes without guilt. Indeed, they quietly voiced the same disgust with their national systems of corruption as the civilians whom their older colleagues regularly hit up for bribes. I became convinced that police recruits of any culture do not *like* thinking of themselves as criminals. The religions they are raised on preach an opposite code of behaviour. The problem, I realized, was that in societies where impunity reigns, honest cops eventually join the lawbreakers. They absorb the worldview promoted by their chiefs: "They pay us nothing, they expect us to steal, so we'll steal." It is a system of management that ensures almost all cops are guilty of a crime from early in their career onward. Those who dare to investigate official corruption are weeded out as deviants or murdered as rats.

By the end of that decade of overseas reporting I concluded that reforming the police was a key element to reforming systemically corrupt societies. But how, I wondered, do you reform entire police forces so that they stand as a chcck against the predators who are their political masters?

After I published my book on assassinated journalists, *Murder Without Borders*, I was invited to address a conference of RCMP officers at a police-training centre outside Vancouver. I spoke about my experiences in nations run according to the principle of organized crime and the murderous behaviour of their police. At the conference was a veteran officer who believed there was a practical way to reform police forces that oppressed civilian populations. His name was Joe McAllister, at the time a forty-nine-year-old superintendent who had served three years in failing states with a little-known federal unit called the International Peace Operations Branch. In far-flung regions around the world, the unit was attempting to give ruined countries a chance at renewal by transforming their police.

I'd never heard of the unit. I'd known that our officers were training local police in Haiti but not that their postings were worldwide and that every year hundreds of city, provincial and Mounted Police were recruited to train cops in the world's most tormented countries. The unit, run by the RCMP, had a strategic mission: Build honest, professional, civilian police services in countries devastated by war or teetering on the brink of collapse. Its officers—known by the acronym CivPol, for civilian police trainers—were at that moment risking their lives in nine red zone missions, including in six of the top ten countries on *Foreign Policy's* Failing States Index. McAllister himself had been wounded on a CivPol mission in Kosovo in 2000, wounded again in East Timor a year later, and had just returned from Kandahar, Afghanistan, where he had spent most of the last eighteen months travelling roads strewn with improvised explosive devices (IEDs), instructing local police in human-rights-oriented law enforcement.

He was a boyishly handsome and easy-going fellow, but when he talked about his overseas missions he voiced a dedication to justice in the face of danger that reminded me of the journalists I'd just written about. Offering me an explanation for why he and his Mountie colleagues volunteered for such hazardous assignments, he said they believed in an ethical code that was worth dying for. They were members of a force beset by its own scandals and organizational problems, but through their thousands of experiences as police officers, they had come to wish all people could live by one principle. It was an elemental ideal of behaviour that had been prescribed across time and across cultures, from the ancient Hebrews and Greeks to the Prophet Mohammed to the modern framers of our written laws. It was the Hillelian ethic: Do not do unto others what you do not want others to do unto you.

"It's law enforcement's mission to keep bad people from hurting good people," McAllister told me. "That's why I became a police officer twenty-nine years ago; that's why we go overseas—to teach officers the lawful means to achieve that mission within their cultures."

As I began looking into the story of CivPol I met other mission-veterans who spoke in exactly the same terms as McAllister. They were men and women with families who had endured a year of roasting heat, nightmarish scenes of slaughter and assassination threats from criminal cops; and yet, like McAllister, they were volunteering for another year on missions in the most volatile regions of Africa, Asia, Latin America and the Middle East. Canada, they all said, can't be indifferent to the plight of tens of millions of civilians in collapsing countries. Their need to live in safety is exactly the same as our own, and while the countries they live in are broken, they can fix themselves with our help. They *have* to be fixed because the distress of their populations is unimaginable. Canadian cops can help by nurturing police forces that practise universal principles of civilized law enforcement. It was the humanitarian thing to do.

On January 12, 2010, shortly before one of my interviews with McAllister, a 7.0-magnitude earthquake struck Haiti, killing two of his Mountie colleagues, both of whom were helping to build a new Haitian police force at the time of their deaths. They were the second and third Mounties to have been killed in Port-au-Prince; the first was shot to death training police in the city's most dangerous neighbourhood, Cité Soleil. As McAllister emotionally reflected on the officers' relationships with Haitian trainees who had also been killed, and on his own close relationships with murdered Afghan trainees, I realized I was listening to a highly charged, humanist tale of international importance—one that involved idealistic men and women who expressed their deepest beliefs in action. It was then that I decided to write this book.

The Hillelian ethic, and teaching overseas police how to lawfully enforce it, is at the core of Canada's civilian police-training missions— one of the last vestiges of our Blue Helmet heritage. At this writing, Canada ranks sixty-sixth among the ninety-seven nations contributing soldiers to United Nations–sponsored peacekeeping missions, whereas between 1956 and 1992, it was often the single largest contributor—a reputation for being on the side of the angels that Canadians still benefit from around the world. That reputation has been partly sustained by our CivPol volunteers. Since the RCMP's first mission to Namibia in 1989, there have been over 3,500 individual deployments of three thousand Canadian police to more than fifty red zone missions, during which dozens of our non-combatant cops have been wounded, stricken by post-traumatic stress disorder, held hostage and tortured, or killed. They were invited in by barely functioning governments in the wake of genocidal civil conflicts, lost wars, foreign occupations or revolutions (and sometimes all four at once). The shattered governments had asked the international community for help and the international community responded by, among other things, offering to train honest police forces in lands that had been without them for generations. The list of nations that have hosted Canadian CivPol missions amounts to a compendium of the conflict zones of the last quarter century. They include Namibia,

Somalia, Rwanda, Kenya, Guinea, Sierra Leone, Ivory Coast, the Democratic Republic of the Congo, Bosnia, Croatia, Kosovo, Serbia, Macedonia, Haiti, Guatemala, Western Sahara, Iraq, Jordan, Kyrgyzstan, Sudan, South Sudan, Lebanon, Palestine, East Timor and Afghanistan. During their missions, policemen and policewomen from prairie towns and urban centres have trained tens of thousands of local officers, patrolled crime-ridden tropical villages, provided humanitarian assistance in disaster zones, and helped to investigate grotesque human rights violations whose bloody aftermath CivPol members have often personally witnessed, including machete massacres, mass rapes, beheadings and, all too often, the murder of the idealistic officers the Canadians mentored. When Canadian officers return home from these postings, they are transformed people and transformed cops, sometimes in ways little understood by their families, friends and fellow cops.

In the fall of 2010, I set out to profile the Canadian cops and the local officers they trained, concentrating on three lands that were representative of different aspects of the CivPol mission and at the centre of international attention: Afghanistan, Palestine and Haiti. Each of these countries was weighed down with problems specific to its region and culture, but they were all similar in their experience of decades of violence, oppression and corruption, as well as in the amazing resilience of their citizens.

Afghanistan was then enduring a Taliban insurgency that was killing twelve hundred Afghan National Police (ANP) a year, with the government of President Hamid Karzai only kept in place by NATO's military might. It was hoped that the still largely ragtag ANP could become, in the words of the *Washington Post*, "the primary long-term solution to Afghanistan's woes." CivPol volunteers, training police throughout the country, were in a race against time to stand up a force that could protect the population against terrorists, rapacious warlords and the ubiquitous corruption of officials before the withdrawal of NATO in 2014.

Palestine, occupied by Israel, was attempting to reverse its history of corrupt and competing security forces established under President Yasser

Arafat. The governing authority under President Mahmoud Abbas was endeavouring to set up a Palestinian civil police force that might convince the Israelis it could prevent radicals from using the West Bank as a base for terror strikes. The Israelis, believing the Palestinian Authority (PA) was still rife with corrupt officials and radicals, were distrustful of the force. CivPol officers walked a knife edge between the two sides as they trained cops who seethed with resentment at the occupation at the same time as they ardently believed that a clean Palestinian police force would be a pillar of an independent state.

And finally Haiti, at the top of every survey of failing states. The Caribbean nation had been traumatized so often by natural, home-grown and foreign-imposed catastrophes that its public services were almost non-existent. The country was dependent on foreign assistance for survival and safety, and, as in the other countries where CivPol served, its national police force was considered crucial to establishing a functioning state. Canadian CivPol officers, training police throughout the devastated land, lived in rented houses among the Haitian population, and some had been captured and tortured by the same violent gangs who preyed on their neighbours.

My intention as I left Canada was to view the CivPol missions through the eyes of the local cops, their Canadian mentors and the civilians whose lives they affected. Tyranny, terror, poverty, ruin and the humiliations of occupation might be the histories of these lands, but CivPol had a mission to keep these conditions from being perpetuated unendingly by creating a force that would bring all citizens, including the parasitical elite, under the rule of law. I knew I would be dealing with fallible Canadians and a fallible programme run by an imperfect force, but I also knew how urgently police-training missions were needed in the world—a conviction that was shortly confirmed by a world-changing event.

One month into my overseas research, on December 17, 2010, Tunisian police officers confiscated the pushcart of a desert-town street vendor named Mohammed Bouazizi, who then doused himself in paint thinner and set himself on fire in front of the local municipal office. That single act of protest sparked a revolution in Tunisia that spread across the Arab world, and the oppressive behaviour of police was the tipping point for that vast uprising. From Morocco to Yemen, hundreds of millions of citizens could relate to the life story of Bouazizi, who'd been tormented by police officers since he was a child. "The abuse took many forms," Al Jazeera reported, each abusive act embodying the "tyranny that many in the region know all too well." These abuses included repeated fines for the crime of selling fruit without a licence, the money for the fines always disappearing into the pockets of police. Bouazizi's breaking point came when the police slapped him, threw him to the ground and confiscated his pushcart—his only means of supporting his family. Hundreds of thousands of protestors took to the streets of the capital and stayed there until the dictator whom the Tunisian police had served for decades fled the country. When Egyptians took heart from this victory and launched their own revolt against a dictatorial government, they purposely chose National Police Day—January 25, 2011—as their first day of protest, and their main initial demand was police reform.

The corrupt police-states that Tunisians and Egyptians overthrew mirrored scores of others beyond North Africa. When I set out on my research, 73 of 178 countries surveyed by Transparency International on all continents were assessed as corrupt. An understanding of how governments use their police to rule billions of people over millions of square miles is crucial to understanding how more than a third of the world works. It is also crucial to appreciating the idealistic goals of Canadian cops who risk their lives as part of our CivPol missions. On their overseas postings, they witness the intense suffering of innocent people who live under corrupt regimes. It is why Canadian cops are "on a mission"—in both senses of the phrase. They passionately believe that to reform such regimes, you have to reform the police. Who else will investigate and arrest bad people who harm good people with impunity?

When I began this book four years ago, I had no idea I would be documenting what turned out to be the golden age of our CivPol missions.

At the time, there were more than two hundred Canadian police trainers in nine countries, and missions were being added as other countries requested Canada's help. CivPol's recruitment drives urged Canadian officers to volunteer by stressing the life-or-death stakes for the nations where CivPol served and appealing to the highest instincts of officers: "The need for Canadian police assistance has never been greater . . . . Canadian police officers are deployed to countries that have often been ravaged by war or civil strife. Democratic and social institutions have either been destroyed or never existed and the police are often seen as agents of repression and terror . . . . Canadian police officers are legendary for their humanitarian efforts. Participating in a peacekeeping mission will allow you to help those less fortunate and make a positive difference in the world."

Then, in late 2012, Canada began an about-face. One by one, the countries on CivPol's mission-roster were dropped and the number of police trainers more than halved. In early 2013, an entire contingent of officers was trained for Sudan, only to have its mission cancelled just before deployment. As I write this, with the need for police training assistance in failing states as great or greater than it was in 2010, there are just 92 Canadian cops on training missions, in only two countries: Haiti (89) and Palestine (3). CivPol's 2014 budget of $36 million is frozen at the level it was in 2006.

The contraction of CivPol is in large part due to a change in the approach toward foreign aid of Canada's Conservative government. The Department of Foreign Affairs, Trade and Development, which determines CivPol's overseas deployments, has dubbed its new blueprint for foreign assistance "the Global Markets Action Plan." The promotion of trade between Canadian companies and Third World nations now trumps police training. I can only hope that this book, the first ever published about CivPol, inspires us to recognize that long-term commitments made to countries in dire need of our assistance cannot be abandoned for a mandate of "economic diplomacy." For that matter, the CivPol mission could be considered a vital part of that new foreign aid mandate: training police in failing states to uphold universal principles of law enforcement is crucial to fostering honestly run economies that benefit local citizens as well as the Canadian companies that wish to do business with them.

The publication of *Worth Dying For* is timed to coincide with the twenty-fifth anniversary of the RCMP's first overseas police-training mission. That word "mission" derives from the Latin *missio*, which means "to send forth." No matter how haphazardly we live our days, we are all on a mission, sending forth our deeds. We all eventually die at the end of our mission, but few of us go to work every day ready to sacrifice our lives as part of that mission. In Mountie Depot, the historic training academy of the RCMP in Saskatchewan, special areas of the almost two-hundred-hectare grounds are devoted to remembering those who were sent forth on a mission and who sacrificed their lives for it. Ingrained in the heart of every cadet who goes through the six-month training course is the belief that keeping bad people from hurting good people is a mission worth defending with their lives. At the front of the chapel is a memorial book with 234 names of the fallen inscribed in it. There is a cenotaph to the fallen. All the streets are named after the fallen. And the field in front of the main building is hallowed—no one is permitted to cross it except on formal parade or during ceremonies that remember the Mounties killed on duty.

On a visit to Depot before I left Canada, I took note of the two names most recently added to the cenotaph monument: Doug Coates and Mark Gallagher—the two CivPol officers killed in the Haitian earthquake. Coates had run CivPol's deployments between 1996 and 1999 and had been its director at the time he left for his last mission in Port-au-Prince as commissioner of all United Nations police-trainers. Six years before he was crushed to death in that earthquake, he delivered a speech on CivPol at a conference of the Peace Studies Consortium in Syracuse, New York, titled: "Police Training Assistance: The Right Kind of Help."

This book is about the hope, heartbreak and tragedy experienced by Canadian policemen and policewomen as they tried to lend the right kind of help. It is about the local police officers who welcomed that help as they sought to bring their nations back from the brink, often at the cost of their own lives. It is about their countries, still mired in endless crises, and their citizens, still being tormented by cop commanders who betray them. I have tried to examine the mission from every point of view as it was carried forward over seemingly insurmountable obstacles.

The relationships between CivPol cops and the cops they train are almost always complicated by past histories of Western colonial exploitation. The divide-and-conquer strategies of Canada's allies over the centuries are still despised abroad for exacerbating tribal and sectarian feuds that have left local citizens with ongoing legacies of violence, poverty and corruption. Yet, whether they are young villagers showing up for their first day of police training at a remote CivPol compound or thirty-year veterans arriving from faraway Canada to train them, most want to start anew. They all know that the police are the only face of government that civilians notice daily, and much of what they think of government is based on what they see.

If the police protect everyone's property equally, investigate crimes committed against the poor as well as the rich, and arrest lawbreakers without regard to their social status, a government is likely to be trusted by its citizens. If the police enforce the law unequally and break the law themselves without suffering the consequences, then the government will be distrusted. Ordinary people will then join the lawbreakers and the result will be a failed state—which is what they live with now. As Joe McAllister told me, for the citizens of the tormented nations where CivPol members serve, "more failure means death."

PART ONE

AFGHANISTAN

A Lost War but Not a Lost Cause

1

A GAME OF HOOLIGANS PLAYED BY GENTLEMEN

JOE MCALLISTER RETURNED TO AFGHANISTAN for another rotation in the middle of June 2010. He and a couple of middle-aged CivPol officers landed at Kandahar Airfield, which had grown to be the busiest airport in the world in the year McAllister had been away. They stepped out of the hatch of a Hercules transport and winced, as if being hit by an electric field. The superheated summer air was thrashed by the ear-splitting roar of fighter jets taking off, a hundred attack helicopters revving on the runway and the prop buzz of drones circling the arid mountains. Beyond the tarmac fence an unending line of desert-brown fighting vehicles inched along newly paved roads that bordered a thousand hectares of newly raised tents.

The Canadians were beholding "the surge," the massive American military build-up announced by President Barack Obama six months earlier in an attempt to use overwhelming force to drive the Taliban back, hold the cleared areas and help the Afghan government build its institutions and infrastructure. A critical component of this "clear, hold and build" strategy was CivPol's mission: recruit and train thousands of Afghan National Police and accompany them on patrol, mentoring them in the three basic tenets of community policing. *Be part of the community not apart from it. Practise policing by consent not coercion. Encourage the public to become partners in preventing crime, corruption and violence.* These tenets were designed to foster a population that willingly served as the eyes and ears of a nascent police force as it tried to provide protection from fanatics, criminals and corrupt officials. Almost all observers of NATO's nine-year effort to defeat the Taliban in

Afghanistan predicted that unless the ANP became trusted by the community before NATO troops were withdrawn in 2014, the Taliban would end up enforcing the law in Kandahar, not the ANP.

A year earlier McAllister had commanded Kandahar's eighteen-person CivPol contingent, teaching community policing at a time when there had been no cleared areas. In the past few months the CivPol mission had experienced its own surge, and McAllister was returning with a promotion: he would be its national deputy commander, overseeing forty-four Canadian cops training the ANP and Afghan Border Police in Kandahar and along the violent frontiers of seven countries. When he wasn't flying to the remotest reaches of the nation he would be based in Kabul, helping the Ministry of Interior address the myriad problems afflicting the ANP. His reform agenda included "Implementing an Anti-Corruption Action Plan" and "Insulating the ANP from Inappropriate Political Influence." Both reforms required specialized ANP units to investigate corrupt politicians and police without other politicians or police derailing those investigations. It seemed an almost impossible goal. Transparency International had just listed Afghanistan as the world's second most corrupt country, largely because of the unchecked graft of the administration of President Hamid Karzai, whose network of relatives, cronies and tribal chieftains were more interested in protecting their kleptocracy than in supporting a law enforcement mechanism that would end it.

Accompanying McAllister on this rotation was a retired Ontario Provincial Police inspector who would be crucial to McAllister's reform plans. Phil George was among Canada's top experts in polygraphy, wiretaps and surveillance techniques—skills he'd used for years to investigate allegations of corruption against Canadian cops and politicians. George would be working out of the ANP's recently established Major Crime Task Force, mentoring its newly formed antigraft intelligence squad.

Also accompanying McAllister was the new mission-boss, RCMP Assistant Commissioner Dave Critchley, who would be overseeing CivPol's delicate relations with Afghan ministers as McAllister pressed his reforms. Critchley had spent the past three years as the RCMP's federal security liaison at the Privy Council Office, handling government officials at the interface between politics and law enforcement. During their training in Ottawa, McAllister had informed Critchley that the complications of that interface in Afghanistan would be a thousand-power enlargement of anything Critchley had experienced back home.

Critchley was forty-nine, and McAllister a year older; Phil George was fifty-eight. They hadn't slept since leaving Ottawa sixty hours earlier—a typical "travel day" to Kandahar via Frankfurt and Dubai that even much younger CivPol cops found an endurance test. Age and rank did not entitle them to special consideration, however, and they were immediately ushered into a series of orientation sessions run by the military and CivPol. The lectures took place at the Canadian quadrant of the base, Task Force Kandahar, just across the traffic-choked road from where they'd landed. Security briefings on where to take shelter during rocket attacks and where to post themselves if the perimeter was breached were followed by tutorials that included techniques to recruit and train more female police, how to ensure ANP officers received their pay without it getting stuck to the fingers of senior cops, and efforts being made to better protect the provincial Police Headquarters against repeated suicide bombings. At midnight Afghan time—three-thirty in the afternoon Ottawa time—they were shown to a pre-fab trailer to get some sleep. Staring wide-eyed at the ceiling, listening to the F-16s roaring down the runway, they were still awake in the Afghan dawn. They rolled out of their bunks to pack barf bags and earplugs, don helmets and body armour and climb aboard a helicopter for the flight to Camp Nathan Smith (CNS), a square-kilometre fort on the northeastern edge of the city that served as home base to CivPol's training mission in the province. The Blackhawk flew "tactical," avoiding possible enemy fire by unexpectedly changing course and altitude (*ergo* the barf bags), pounding down fifteen minutes after takeoff in a great cloud of dust that billowed over the line of blast walls protecting the Kandahar Provincial Reconstruction Team (KPRT) building, where CivPol had its headquarters. The exhausted cops grabbed their gear and jumped off to the waiting handshake of RCMP Superintendent Vic Park, who in March had assumed McAllister's old post as CivPol's contingent commander.

As he did with all VIP arrivals, Park gave Critchley an overview of the base's history and a situation-report on current conditions. The brick-walled fort occupied the site of a one-time canning factory. During the Taliban reign in the 1990s the factory building had been converted into a jail and torture chamber, with frequent executions taking place against the outer walls. American Special Forces, entering the compound in late 2001, had discovered in the dark corner of one of the former cells two tiny Pashto words scratched into the plaster. *Alhamdulillah fidya.* "Praise be to God, save me."

The Americans converted the compound into a fort, gravelling it over with coarse sharp rocks—the reason even civilians posted by the U.S. Agency for International Development to the newly built KPRT wore combat boots stiff as planks. When the Canadians replaced the Americans in October 2005, they named the fort Camp Nathan Smith, in honour of one of their soldiers killed by U.S. friendly fire in 2002.

Over 450 Canadians were based at CNS, including thirty-two CivPol officers, a detachment of 350 Canadian soldiers and about eighty civilians from the Department of National Defence, the Canadian International Development Agency (CIDA) and the Department of Foreign Affairs. Outside the wire, under the protection of the camp's soldiers, the full Kandahar team was attempting to reconstruct the war-ravaged province by training police and prison guards, building schools, roads, government centres and irrigation networks, as well as mentoring Afghan politicians in the principles of democratic governance and human rights. Most of the soldiers slept in Quonset tents on the other side of the base, while the civilians and CivPol bunked in trailers or plywood barracks just east of the landing zone and shooting range. The fort was quieter than Kandahar Airfield, Park said, but not by much. During their first days at CNS most cops felt like they were camping in a gravel pit beside a steel mill during hunting season. The power and sewage plants whined twenty-four hours a day, Chinook, Apache and Blackhawk helicopters were constantly taking off and landing, mortars and sniper fire from the surrounding rooftops and mountains triggered sirens at all hours, patrol convoys of armoured vehicles were always roaring to life, and ANP shooting practice crackled and echoed within the walls on most afternoons. Still, it was better than what was outside. When they rolled in from a month of training cops in Zhari or Panjwai, CivPol cops thought they were returning to the lap of luxury.

Camp Nathan Smith was McAllister's home turf, of course, and even without sleep he felt as if he were back in the office. After emotional reunions with his Afghan translators and cultural advisors, McAllister asked Park to take him and his colleagues over to what he considered the fort's beating heart—CivPol's Police Training Centre, in the middle of the base. In his year at home, amidst all the bad news coming out of Afghanistan, whenever fellow Mounties had asked McAllister what CivPol had accomplished in four years in Kandahar, he'd always answered that there were two "pieces" of the mission that would leave a lasting legacy in the south. The first was the Training Centre, where the ANP attended CivPol's classes, and the second was the mentoring that CivPol performed while embedded with the ANP across the province.

The Training Centre, built by the Department of Foreign Affairs under CivPol's direction and first opened in May 2008, was a fenced-in campus about the size of two football fields, containing a mosque, a gym, a barracks, a dining hall, several wood frame buildings for scenario-based training and a long portable lined with classrooms. CivPol's approach was to teach contemporary policing skills geared to a force that was technologically stuck somewhere in the 1940s, three-quarters illiterate, and doing its job in the middle of a war. Early each morning a rotating roster of sixty male and female junior cops arrived for half-day tutorials on literacy and "handcuffing 101," and then went to work on the streets, mentored by CivPol officers. Another rotating roster of fifty experienced Afghan patrolmen, NCOs and commissioned officers lived on campus for anywhere from two weeks to six months, taking the more advanced courses, which included condensed versions of the training Mounties received in the Regina Depot. At the core of each course, and of the entire programme, was the ethics-, values- and human rights-training that CivPol taught as the foundation of a community-based police force. In most classes an ANP senior officer took part in the instruction, since the school was as much about "training the trainers" as it was about training the recruits. When the bulk of NATO forces left Afghanistan, these senior officers would run the school.

After observing a couple of classes and chatting with the young recruits, McAllister, George and Critchley were introduced to the CivPol officers who constituted the second "piece" of the mission. Most of the CivPol cops in Kandahar served at least part of their nine-month tours based at primitive ANP substations, attempting, in Park's words, "to connect the ANP to the community." Among the officers were the first two female Mounties to be posted outside Camp Nathan Smith. Candice McMackin, thirty-seven, and Karen Holowaychuk, forty, both corporals, had been living since March in desert substations in the most dangerous reaches of Kandahar. Born and raised in small prairie towns about as far as you could get in climate and culture from southern Afghanistan, they patrolled in fifty-degree heat with all-male platoons of ANP through remote villages, explaining how to interact with locals as if the locals were the equals of the police, and demonstrating by their professionalism that female cops were the equal of male cops. At checkpoints they coached nineteen-year-old recruits on how to search vehicles for explosives, and in the aftermath of blood-soaked suicide bombings they instructed their students on how to administer first aid, carry victims into vehicles, gather evidence and interview witnesses.

Listening to the two women and their colleagues matter-of-factly report on their perilous duties, Critchley felt himself overwhelmed with emotion. He'd never been on a CivPol mission or even to a war zone, and his own short experience of what his officers were facing suddenly hit him. Because they'd been selected for duty in Afghanistan according to CivPol criteria—the desire to help people in danger and the ability to picture positive outcomes to dangerous situations—Critchley was not surprised when they told him the mission was worth its risks and that they believed they were making a difference. But he couldn't help asking himself: *How am I going to handle it if one or more of them gets killed on my watch?* "At any step they could have been blown to bits," he said when I met up with him a few months later at CNS. "They patrolled with the ANP eight hours a day, day after day, carrying forty pounds of body armour and gear. How did they do it? It was so hot I couldn't stand outside for five minutes. The love and awe I felt for them almost brought the tears to my eyes."

Critchley was a tall skinny cop with a pale complexion definitely not suited for the sun of Kandahar. He'd spent the last three years behind a desk in Ottawa and was not in the same shape as George, who in his career had served nine years on the OPP's Underwater Search and Recovery Team, or McAllister, who'd once been a member of the RCMP's elite antiterrorism unit, trained to the standard of Navy SEALs. Park, a former colleague of McAllister's on the antiterrorism unit, and a second-degree black belt in Taekwondo, suspected Critchley's emotional reaction might be due to the disorientating combination of heat and sleeplessness that affected all new arrivals. After dinner, he took Critchley aside. "Dave," he said, "we got you a VIP room—it's in the building right over there. You'll have some privacy tonight."

"So we walk over," Critchley remembered, "and it's just a big warehouse. They built this cubicle in a corner out of plywood, no ceiling and no bigger than the bed. And I look at the pillow and it's covered in dried blood, somebody had slept there with a head wound. So I take out a clean T-shirt, I wrap the pillow and I lie down on a mattress that sends up this cloud of dust. The air conditioning's not working and the warehouse is like an oven. And my mind's going, *This is the best these folks live with?* And yet no one uttered so much as a word about needing better conditions."

The next morning Critchley, McAllister and George boarded a Chinook for the trip back to Kandahar Airfield, and then an afternoon flight to Kabul. George was dropped off in the compound of the Major Crime Task Force on the desert flats north of the Kabul airport.

McAllister and Critchley drove south to the centre of town and moved into reinforced-steel containers on the grounds of the Canadian Embassy. "Absolute luxury compared to the south and what our team endures down there," McAllister wrote me in an e-mail. "That said, Kabul is still a dangerous place and we travel in armoured vehicles wherever we go. With luck, good work and the will of Allah and of the people, maybe before we leave here Afghans will be able to walk down a street without looking around for the boogie man. At least that's the goal and we'll work hard at it. I'll fill you in on some of advancements on the police end of things, and the overall mission, when you get here."

As I went through the reams of government paperwork necessary to join McAllister and accompany his officers on their missions, I weighed CivPol's chances of connecting the ANP to the community. There was a passage I'd read in *Fifteen Days*, journalist Christie Blatchford's account of the experiences of Canadian troops during their first deployment to Kandahar in 2006, which all but blamed the ANP for the explosion of the Taliban insurgency that June. The ANP "were alienating themselves from the local population because of the way they operated," a major named Nick Grimshaw had told Blatchford. "Not only were they rounding up fighting-age males, but they were extorting money, stealing food, stealing motorcycles, without any regard for any ounce of professionalism, without any investigations. It was completely by the discretion of the ANP commander on the ground." The locals stopped cooperating with the ANP, then turned against them, in some cases joining the insurgency, and the Canadians became "guilty by association." The ANP's blatant abuse of power and trust, Grimshaw concluded, was "part of the reason things kind of went south during our tour."

CivPol had five officers based at CNS in 2006, a contingent that was increased to ten by the time McAllister arrived for his first nine-month tour in November 2007. By then Kandahar had become among the most dangerous places in the world. With only 2,500 Canadian troops defending the province's 54,000 square kilometres of mountains and desert, organized units of Taliban fighters, some groomed in Pakistan, found it easy to infiltrate the same ground again and again, seeding roads with improvised explosive devices, blowing up schools and government buildings, beheading teachers and assassinating Afghan police in a kind of reverse form of natural selection: honest officers trying to stop the Taliban at checkpoints were killed; corrupt officers taking bribes from the Taliban survived. The police force, shattered during the civil war of 1992–96 and then replaced by the Taliban's religious police, had only been officially reconstituted by the Ministry of Interior and NATO in 2003. Four years later, it had little effective command structure and almost no training. Most Afghans, not knowing what to expect from the ANP, remained mummy-faced at the sight of a cop, too distrustful to pass on crucial information about the politicians, militants and other cops who made their lives miserable. By early spring 2010, the Taliban were on the attack in three-quarters of the country and the ANP were still being blamed.

A month before McAllister landed in Kandahar for his latest tour, National Public Radio interviewed U.S. senator John Kerry, who had just returned from a fact-finding mission in Afghanistan. The radio host related to Kerry that a Taliban commander had told an NPR reporter that his fighters regularly bought their weapons on the black market from the ANP. "The police situation in Afghanistan is probably the single worst link in the whole chain," Kerry admitted glumly. "We've known that for some time. There is no surprise about it at all. And I think there are a number of plans on the table right now to try to deal with the police situation. It has really been the most difficult, least productive of all of the efforts over there thus far."

When I e-mailed Kerry's assessment to McAllister, he wrote back: "The police in the countries we serve are *always* the worst link in the chain or we wouldn't be there." Helping countries like Afghanistan pull themselves out of the places they were stuck "will take years, maybe decades. I fully expect the link will break again and again until it gets fixed."

Five months later I boarded a Lufthansa flight for the two-day haul to Afghanistan, long enough to read through a printout of the on-line manual studied by CivPol volunteers before deployment. In theory, CivPol had a plan that could at least begin an evolutionary process of national reform in the broken countries it served. "Civilian Police Tasks and Responsibilities"—the introductory chapter—stated: "Changing the attitude and behaviour of host country police is the most important objective of mentoring as well as the most difficult one." CivPol officers were to teach local officers that in a democracy, power was held by the public, that all were equal before the law, that the police served the community "in partnership with the community and with the support of the community" and that "the police were responsive and accountable to the community." CivPol would know it was making progress when it observed "police participating in the community and responding to the needs of the community, and the community participating in its own policing and supporting the police."

This symbiotic relationship was captured by the compound noun from which CivPol derived its name and mission. In contrast to a police force that viewed itself as an army of occupation keeping control over hostile civilians, "civilian police" concisely defined cops as being on the side of civilians because cops *were* civilians. In the words of Robert Peel, a nineteenth-century British politician honoured in western police academies as the founder of modern civilian policing: "The police are the public and the public are the police."

Most of what is contained in CivPol's training manual for its officers rests on Peel's definition of an ethical police force. In 1829, serving as British home secretary, Peel disbanded the private guards and gangs of hired thugs arbitrarily imposing the whims of lords and factory owners upon Londoners and founded the capital's Metropolitan Police Force, which he staffed with a thousand ordinary citizens who were trained to impartially enforce written laws that the cops themselves were subject to. Peel's prescription for running this department was a revolutionary statement of civic equality, a set of rules that put police in their proper place in civilian society. To Peel, there was nothing special about the police. They were "only members of the public who are paid to give full-time attention to duties which are incumbent on every citizen in the interests of community welfare and existence." While the basic duty of the police was "to prevent crime and disorder," the ability of the police to perform that duty was "dependent on public approval of police actions." To secure that approval, police had to obtain "the willing cooperation of the public in voluntary observation of the law." *Voluntary* observance was stressed by Peel, not force: "The degree of cooperation of the public that can be secured diminishes proportionately to the necessity of the use of physical force," he wrote. Therefore, a cop's daily job was to "maintain the respect of the public . . . by constantly demonstrating absolute impartial service to the law. Police use physical force . . . only when the exercise of persuasion, advice, and warning is found to be insufficient." Peel concluded his list of civilian policing principles with a stern advisement. "The test of police efficiency is the absence of crime and disorder, not the visible evidence of police action in dealing with it."

Over the next half century these "Peelian principles" were adopted in big cities across Britain, Canada and the United States. It soon became evident, though, that Peel's principles would last only as long as they were actively pursued by civilian governments. Perhaps more than in any other profession, the daily encounters police officers have with the worst of humanity breeds in them cynicism, even nihilism. As son follows father into the subculture of policing, a new generation of officers reverts to the idea that they are part of a brotherhood separate from civilian society, and their old brutal methods of enforcing the law become acceptable to some officers and tolerated by others. In such a climate of lawless law enforcement, political bosses caught with their hands in the till find it easy to bribe the police for special favours and then return those favours by giving the police impunity when the cops themselves steal from the public. The list of corruption scandals that have rocked urban administrations working in conjunction with their police departments includes every major city in North America, often multiple times.

In the mid-twentieth century, big-city progressives realized that in order to maintain Peel's principles, police reform would have to be orchestrated through continual community oversight by independent civilian police boards and civilian complaint commissions. The police resisted at first, but then, in the 1980s, the situation on the ground changed radically when the crime rate peaked with the crack epidemic and police departments from Los Angeles to New York and Toronto admitted that, unless they became one with the community again, they would be viewed as occupiers of high-crime neighbourhoods, passively resisted with resentful silence by average citizens and forcibly resisted by criminals. The consequences would be mortal: police would be left without the intelligence they needed not only to enforce the law but to protect themselves. The new textbook name given Peel's philosophy was "community-based policing," and it was taught in police academies across North America as *the* model of law enforcement and crime prevention. Henceforth, police would no longer race from emergency to emergency, mostly appearing to the public as anonymous, car-bound robots. They would get out of their squad cars and become recognizable individuals in the community. In other words. they would be Peelian beat cops, meeting regularly with local groups to learn their needs and work out strategies of law enforcement that would best meet those needs. Neighbourhood residents would again become the eyes and ears of the police, and the police would concentrate their efforts in the direction the residents pointed—a modus operandi dubbed "intelligence-led policing." With the adoption of such methods, the record-high crime rate plummeted, and study after study has since confirmed that "public safety is strongest when local cops and local community leaders work hand-in-hand."

The ascent of community policing in North America coincided with Canada's first CivPol mission in 1989. Namibia had just won its twenty-five-year war for independence from South Africa and had requested United Nations help to train a police force before the country's first elections. Canada responded to the United Nations' request with 110 Mountie volunteers. They left Canada on October 17, 1989—now considered

CivPol's anniversary date—landed in the capital, Windhoek, and fanned out across the desert scrublands, where thousands of disorganized tribal militiamen roamed. In the tense weeks leading up to the elections, the Mounties, untrained in peacekeeping but trained in community policing, conducted courses for the indigenous police who had served under the occupying South Africans. One of the most crucial concepts the Canadians communicated was that in a democracy, the losing side in an election always has another chance, and that the sworn duty of a democratic national police force is to protect the defeated side's rights, including its right to be heard before, during and after an election. CivPol then set about building bridges between the Namibian police, villagers and militias by arranging community meetings in which the police listened to the needs of all parties and worked out ways of addressing those needs. The militiamen supported different candidates than those favoured by villagers, yet under the watchful eyes of the Namibian police the elections were carried out peacefully and declared free and fair by UN observers.

CivPol has been exporting community policing around the globe ever since. Today, at the Canadian Police College in Ottawa, each CivPol recruit is taught that "community policing is a *key* approach for civilian police in Peace Operations," and much of what they learn matches Peel's principles of ethical policing. Everything McAllister told me he would be attempting to do in Afghanistan in 2010 and 2011—everything he had done in Afghanistan, East Timor and Kosovo in the previous years; indeed everything Civpol did around the world—represented an effort to advance the crucial mission of civilian policing that rests on consent, not coercion; being part of the community, not apart from it.

Opposite the baggage carousel at Kabul International Airport I ran into a platoon of Afghan Border Police who had set up an x-ray machine to check bleary-eyed passengers for contraband. "You are carrying alcohol?" the captain overseeing the Border Police asked me as the interior of my Safari bag appeared on the x-ray screen.

"Just water," I said.

The captain looked askance at my bag as it trundled through the rubber strips and slid down the ramp, at which point he told me to follow him.

He led me to a line of search tables separated by dingy divides where he unzipped my Safari bag and discovered my two Ziplocs bulging with water bottles. "Two-five," he said softly as he rummaged further into the bag.

"Eleven-eighteen," I replied, thinking he'd misread my visa stamp.

"Two-five," he repeated, digging deeper. I reached into my pocket, palmed a five and placed it in front of his eyes. He scowled at my stinginess but took the money anyway. That was my first encounter with an Afghan policeman.

Outside, the early morning air smelled exactly as McAllister had described it. With no sewage treatment plants, Kabul had the worst-smelling and most unhealthy particulate pollution on earth, the result of the smoke from the millions of pounds of feces burned every night in municipal furnaces. From the plane I'd seen a brown cloud suffocating the 1,800-metre-high urban valley in the dawn light. The advice McAllister said he offered newly arrived CivPol cops was simple: "Don't breathe."

The hotel I'd booked for myself was the storied Gandamack Lodge, where the third wife of Osama bin Laden had once lived and which was now run by a former war photographer named Peter Juvenal. Walled from the street and guarded by hired guns, the Gandamack was as secure as any hotel in Kabul, but my ride to it wasn't in sight. A driver from the hotel was to have met me at the airport, holding a sign with my name. I turned to a couple of Afghan border cops guarding the breezeway. "*Salam aleykum*," I said. "Is this where I meet my car?"

"*Salam aleykum*," the older one replied. "Cars outside." He lifted his AK-47 toward an opening in the high wall across the lot, blocked by a cross-arm barrier and flanked by sand-bagged guard houses. Beyond the guard houses was a sea of black-haired heads and Toyotas parked every which way.

"Is it safe for me out there?" I asked.

The older cop said something in Dari to his young companion, who slung his rifle and hitched his head to follow him. I pulled my roller bag after him over the lot's broken-up concrete, through the gate and into the pressing crowd of males—not a woman in sight, even in a burka. Almost all the men were wrapped in woollen *patus* as they milled about street stalls or stood stamping their feet beside taxis, looking as if they were freezing in their thin pajama pants and open sandals. I climbed onto the plinth of a flagpole, and with infinite relief saw a man deep in the crowd beside a Corolla, wearing a sports jacket and holding up a sign with my name.

"*Tashakor! Tashakor* so much!" I said to the young cop as I jumped down from the plinth.

In his torn uniform jacket and oversized hat, the border cop looked almost as poor as the civilians around us. I offered him five dollars.

"No money," he replied, flipping both hands away from him like flapping wings. "You are safe, so I am happy."

That was my second encounter with an Afghan policeman.

"There's far more guys like him than the other," McAllister told me a couple of days later as we drove through the ANP's "Ring of Steel" checkpoint guarding Shirpur Square in downtown Kabul. There'd been an alert that morning about suicide bombers on bicycles so McAllister was wearing body armour under his Mountie fleece jacket, adding a couple of inches to his already muscular torso. When I mentioned that everything I'd been reading about the ANP indicated that police corruption was top to bottom, he replied, "Not to excuse the first cop you met, but can you name me one force in the world that doesn't have corruption?"

His driver, Obai, moved his eyes to mine in the rearview mirror. "I would like to hear of such a force myself," he said, laughing.

"The RCMP?" I offered from the backseat.

McAllister swivelled his shoulders to face me. "What do you call corruption? Is it, 'You're my buddy so I'm going to give you that job?' That happens in our organization. We can't even eliminate it in our own country. And we have no excuse for not eliminating it. The Afghans at least have an excuse. You'll get down to Kandahar, you'll see most of them don't even ask for money at checkpoints."

"They ask for food!" Obai said. "Give me that watermelon. Give me those pomegranates."

"They're starving!" McAllister said. The cops in Kandahar, he explained, were only receiving a fraction of their $150-a-month pay and went for days without eating. "There's no banks outside Kabul, so the government gives the cash to the provincial commander, who gives it to the district commanders, who gives it to the substation chiefs, who distribute it to their men—whatever's left. So they're not asking for food because they're corrupt. If you've got a wife and six kids with no food at home and you're not getting paid and not eating yourself, you ask for food."

He turned back to the road, lifted his hand to wave at a parked M-RAP fighting vehicle as we entered the heavily defended neighbourhood near the headquarters of the International Security Assistance Force at Camp Eggers. "We're trying to fix the problems with getting them their pay because that negatively affects how the population relates to them," McAllister said. "Once they bring the population onside, they start to get intelligence and that helps them deal with the security issues."

"Education and security are No. 1," Obai said. "Education for the children, security for them to get professions, start businesses."

"My experience," McAllister said, turning around to face me again, "is that the rank and file ANP are willing to take tremendous risks to build a society where their children can get an education, become professionals, start businesses." For evidence he pointed to the almost four thousand Afghan police who had been killed in little over three years, most of them as they stood their ground at checkpoints. No country in modern history had lost that many police in so short a time. "Canada has built fifty schools in Kandahar," he went on. "They're all full. The Taliban want to blow them up and the police want to stop them. They know that once their kids are educated they'll have economic opportunities for the first time in thirty years. They think it's worth their lives to do their jobs for the sake of their kids."

For a pensive moment McAllister looked down Akbar Khan Road, jammed with Toyota Corollas and bicycles manoeuvring in the canyon made by high walls topped by razor wire either side of the street. "We have huge challenges with the top tier of the ANP," he said, "but one of the best cops I've ever worked with in my life was the police chief of Kandahar." His name was Matiullah Qati Khan. "Matiullah *knew* he would get killed for doing his job. He never thought of himself as anything more than just a cop doing his job. I mentored him for almost a year before he was murdered."

He remained quiet for a moment, then pointed through the windshield. "Our embassy's just around the corner. On the left here is our supermarket."

The supermarket was a modern-looking place, with the word FINEST on its big green marquee above picture windows. It catered to embassy personnel like McAllister who went there to stock up on nachos, chocolate and ice cream. Out front, a crowd of Afghan boys in pajama pants and sandals hawked cell phone cards to the shoppers. I would think of those boys when the Finest was blown up by the Taliban a little while later. They were targeting guys like McAllister but only succeeded in killing five embassy cleaning ladies and four of the young hawkers.

After we were waved past the guard houses at the entrance to the embassy compound, McAllister told Obai he'd call him on his cell when he needed to take me back to the Gandamack. As we walked between tall Hesco barricades that protected the parking lot, he said, with a sigh of exhaustion, "Terry, we're fighting so many wars at the same time here. The Taliban, narcotics, low-level corruption, high-level corruption. But there's a difference between a cop saying, 'Twenty bucks or you're not going through,' and the stuff that's going on at the top. The problem for us is that some of the biggest crooks in the country also fight the Taliban. The moral question is: how do you deal with people like this, in a country like this? Or do we?"

We walked in silence past the glaring white embassy building, built a few years ago out of chiselled stone cut from the surrounding Hindu

Kush Mountains. As we came abreast of the rec centre, he said, "Despite our best efforts, the rule of law here is constantly being subverted. But there *are* people in high positions who I not only trust with my life but who are working with every fibre of their being to turn this country around."

In my time with McAllister in Vancouver he'd shown two moods when discussing the Afghan CivPol mission. The first was full of positive-thinking optimism, which was the one he usually showed the world. The other was full of grief and disappointment, which he tried to hide from most people. His grief was over his many Afghan and Coalition friends killed in Kandahar—most by the Taliban but some by Afghan police. His disappointment was over the reversals that followed almost every CivPol success.

Overlaying both moods were his transparent humanism—he didn't judge people, just their actions—and an epigrammatic sense of humour that left a lot of room in the world for every type of person. He was a lifelong rugby player and one of his two favourite sayings was, "Rugby is a game of hooligans played by gentlemen." He employed it whenever he described the gentlemanly behaviour of Canadian police in this hooligan war. He employed his other favourite saying now, when I thanked him for offering to get around regulations and lend me a set of Mountie body armour for my trip to Kandahar. "No problem. A friend helps you move; a good friend helps you move the body."

McAllister's dad had been in the habit of summing up human relations with aphorisms like that, too. Before he'd died of alcoholism, when Joe was sixteen, John McAllister had been a naval ward officer. He'd served during the time when Canada had frequently committed its ships and troops to UN peacekeeping missions. One of Joe's first memories, growing up in Victoria, B.C., was visiting his dad's warship in Esquimalt Harbour on family day, shortly before John had left for a six-month tour as part of the United Nations Cyprus peacekeeping mission. "My parents always said, 'The United Nations is a great deal for the world,'" Joe had told me. "From a very early age I was taught to contemplate that name. *United Nations*. It really says it all."

While his father had been away on missions, his mother, Hilda, had given Joe geography lessons, teaching him that the world's nations were like houses on a block in a neighbourhood. "If there was a family on the block whose house had burned down," he said, "or the dad wasn't there and the kids were disadvantaged, I was taught that everybody on the block should try to help." He actually couldn't remember a time when he didn't believe he was supposed to put his own needs aside to help others. When he was in high school he had thought about becoming a teacher, but, he said, he wasn't the academic type. He'd joined the police after a year of college because "that was a profession where I could go to work every day and help others. I joined CivPol for the same reasons."

Not that he hadn't paid a price for his commitment. In Kosovo, a mob of angry Serbs had smashed his face and driven his front teeth into the back of his throat. In East Timor, radicals had attacked CivPol quarters and he'd wound up with a severed artery whose bleeding was staunched during the assault by a Toronto cop using a tourniquet. After his last tour in Kandahar he'd gone through four months of psychological counselling. "I have strong emotions about the mission, about the people we lost," he said. "Things bring tears to my eyes that never did before. I manage it, I live with it, and continue on. We have a mission, a job, and people depend on us."

We walked past the embassy rec centre to his "man-can"—the steel trailer he called home. On the walls he'd hung pictures of his mother and his twenty-eight-year-old son, daughter-in-law and grandson. He'd married just after he'd joined the Mounties, when his wife had become pregnant, and had divorced two years later. Beside the picture of his mom was a photo of his second wife, Jennie Chen, a Canadian diplomat he'd met in Kandahar in 2009, married a year later, and hadn't seen in four months. She was now based in Washington, D.C. "We're on the phone and Skype, and try and stay close in spirit," he said, "but it's hard, no question it's hard. Lots of tears when we talk."

We wandered back to the rec centre, crossed the patio lined with dozens of little Canadian flags and sat down inside on leatherette couches beside a wall on which hung three framed jerseys, from the Vancouver Canucks, the Calgary Flames and the Montreal Canadiens. I took out a notebook and said I'd like to talk about his relationship with the Kandahar police chief, Matiullah Qati Khan. I said my intention was to concentrate on the working relationships between Canadians and the ANP as they tried to create an honest police force in a country like Afghanistan. I would visit the places he told me about and talk to the people he and the chief had known. "I'd like to put it all together so that people can get an idea how your mission started, what you've gone through, why you came back, and how you and your colleagues are progressing now."

"I wouldn't start with what *I* go through," he advised me. "I'd start with what the *Afghans* go through."

2

A COP LOVE STORY

IN NOVEMBER 2007, when McAllister had arrived for his first Kandahar deployment, the ANP were being killed at three times the rate of the Afghan National Army. The reasons became evident to him on his first trip outside the wire. "They were hired off the street and told to stand there and hope for the best," he wrote in an e-mail home. Most ANP dressed for duty in threadbare *shalwar kameez* and open-toed sandals, patrolled in unarmoured pickups and stood at checkpoints without radios, bullet-proof vests or even ammunition. Every day they were being kidnapped and beheaded, blasted to bits by car bombs or gunned down in ambushes.

Their living conditions were as abysmal as their working conditions. Their *tashkeels*—or detachments—were based in district substations that were little more than mud-walled compounds, with no electricity, running water or jail cells. In the middle of the compounds stood their "headquarters"—usually a steel shipping container that in summer became a solar furnace. Because of the danger of commuting to their families, the ANP lived in their substations for months at a time, sleeping on straw on the floor of the container. In the most remote substations they often ran out of water, and from May to September an appalling number of them died of heatstroke and thirst.

It was little wonder that 15 percent of the ANP were deserting every year. Some took jobs planting and harvesting the year's poppy crop, for which they were paid $100 a month—promptly and in cash. By contrast, in 2007 the salary of a patrolman was only $70 a month, and even this starvation wage was rarely received without a percentage being stolen by the chain of command above him. Only one group of patrol-men received their pay on time. CivPol called them "ghost police"—ANP officers who'd been killed by the Taliban but were kept on the payroll by their commanders, who pocketed their post-mortem wages.

Not surprisingly, those at the top of the law enforcement and government pyramids lived quite well. The provincial police chief, Sayed Saqib, was a barrel-chested man with an aggressive bearing who was suspected by CivPol to have used inappropriate influence to attain his position and then employed his power as chief to garner a share of the taxes charged by police at highway checkpoints in the province. He and his circle of allies worked out of Kandahar's five-storey Police Headquarters in District One, a reconstructed area in the middle of the city. A few blocks northeast stood the manicured and well-defended grounds of the grand, white Governor's Palace, fronted by an arcade that faced the city's only lawn, mown to a putting green polish. Handsome as a Bollywood movie star and always stylishly dressed, Governor Asadullah Khalid was appointed in 2005, at the age of thirty-eight, by his close ally, President Karzai. According to later reports by *The New York Times,* Western officials became "troubled by allegations of torture and drug trafficking against Mr. Khalid" during his first two years as governor. In the rural districts, Khalid became notorious for "rudely throwing his feet on the table during meetings with elders." Like Chief Saqib, Governor Khalid was detested by Kandahar's tribal elders.

Six months before McAllister arrived in Afghanistan, Kandahar had actually had an honest police chief named Esmatullah Alizai, who was arresting officials tied to the heroin trade that helped fund the Taliban insurgency. When Alizai attended community *shuras* held by the chieftains, he listened to their complaints about government corruption and did what he could to address the worst offenses. Since good relations between the chiefs and the ANP were crucial to fighting the insurgency, RCMP Superintendent Dave Fudge, CivPol's contingent commander of the day, was shocked to be informed by an Afghan official that Governor Khalid wanted Chief Alizai fired. In his book *The Savage War,* journalist Murray Brewster reported on a meeting between Fudge and the official, in which Fudge was informed that the governor was "involved in drugs, all drug dealers like him," and that if Chief Alizai wasn't fired he would probably be assassinated. "This man will kill him," the official said, referring to the governor. A summary of the meeting was eventually sent to Ottawa: "Discredited with the population, not respected by tribal elders, corrupt and dissolute, dangerous and self-serving, [Governor Khalid] discredits us through association, undermining our efforts to build public support for the Karzai government and NATO's presence in the south." In truth, Governor Khalid was greatly favoured by the president, and on July 1, 2007, he got the chief he wanted. Alizai was fired for doing his job and replaced by Sayed Saqib, who would cause the CivPol mission no end of grief.

One of Esmatullah Alizai's last acts before being removed was to promote an idealistic ally on the force to head the ANP's policy section. Matiullah Qati Khan had joined the Afghan police in the late 1970s, when he was a teenager, and had tried to uphold the law in Kandahar through all the ensuing wars and under all but one government. The exception was the five-year-reign of the Taliban, when Qati had been a hunted man. After the Taliban government was toppled and the ANP was officially reconstituted in 2003, Qati rejoined the police, was commissioned a major, and, under Esmatullah Alizai, moved into the new Regional Command Centre as a colonel.*

Matiullah Qati's promotion to policy chief effectively put him in charge of drawing up reform plans for the ANP. Over the next several months he submitted lengthy reports to Chief Saqib. These reports recommended ways to improve the lot of the rank and file in their substations, advocated that district commanders meet weekly with elders, pushed guidelines that would ensure money destined for ANP officers was kept out of the grasping hands of officials, and recommended the formation of anticorruption and internal investigation squads.

---

* In the text I will most often refer to Matiullah Qati Khan by his middle name rather than his last name to distinguish him from an infamous highways chief in the region, also named Matiullah Khan.

The reports would eventually bring Qati to the attention of CivPol, and subsequent investigations of his integrity by Canadian military intelligence showed him to be completely clean. He lived with his wife, young son and daughter in a small house he rented from a local business-man in a poor district of the city. He paid the market rate for rent—about $50 a month—and, unlike other senior ANP officers, kept no second or third wife. Indeed, his continuing tenure at Regional Command called into question the notion that not one honest man could survive in the upper echelons of the Kandahar ANP. Qati obviously could, although the chances of his rising to an executive position where he could actually carry out his proposed reforms seemed slight.

To the unending exasperation of CivPol, the fight against govern-ment corruption and the fight against the Taliban were treated as two separate issues by U.S. intelligence officials and by the generals who actually ran the war from Kabul. They considered it naive and counter-productive to try to take on both problems at once. President Karzai had extended his influence through a patronage system that encom-passed the whole country. He'd brought warlords and power brokers over to his side by giving them immunity from prosecution for theft and human rights abuses; in return, Karzai's appointees promised to fight the Taliban. Without that arrangement, his regime probably would not have had the power to exert control in a nation with poor infrastructure that was larger than France. Once the Taliban had been defeated, the military leaders felt, the Coalition could turn its attention to reforming the systemic corruption in provinces run by governors like Asadullah Khalid.

Indeed, in his two years in power, Khalid had demonstrated his fierce anti-Taliban sentiments by proving effective at extracting information from Taliban prisoners and then organizing operations that had suc-ceeded in hunting down and killing hundreds of mid-level leaders who executed the astounding violence in Kandahar. There might have been some logic to Karzai's arrangement with the fighting governor, except that, month by month, the violence in Kandahar continued to rise. To CivPol, the reasons were clear. The first was that Khalid's brutal and corrupt regime, employing torture to gain information, created more terrorists locally than it killed; the second was that the Taliban's senior leadership and training camps were not in Kandahar. They were across the border in Pakistan, in and around the teeming city of Quetta, where Taliban leaders such as Mullah Omar lived under the protection of the ISI, Pakistan's intelligence service, which viewed the Taliban as allies in Pakistan's decades-old rivalry with India for influence over Afghanistan.

Between their strategy and training sessions that coordinated the violence in Kandahar, the Taliban commanders turned their talents to recruitment propaganda, penning nostalgic poems extolling the beauty of their homeland, which was occupied by the infidels and their corrupt Afghan collaborators. The poems were then recorded by fighters as jihadist *nasheeds*—Islamic chants—and used as soundtracks to videos whose storylines featured third-act climaxes involving group behead-ings of Afghan cops against a backdrop of Kandahar's red rock moun-tains and vast desert plains. The videos were shown in Afghan refugee camps in Pakistan and posted on Taliban websites, accompanied by calls for patriots to join the fight. Thousands of refugees, fed up with life in the camps, and thousands of Kandahari villagers, fed up with paying kickbacks to the government, heeded the call.

Mentoring the ANP amidst Kandahar's Wild West landscape, some CivPol officers shared the Taliban's awe at the austere beauty of the country and could see why it would figure as the holy subject of the jihadists' *nasheeds*. Others thought Kandahar the most desolate and physically uncomfortable place this side of Mars. Canadian cops faced harsh conditions in the jungles of the Congo, the baking scrublands of Sudan and the slums of Haiti, but CivPol's operations chief in Ottawa knew that Kandahar was the roughest posting on the organization's roster of deployments.

The RCMP eventually tried to prepare CivPol officers for a Kandahar posting by having them spend two summer weeks south of Death Valley, in the middle of the Mojave Desert, where the U.S. military had built a replica of a Pashtun village for scenario-based training. The terrain looked almost the same as Kandahar, the latitude was almost the same, and the forty-five-degree August air was nearly as hot. But the ersatz village in Fort Irwin couldn't replicate the dust. Kandahari sand is a light beige talc with the abrasive consistency of ground glass. Each step puffs up little clouds of it, rolling vehicles produce six-metre walls of it and a single helicopter sandblasts two hectares. In Kandahar there was no way to keep the desert grit out of even an air-conditioned hospital trailer, never mind a tent. It infiltrated sleeping bags, chafed the groin and turned toilet seats into emery boards. There wasn't a clean window in the province.

Nor could the Mojave training base prepare CivPol cops for the number of times they would encounter dismemberment and death on a typical Kandahar rotation. On November 18, 2007, four days after McAllister began his tour in Kandahar, he attended his first ramp ceremonies, held for the 72nd and 73rd Canadian soldiers killed in the province. Some time later, his armoured convoy passed a Canadian patrol tending to the aftermath of a suicide bombing. He'd learned to keep his professional bearings in the face of horrific road accidents and domestic murder-suicides involving whole families, but the glimpse of opened-up bodies and the blood-curdling screams of Afghan women and children were of a different order than anything he'd experienced at home. It took some time before McAllister was able to "professional-ize" his emotional response to the premeditated targeting of civilians and the regularity of the carnage in Kandahar, pushing his initial reactions aside to deal with another day.

McAllister was then serving in two capacities that required him to be constantly on the move: he was CivPol's senior advisor to the military at Kandahar Airfield, coordinating the building of police stations in battle zones like Zhari and Panjwai, where he advised soldiers on the training of the hundreds of new ANP officers that CivPol's scant ten officers couldn't train on their own; and he was keeping CivPol's contingent commander, Lou Racz, abreast of the extreme security issues that faced Canadian police travelling in the province.

In late January 2008, McAllister hitched a ride in a military convoy to the western edge of Kandahar City, territory he hadn't yet covered. He was headed to inspect Sarposa Prison, an eighty-year-old stone fortress that held several hundred captured Taliban fighters. The prison was guarded by Afghan officers trained by personnel from Correctional Services Canada, who were based with CivPol at Camp Nathan Smith.

It was taken for granted by CivPol that the prison was on the Taliban's list of targets, but Sarposa had walls ten metres high, with guard towers offering sweeping views in all directions, making frontal assault difficult. The prison's weak points were its senior staff and the street cops guarding its approaches. The boss of the street cops, ANP Chief Saqib, was "incompetent" and a "crook," according to McAllister, and the warden of the prison was known to be more interested in selling contraband to the prisoners and extorting money from their families than in prison management. The prison's thousand inmates lived fifteen to a cell in dark catacombs, with light from barred windows high above sending shafts of sun through clouds of steam rising from dozens of cauldrons of boiling soup.

Stories about the torture of Taliban detainees in secret facilities run by Afghanistan's intelligence service, the National Directorate of Security, had been headline news in the Canadian media since May 2007, but no reporter had alleged that the torture was taking place in Sarposa Prison. (McAllister was still new to the country and hadn't yet encountered direct evidence of the beatings of prisoners in ANP stations, a practice he would later try to end.) Aside from their medieval cells, the prisoners' daytime treatment, monitored by a Canadian corrections officer named Rob Cater, seemed humane. They had free access to the yard between sunrise and sunset and, on McAllister's visit, the yard was full of pious Taliban at prayer, their carpets laid out around a little mosque. Amazingly, along the wall of the yard McAllister saw a line of pup tents being used for conjugal visits. "Interesting concept," McAllister wrote his Mountie buddies back home. "The prisoners get to conjugate with their wives for an hour and then go back to jail. That helps when you're doing ten years in a dungeon."

After his tour of the prison interior, McAllister climbed several flights of stairs to reconnoitre the surrounding terrain from the roof.

East of the prison, past the swirls of razor wire and solar panels donated by Canada, was what looked like a desert village with half a million people in it. Kandahar City had been founded by Alexander the Great 2,400 years earlier, but its domestic architecture had changed little in all that time. Filling the valley floor and flowing halfway up the sides of the parched mountains were a hundred thousand concentric yellow squares, each one an adobe flat-roofed house within a high-walled *qalat* compound. Almost every family in the city followed the ancient custom of building a little fort to protect itself against the invasion of enemies and the gaze of males unrelated to the women cloistered within. The architecture was a manifestation of the primacy of clan, family and honour in Pashtun tribal culture. Reflecting the central importance of Islam, the tight grid of dwellings was interrupted every few blocks by the punctuation points of minarets and their accompanying mosque domes—about one mosque for every fifty houses.

Given the number of loner criminals McAllister had dealt with as a cop in Canada, he could appreciate how family and faith could act as restraints on misbehaviour in poverty-stricken societies. It was a matter of balance, though. While he had seen beautiful expressions of Pashtun tribal culture, including infinite hospitality, compassion, honesty and fairness, he had also seen evidence of the culture's murderous side: blood feuds that had gone on for decades, amoral predation by clan chiefs, honour killings and violent intolerance of ethnic differences.

The immediate and dire problem for the locals was the thousands of Taliban fighters who followed the Muslim world's most fanatical interpretation of the Prophet's teachings. One of those supposed interpretations, *mustabahu d-dam*—"blood that is permitted"—meant that holy warriors had the right to kill Muslim civilians who were deemed to be working against the Taliban's reading of the Koran. Lately, sometimes with the support of the local mullahs and sometimes against their wishes, Taliban emissaries had been putting up posters at the entrance to the mosques: "Don't Let Your Daughters Go to School." It was a warning to the three-quarters of Kandahari families who were trying to give their daughters a *haram* education by sending them to

Coalition-built schools. The Taliban doused the faces of the girls attending the schools with acid, blew them up inside packed classrooms, and kidnapped and beheaded the local carpenters hired to build the schools.

On the city's far eastern edges were the two forts whose mission was to stop these atrocities, each by different means: Camp Nathan Smith in the northeastern suburbs, and Kandahar Airfield to the south. Even at this distance of eight kilometres McAllister could hear the roar of F-16 afterburners and see the grey specks rising from the airfield, as the jets headed in echelon toward the mountains, followed minutes later by the thumping of 500-pound bombs. He knew that if twenty-first-century NATO airpower could win the battle for Kandahar, victory would have been declared a long time ago. In battle, the Taliban wore *shalwar-kameez*—called "man-jammies" by Westerners—their protective armour nothing more than a mulberry bush or a grape hut. It wouldn't be an air force or an army that would put an end to Taliban influence, he felt. It would be a civilian police force living among a population who knew what went on in their own warren of neighbourhoods.

Looking west and south from the prison roof, away from the city, McAllister beheld a scene that reminded him of the Bible illustrations in the Catholic school he'd attended as a boy in Victoria—complete with men in sandals and shawls tending goats against a desert backdrop. Beyond a patchwork of pomegranate orchards and vineyards irrigated by a dam that had been restored by Canadians, the western Registan Desert began, heralded by a saw-toothed, red mountain jutting out from a tawny plain. Past the scree-face of the mountainside, lonely buttes marched off into the dusty infinity. The buttes, each a replica of its neighbours, became shorter in the middle distance, and shorter still in the far distance. The explanation was that the curve of the earth was dropping into emptiness and taking the land with it. If McAllister looked at the view long enough, he felt the curve of the entire planet.

The Taliban—the free ones who were not in the prison yard below— controlled that disappearing landscape, and nothing the Coalition did seemed able to destroy their jihadist zeal to re-establish their old religious rule in the city where their movement had been born. What chance, McAllister wondered, did the seventy thousand or so bedraggled and illiterate ANP have of enforcing the law throughout Afghanistan? NATO countries had recently promised to triple the number of police in three years and make sure they were all properly equipped and trained. However, among the total of forty-two nations that comprised the Coalition, the United States was still the dominant military player, and its senior officer corps viewed the Afghan police as an auxiliary to the Afghan National Army—a back-up security force rather than a national law-enforcement agency. As a result, the vast majority of American equipment and training had gone to the Afghan army.

McAllister had begun making the case to Canadian generals at Kandahar Airfield that the U.S. military had it the wrong way round: the police should be given priority. By patrolling the country's cities and towns, a competent, well-equipped police force could develop personal relationships with locals, who would then report terrorists in their neighbourhoods. The Afghan army, on the other hand, whizzing through cities in their closed military vehicles and using massive firepower to kill rather attempting to obtain information, could never develop a comparable network of informants. If the goal was to foster a sympathetic civilian population that trusted its government to provide protection from fanatics, criminals, warlords and corrupt officials, then Afghan community policing would be the most direct route to that goal. "Police are the *key* to fighting an insurgency," McAllister wrote home in an e-mail. "The Coalition can clear any place they want pretty much at will; it's the hold portion that we haven't been able to expand on because we need an indigenous police force for that. That's why we're here."

Sarposa Prison had been built in 1929, during the last year of the decade-long reign of a reformist king named Amanullah. After a war in 1919 against the British that had finally liberated his nation from eighty years of colonial interference, Amanullah had toured Europe and returned home convinced that, to avoid being recolonized, an independent Afghanistan had to modernize rapidly. He set about importing machinery for factories and building roads and schools for both girls and boys.

Then, as an example to Afghan women, he boldly presented his wife, Queen Soraya, unveiled in public, allowing her photograph to be printed on the front pages of newspapers. That was too much for the country's conservative tribal chieftains, who rose in revolt, from Badakhshan in the north to Kandahar in the south.

Amanullah soon needed a fort in Kandahar that could hold a thousand captured rebels and withstand attempts to free them. His engineers chose a spot three kilometres beyond what was then the city's edge, on the west bank of the Panjwai River and at the beginning of the eight-hundred-kilometre dirt road that crossed the desert to Herat. Attackers from the city would have to approach the fort along exposed ground and then cross a narrow bridge, where guards could cut them down with Enfield rifle fire from the top of the east wall. Guards on the west wall would be able to spot the dust cloud of an attacking force approaching when it was still half a day's ride away.

Sarposa's supposed invulnerability made it a spectacularly tempting target for the Taliban. In the spring of 2008 they began manoeuvring to capitalize on the incompetence and corruption of the prison warden by smuggling cell phones and handguns to jailed senior insurgents. On the thirty-degree evening of June 13, 2008, Sarposa held four hundred captured Taliban plus another seven hundred common criminals. At nine o'clock, ten of the forty prison guards were squatted as usual by the main prison gate, eating their supper of flat bread, rice and mutton. At ten past nine they heard small arms fire and explosions coming from the direction of a police checkpoint half a kilometre east and from a police barracks defending the western approach on Amanullah Road. Taliban attacks on these outposts were almost routine at night, and the guards at the gate continued eating their supper. Ten minutes later a tanker truck roared past the heavily engaged east checkpoint and detonated almost two tons of explosives at the main entrance of the prison. The steel front gate was blown inward and the ten guards on the other side were incinerated in the fireball. About twenty Taliban then stormed the prison yard, their machine guns and grenade-launchers blazing. The assault was so sudden and concussive that the prison guards still standing fled for their lives. At that point, a dozen more Taliban rode motorcycles into the compound. While the ground fighters emptied their Kalashnikov clips at the guard towers, the motorcyclists dismounted and ran into the prison, blasting locks with their machine guns in the main wing and then running through the corridors, following the cell phone instructions of Taliban prisoners who informed them of where they were being held. With a phalanx of Taliban leading the way, almost every inmate in the prison escaped through the blown gate. The top Taliban among them were ushered into waiting vehicles, some entering the city and others heading west and south into the world that dropped away.

The Sarposa Prison break—the largest in history—marked a turning point in McAllister's mission. By then he had volunteered for another tour and had been promoted to contingent commander of CivPol's eighteen police trainers in Camp Nathan Smith—a number that, thanks in part to his lobbying, had almost doubled since he'd arrived. Within a week the Taliban launched a reinforced campaign of ambushes, rocket attacks and bombings throughout the province which never really let up for McAllister's remaining time in Kandahar.

"The prison break caused a series of events that just kept cascading afterwards," he explained to me. The first of those events occurred on June 21, a week later. "I had a very good friend, Jim Walton, a U.S. police mentor. He and three other police mentors I knew were killed by a massive car bomb—"

He stopped in mid-sentence, looked to the side and clicked his tongue, shaking his head at the concrete walls of the rec centre where we were talking.

"Are you crying?" I asked.

"Oh, I always get choked up over this," he said. "Gimme a minute."

He stood up, put his hands in the pockets of his cargo pants and looked across the embassy compound to the gravel road that led to his reinforced-steel quarters. Then he turned and contemplated the wall where the framed hockey jerseys were displayed. He remained quiet for another minute, looking at a map of the world. He was wearing his grey Mountie service shirt, the Mountie logo on one sleeve, the CivPol patch with a Canadian flag on the other. In all but one of the pictures I took of him that day, he appears fit and handsome. The exception was the picture I took of him now. For that one moment he looked like an old man.

At last McAllister sat back down, put his forearms on his knees and stared at the linoleum floor. "Jim lived with us at Nathan Smith," he said. "I remember he joined us for a floor hockey game after Sarposa. The next day Jim and his guys headed out to train ANP in Zhari District. They were all killed by an IED. I wrote a letter to his wife. I tried to express that Jim knew why he was here. We were attempting to train police to protect the schools and we were racing to do that."

The Sarposa breakout ensured that the CivPol team lost that race— at least for a while. As part of the cascade of events that unfolded in the wake of the breakout, several teams of Taliban launched coordinated attacks on teenage girls and their female teachers as they walked to school. "They yanked back their headscarves and sprayed acid into their eyes and faces," McAllister said, describing one attack against a dozen girls and four teachers. "It wasn't the usual splash and run; they were trained with spray bottles."

The prison warden was soon found to be complicit in the breakout and was arrested. Chief Saqib, a scrupulous accountant in so many other areas of his jurisdiction, was apparently unaware of the bribes the warden had received to facilitate the Taliban attack. His incompetent response to the catastrophe did not redeem his lack of oversight. "Saqib couldn't get organized. He didn't have anybody to sort it out, didn't have any plans, didn't chase the bad guys down," McAllister said. When corrections officer Rob Cater and a Canadian Quick Reaction Force arrived on the scene that night, they discovered that the ANP had become distracted from their duties by the opportunity to loot the paltry possessions of the escaped prisoners.

The prison breakout made headlines around the world, causing such an embarrassment to the Karzai government that Saqib was fired on June 26 and Governor Khalid was informed by Karzai himself that, because of his "poor stewardship," he too would have to go. The Ministry of Interior then began quickly searching the ANP's senior ranks for Saqib's replacement. To its credit, the ministry put Matiullah Qati Khan at the top of their list and on June 29 he was appointed. A couple of days later McAllister drove into the compound of Kandahar's Police Headquarters to meet with the new chief for the first time. Qati was a short, slightly built man with a trim beard, and when McAllister walked into his office he stood up from behind his desk with a gentle, almost bemused expression, as if he too were surprised at his elevation to command. Unlike Chief Saqib, who rarely had worn anything but his medal-bedecked and epauletted parade uniform, Qati wore the simple blue fatigues of the low-ranking ANP officers in the halls. Not five minutes into their first cup of tea, as forthrightly as McAllister had ever heard an Afghan address him, Qati quietly stated that CivPol would be dealing with someone different than Saqib. "I didn't buy my position," Qati said, looking from the interpreter and directly into McAllister's eyes. "I was promoted because of my record, not because I am corrupt."

Qati offered McAllister another cup of tea, and the Mountie listened as the new chief explained that it might take him years, but he would break the long pattern of corrupt leadership and train a police force that could protect civilians against the violence. At the end of their meeting, Qati extended his hand. "With your help I will change things here," he vowed.

"I told him my help was what he had," McAllister recounted, "but to tell the truth, things were such a mess in Kandahar, and so dangerous, that I was really worried for him. He was such a gentle, humble guy. He always wore those same work clothes, even on visits to the Governor's Palace or when I brought him to meet our minister of defence."

McAllister glanced to the side again. When he looked back at me, his eyes were once again brimming with tears. "His men were getting killed by the dozen. He was definitely not religious at all and the Taliban just hated him. Had the Taliban killed him, he expected that. But he never expected what actually happened."

The six-thousand-man Kandahar force that Matiullah Qati inherited was in a shambles after a year of Saqib's leadership. A hundred new cops were being recruited every month but their selection was not based on merit, their training was not mandatory and their performance was not monitored. After being assigned to substations, the first lesson the recruits learned was that their loyalty was not to the law but to their district commanders, who made up the law as they went along. Among these commanders were former warlords whom Saqib had allowed to get away with just about anything. They extorted road taxes from the civilian population, provided protection services for drug traffickers and set reprehensible standards of predatory cruelty, including, in some cases, keeping village boys as personal sex slaves. To the locals, it seemed that the ANP operated in a leaderless vacuum, with some officers racing into the gunfire of the Taliban to help victims after an explosion, while others in the same unit demanded bribes in order to take action, and still others simply fled the scene. From Zhari in the north to Spin Boldak in the south, officers were neither rewarded for valorous behaviour nor penalized for corruption or cowardice.

In addition to reversing this dysfunction and criminality, Qati had to find a way to end the role the force played in protecting Kandahar's political bosses. Governor Khalid would be gone as of August 1, but above him during his reign had always stood President Karzai's half brother, Ahmad Wali Karzai. Since 2005, AWK had served as the head of the Provincial Council, which made him the "unrivalled strongman of Kandahar," according to a cable sent to Washington from the U.S. embassy in June 2009.

The cable was made public by Wikileaks in December 2010, when I was covering CivPol in Kandahar. Reading it in my bunk at CNS gave me a picture of the impossible odds Matiullah Qati had faced in reforming the Kandahar police. AWK used "state institutions to protect and enable licit and illicit enterprises," the cable stated. His "overriding purpose" was "the enrichment, extension and perpetuation of the Karzai clan, and along with it their branch of the Popalzai tribe. This applies equally to his entrepreneurial and his alleged criminal activities." The alleged criminal activities included AWK's involvement in the poppy trade, although his entrepreneurial schemes were even more damaging to the province. These schemes often involved the personal use of Western funds that should have been benefiting the population but instead were siphoned to build his business empire, giving him controlling shares in construction, real estate and agricultural development projects. The cable ended with an overall judgment of AWK: "The coalition views many of his activities as malign, particularly relating to his influence over the police."

CivPol's approach to AWK and his ilk followed diplomatic protocols worked out in other failing states controlled by corrupt power brokers. Publicly, Canadian officers were required to keep their mouths shut, particularly when the power brokers declared that all the allegations mentioned in the press were unproven rumours fabricated by political opponents. In private, CivPol commanders tried re-educating and reforming the most malfeasant officials; failing that, they lobbied federal officials in the capital to remove the officials; failing that, they attempted to build a base of honest police officers beneath the thieving satraps to thwart or limit their corruption. This last was their approach in Kandahar.

The fallout from the 2008 Sarposa Prison breakout made it clear to AWK that the Coalition would not allow the ANP to continue its descent into ungoverned irresponsibility, and as a result he had approved the minister of interior's choice of a respected cop with an unblemished record to replace Saqib. According to one member of the Provincial Council I talked with in Kandahar, AWK had his own Machiavellian reasons for going along with the appointment. By birth, Matiullah Qati was a member of a tribe called the Achakzai, a secular group allied with AWK's own Popalzai tribe, and he may have figured there was a chance that Qati would become transformed by the benefits of his job into someone with whom AWK could do business. On the other hand, if Qati remained incorruptible, he would probably be killed by his own police before he got too far along with his plans for reform. Eventually the Taliban would surely kill him, given their successes in assassinating other senior officers. In the meantime, AWK would reward Matiullah Qati's efforts with praise, and approval if he was promoted in rank— handing the Coalition the kind of bauble they liked to show the press as they made announcements about improvements in governance.

Qati was completely aware of this cynical speculation about his professional future and his short lifespan. The idea that he would be tempted to betray his ideals made him laugh. Given the state of the force he had to work with, he knew there wasn't much he could do about the high-living political figures above him. So many people at so many levels were hooked into the province's skein of corruption that Qati estimated it would take half a decade to build up a force that could even begin to unfasten them. What he could do in the short run was remain unyielding if the politicians tried to inhibit reforms that would improve the lives of his fellow cops and his fellow citizens. Because of the manner of his appointment, he owed no favours to the governor or to AWK, and from the moment he became chief, he announced that he was outside Kandahar's patronage system and would someday reverse it. "I am affiliated with no one," he told McAllister. "My loyalty is only to the law. I will reform the ANP so it enforces the law." As for the possibility that he would be assassinated while doing so, he said, "Only God knows the time of our deaths. Altering that moment is not in our power."

It is often said that Afghans are constantly switching sides for their own benefit in their never-ending blood feuds, civil wars and holy wars against invaders. But the paradigm does not apply to Matiullah Qati Khan. He always remained on the same side, even as the world switched sides around him. From the time he joined the police at the age of eighteen, in 1978, a year before the Soviet invasion, to his murder thirty-one years later, Qati's animating ideals were secularism, honesty and the protection of the people against religious and criminal predators. He fought to uphold these ideals regardless of who was in power.

He was raised by a left-wing father who sent him to a Kandahar high school built by the U.S. Peace Corps during the Kennedy administration. When the communists came to power in Kabul in 1978, Matiullah and his father backed the revolution, and when the communists invited the Soviets in to defend the revolution, they backed the reforms the Soviets promised. Unnoticed during the West's reporting of the subsequent atrocity-filled years is the fact that, initially, there were thousands of secular and left-wing people in the Islamist south who wanted medieval Kandahar upended. Qati was just one who rejected the label of collaborator and called himself progressive; the reforms the Soviets promised were not very different from those promised by NATO when its armies arrived in 2001. They included universal education, the reordering of gender relations, ending tribal nepotism and ridding the country of the fundamentalist superstitions that governed many parts of Afghanistan outside Kabul. Matiullah Qati received forensic training and an academic education from the Soviets and rose through the ranks until he witnessed something that caused him to realize the Russians were abandoning their shared progressive goals.

A colleague of Qati's, an ANP colonel named Rahim, told me that in 1984, Qati was fighting around the border town of Spin Boldak against Islamist mujahedin when he witnessed a massacre. "Usually the mujahedin were *shahids* [martrys], but some were not so brave and sought to surrender," Colonel Rahim said. "They came out from behind their rocks with their hands up. But the Russian commander gave the order to fire. Matiullah saw many men mown down."

He confronted the Russian commander, who knocked out his front teeth with the butt of his gun and said he would execute Matiullah Qati if he criticized him again. "I don't know how long afterward, but Matiullah then joined a faction of the mujahedin," Colonel Rahim said. "He reasoned that the Russians had violated his ideals and to keep his ideals he must now fight them."

According to Rahim and others I spoke to, Qati never fled across the border to Pakistan to find safety in a refugee camp, as millions did. He stood and fought the Russians until, five bloody years later, Soviet leader Mikhail Gorbachev announced the war was ending. Kandahar was then taken over by mujahedin warlords. One Kandahar provincial councillor I spoke with said that Qati told him he despised the "pirates" who had occupied the city and for the next several years he tried to assert his old role as a policeman to stop the pillaging of the city and the rape of young boys.

The communists had held onto power in Kabul until 1992, when they were finally overthrown by the mujahedin. A four-year civil war then broke out between the victors, which all but destroyed Kabul. Down in Kandahar, the recently named Taliban—"religious students"— secured Pakistan's backing against the warlords and won the province, then marched north to seize Kabul in September 1996. The long night of the Taliban then descended on the country, with their al-Qaeda allies, headed by Osama bin Laden, setting up their jihadist training camps near Kandahar City. During this period, Qati—hunted by the Taliban as a secularist and former Soviet collaborator—went to ground. After the 9/11 hijackers brought down the Twin Towers, he joined a militia of anti-Taliban Achakzai fighters, and when U.S. forces defeated the Taliban, he put his name forward to the American-backed Karzai government as a veteran policeman who wanted to uphold the law in his hometown.

"Our Provincial Police Chief got promoted to General," McAllister wrote home two months after Matiullah was sworn in. "The more I work with this guy the more I like him. Last week there was a massive IED placed outside his residence that our Canadian Forces went and defused. He was very thankful for our help but laughed at the bomb. He is very honest about the challenges he has internally with his men and I like that. He knows they have drug and corruption issues and is doing his best to deal with those. Mind you, it takes a presidential order to fire a policeman here so he knows it's a battle to fight."

By then McAllister and Qati were holding regular meetings at Police Headquarters and at CNS, marking the beginning of the first methodically coordinated attempt by Afghans and CivPol to reform the ANP in Kandahar. During that summer they drew up a list of their goals. Among them were setting up a system of district-based community policing; establishing supervisor responsibility for the misdeeds of officers, from chief all the way down to patrolman; radically expanding ANP training and equipment disbursement; tripling pay for police so it was on a par with the Afghan National Army; protecting women and recruiting female cops; and, most important for Matiullah Qati at the moment, ensuring that wounded police had access to Afghan military hospitals.

"See, the biggest problem for his guys was that the army got everything, the police were getting nothing," McAllister explained to me. "The army got a brand new hospital—Matiullah's policemen, if they got shot up, the military wouldn't let them in, they had to go to the local hospital. And in one bed there's an insurgent and in the next bed there's his guy. So we made a deal saying that if the police get hit, they go to the army hospital. I promised we would do that for him."

In his devotion to the welfare of the much-maligned rank and file, Qati was different from all other chiefs who had come before him. From his first meeting with McAllister he made the point that what he needed most from the coalition was for its senior officers to lean on the government in Kabul to change its mindset toward the police. The young ANP recruits may have been illiterate and untrained but, he said, most of them were anxious to prove themselves as defenders of their country. He pointed out that they threw themselves into the line of fire without a thought for their safety, fought to the death to defend dilapidated compounds after their commanders had fled, and remained at their remote guard posts without water even as they died of thirst. To Qati, their ability to suffer unspeakable hardship for so little money meant they were imbued with ideals that reflected his own. The more he travelled the province and gathered them in groups to explain his upcoming changes to the force, the more he became convinced that they accepted him and his plans for reform. The sincerity and honesty of these young recruits and their potential to form a professional force were at the heart of his belief that the mission to reform the ANP had a chance of success.

Three of the young recruits that Matiullah Qati addressed during his first weeks on the job were named Atul, Janan and Mirzal. By the time I met up with them two years later at CNS, they'd all been promoted to 3rd sergeant and were attending a six-month officer-training course at CNS. I sat down with them after shooting practice one day near the ANP bunkhouse. Atul had been wounded by the Taliban in two fire-fights, the first by a bullet that had ricocheted into his eye and the second by shrapnel from a rocket-propelled grenade that had entered his knee and arm. In both cases he had been refused treatment at the Kandahar military hospital and had gone to Pakistan to seek medical attention, which he had paid for out of his own pocket. He was recuperated now—a fit twenty-four-year-old, wearing a trim uniform.

He spoke a little English and tried to explain what Qati had said to their *tashkeel* at the substation in Panjwai East. "Do not care what your bad brother does," he recalled the chief saying. "You will not learn from him. He will learn from you. Your bad brother will feel shame doing bad deeds in front of your eyes. If there are ten good brothers and ten bad brothers, the ten good brothers will become twenty good brothers. The bad ones cannot live with the shame they see in your eyes. If they try to take money, you do not take money and they will feel too ashamed to continue taking money. If they want to run away, you do not run away and they will feel too ashamed to run away. In such a way we will make an ANP that protects our people."

He added: "I myself tell these words to patrolmen. When I am an officer I will tell these words to corporals and sergeants. If enough officers have been trained in this way, then Afghanistan will change. That really is my hope."

When his buddies asked him what he had said to me, he offered them a translation. They listened in silence, nodding, then began explaining their own point of view. The most important factor in making a functional police force, they both said, is good commanders. "The men will behave the way the commander behaves," Atul translated. "If the commander is bad, the men will be bad. If the commander is good, the men will be good."

I asked what their experience was with their commander in Panjwai East. They all glowered. "Thief!" Janan said in English. "Stole money!" Mirzal said.

I asked what Matiullah Qati had done about that. "Fire him," Mirzal said. "Our hope is our fired commander will spend all future time in hell with the Taliban."

In addition to the meetings McAllister and Qati held at Police Headquarters, they also had weekly dinners together at CNS in the air-conditioned tent-cafeteria opposite CivPol headquarters. The dinners were designated as a time to forget the violence and corruption they encountered daily beyond the walls and to get to know one another.

"We would just talk as men, talk as fathers, talk as people," McAllister told me. "How's it going? How's the wife and kids? What are you gonna do when you retire? And it was really nice and relaxing, there was no pressure, we didn't ask one question about the insurgency. Once, I was talking about my family and Matiullah reached over and took my hand, just held it. He said he was very grateful to me for coming all this way to help him with his job. So I knew I'd made a friend. In CivPol, to work with someone honest at the top who believes you're there to share a model of policing that could work in his culture, that's half the battle."

On November 10, 2008, Matiullah Qati and McAllister drove into the compound of the newly built headquarters of the Panjwai ANP, about fifty kilometres southwest of Kandahar City. Built under the supervision of the Canadian military and CivPol, the headquarters had high brick walls, thick wooden guard towers, porta-potties, running water and sleeping quarters for all the ANP stationed there. It was one of many stations and substations being built to military standards all over the province to replace the unlivable compounds where the ANP cowered. Directly beside the fort, the Canadians had also built a civilian district headquarters. Clan and family elders had already begun holding their town council *shuras* there, and McAllister and Qati had timed their trip to Panjwai to attend one. The main topic on the agenda was the ANP in Panjwai.

In Afghan *shuras* about a quarter of the time is taken up with formal greetings among the chiefs, clan leaders and government officials in attendance, each individual going through a ritual of questions and good wishes that are precisely pronounced, answered in the affirmative, and then re-asked and answered in the affirmative. ("Peace be with you. How are you? Is your household doing well? Is your health doing well? Is your soul doing well? I wish you a long life. I wish your household prosperity. I wish your soul many blessings.") The long ritual of greetings had evolved over many centuries to defuse aggression between clans competing over scarce resources in the desert, and though they tended to drive Westerners batty, they were not so very different from the small talk that takes place before a business meeting in Canada, the difference being that in Afghanistan the ritualized socializing is part and parcel of a *shura*, rather than a hallway preamble. In addition, the order of the questioning and the good wishes establishes seniority in the district: in the case of visiting government officials, the district chief addresses his first greeting to the most senior federal official. This etiquette lets it be known that the district chief is in charge of his home ground and that, while the federal official may be the honoured guest, he comes second in these parts.

Despite all the initial formality, Afghan chiefs proceed very abruptly to what's on their minds. The new ANP headquarters and district council building had been built on open ground a kilometre outside of town. While this position ensured that the two buildings could be better defended against attack, it also allowed the ANP officers more opportunity to charge road taxes to district leaders making the trip and passing through ANP checkpoints. Was Matiullah Qati Khan aware that his officers were still charging these road taxes? Was he aware that the officers smoked marijuana at these checkpoints? Was he aware that the officers at the new headquarters could seldom be bothered to leave the fort to answer emergency calls for help? Was he aware that the district commander of Panjwai East substation was utterly corrupt?

On the rare times Sayed Saqib had attended district meetings he had usually dismissed such complaints on the grounds that there was scant evidence to back them up. McAllister listened carefully to the translation as Qati stood to answer the allegations. Qati referred to McAllister and said that with the help of CivPol he was taking steps to address each of these ANP deficiencies. He then explained how he was taking those steps. Until recently there had been no drug tests, he said, but now they would be done regularly; he would personally oversee an anticorruption task force to crack down on road taxes.

Henceforth, Qati said, he would accept responsibility for the actions of every district commander under him; every district commander would accept responsibility for the actions of his senior officers; every senior officer would accept responsibility for the actions for his junior officers; and every junior officer would accept responsibility for the actions of the rank and file under him. All commanders and senior officers would attend a training seminar on "performance measures and accountability." Both positive and negative behaviour was to be recorded, and, in McAllister's words, a "three hits/three strikes" scheme was to be put in place: "Three serious issues against Matiullah's men and he fires them," McAllister recollected. "Three solid actions that impact the community or save lives, they get a reward."

Matiullah Qati added that he had designed "motivational posters" that were going up in all police stations, providing clear illustrations of police codes of conduct, which could be pointed to when officers violated their mission. For the illiterate officers, some posters took the form of cartoon strips that gave the history of policing in Afghanistan according to precepts of justice and fairness set down in the Koran.

McAllister and CivPol were key to helping Qati redress a serious charge made by the local chiefs. "The police chief in Panjwai East was corrupt as all hell," McAllister told me. "The *shura* wanted to get rid of him. We had evidence the guy was stealing money from his men, he was lying, cheating, cooking the books, and we wanted to get rid of him too. So we gave Matiullah all the documentation, and after the *shura* he went over to the Panjwai East substation and he fired the guy. The Panjwai *shura* was very impressed with that."

To impress them even more substantively, however, a far worse offence had to be stopped. On the ride back to Kandahar, McAllister brought up what was for him, and for all of Kandahar, an urgent issue: some of Matiullah Qati's ANP commanders were pedophiles.

Throughout the world it's taken for granted that even the most corrupt police forces will bust pedophiles. Not in Kandahar, where it was considered acceptable for senior ANP officers to keep adolescent male sex slaves. The exploited children were known variously as "chai boys" or "dancing boys," and there were dozens of them in police stations around the province. They were "recruited" into the ANP as young as nine years old, then forced to don make-up and female clothing, dance at parties and submit to being sodomized by their owners. While usually conducted with some secrecy in other parts of Afghanistan, *bacha bazi*—"boy play"—was openly celebrated as a cultural tradition in Kandahar. Pederasty was not illegal and officers could not be fired for practising it. The only time it had gone out of favour was under the Taliban, who had beheaded its practitioners—an act of justice that ordinary citizens had cheered. Since many of the current district commanders within the ANP were former warlords who had fought the Taliban in the 1990s—in part to keep their dancing boys—they considered *bacha bazi* as a perk of their command. (It would not be officially condemned by the Karzai government until 2011.)

One of the worst spots for *bacha bazi* was Zhari District, under the command of an illiterate senior officer named Bizmullah Jan, who refused to hire literate officers because he distrusted them. Bizmullah had been one of the warlords who'd ferociously fought both the Russians and the Taliban, and his tribally affiliated officers were intensely loyal to him. While Bizmullah himself did not have a dancing boy, many of the men who worked for him did. Over a planning session at Police Headquarters a couple of weeks after the Panjwai *shura*, McAllister and Qati planned a child rescue operation throughout the entire district, which the military expected would be almost as dangerous as an operation against the Taliban. The next week they mounted up an armoured Canadian Forces patrol and went from substation to substation seizing the boys. "We almost went to guns against this one particular police station when we took their chai boys away," McAllister told me. "They reached for their guns, I reached for mine and the military reached for theirs." There was a breathless ten-second Mexican stand-off, broken only when Matiullah Qati stepped between the two sides and "started yelling and screaming at his men about the shame they were causing the country and the ANP. 'You can't have these kids in the camps. You cannot!'" The Canadian soldiers kept their guns on the ANP as McAllister and Qati led the children to the armoured vehicles and put them aboard.

"How did you feel when the cops you were reforming showed they were willing to kill you to retain their right to rape boys?" I asked McAllister.

"Put it this way," he replied. "We had all these benchmarks, and here were all these district commanders doing this. It was so sick I can hardly stand to think about it."

As they drove back to Kandahar with the rescued boys, McAllister discovered that firing Bizmullah Jan would not be as straightforward as firing the commander of Panjwai East. Qati might have been a man of ideals, but he was no saint when it came to choosing between protecting the ANP against Taliban attacks and sacking a corrupt commander who knew how to fight the insurgents.

"Bizmullah told Matiullah that if he got fired he'd fuck off with everything—his men, their guns, their cars, their equipment—leaving a huge hole for the Taliban," McAllister recalled. "So I said to Matiullah, 'That doesn't matter! His commanders have chai boys. He's not running his shop, he's illiterate, he won't have people around him who are literate.' Matiullah said, 'Listen, he's a mujahedin warrior; the people around him are loyal. If I lose him, I'll lose half the police out there and the whole district will be exposed to the Taliban. I have no short-term solution to that.'"

Matiullah Qati argued for an Afghan solution to this Afghan problem. Bizmullah should stay on as commander of Zhari until after the upcoming fighting season in the late spring and summer, when the Taliban, having harvested their poppy crops, launched their most ferocious assaults. McAllister couldn't agree to leaving Bizmullah Jan in place that long, even with the chai boys removed. A couple of weeks later, a Canadian military patrol stopped in at Bizmullah's headquarters and discovered a prisoner who'd been badly beaten. The soldiers handed the prisoner over to McAllister, who took him to the attorney general's office, where he demanded that an investigation be opened on Bizmullah Jan. McAllister then showed up at Matiullah's office, and told him, "Listen, one of his officers beat a prisoner, and Bizmullah's done nothing about it. *Ya gotta fucking remove him!*"

To McAllister's surprise, Matiullah got tearfully upset at him. "Yeah, I gotta remove him, I *have* to remove him, because *you* tell me to and I love you and you're my brother, but it's so difficult for me to remove him."

"No, no, no!" McAllister shouted. "You can't remove him because *I* tell you to. You have to remove him because it's the right thing to do. You have to understand the rationale to remove him. Don't remove him because I said to, don't remove him because *Canadians* tell you to remove him. You have to have an Afghan reason to remove him."

In the end, they compromised. There was a district substation to the south of Zhari HQ that, in military jargon, "needed a strong bill of security." Bizmullah Jan was demoted and he and his men switched stations. Now the issue for Qati was that, without a reliable, if corrupt, fighter in Zhari HQ, his left flank was exposed. When four of his men were blown up by an IED, he was furious. By then he had lost another two hundred police and he himself had survived another IED, which exploded near his office window, demolishing the first floor of the Police Headquarters around him. Replacing corrupt warlords with cops who were nowhere nearly as skilled as fighters had had its consequences.

At a meeting at headquarters, McAllister could tell right away that something was on Matiullah's mind. When he began asking him questions about performance ratings in substations, the chief blew up. "Are you a fucking journalist? You just write notes all the time! You want a story, I'll give you a story." And Matiullah proceeded to tell McAllister about the four men who'd just been blown up by an IED. Three had lost limbs and the fourth had a hole in his skull, but when their buddy took them to the nearby army hospital they were stopped at the door and told to use the civilian hospital half a mile away. There, they were placed in beds beside Taliban. Qati shouted that he'd done his part, but McAllister had not delivered on his promise to make sure that Qati's men were treated the same way as the army if they were wounded.

McAllister remembered thinking Matiullah had a right to be irate: "His men were getting wasted all the time. And he was trying to do good for his men, give them medical treatment, give them equipment— really, really working hard for his men, knowing that they were getting killed by the fucking dozen, and meanwhile doing all the things we had advised him to do, and here we'd let him down. I took it up with the Canadian military, but it was the Afghan army that had to change, and they said they didn't trust the ANP to be in beds next to their soldiers."

"How did he explain this failure to his men?" I asked. "His popularity must have suffered."

"Oh, he was out there on his own and he knew it," McAllister replied, "not just from that but from *all* the changes he was making. He was getting it from all sides from the very beginning. For instance, he was hiring more female officers. When the Taliban put his female officers under threat, he moved them all into a compound and he assigned guys to watch their houses. The Taliban had him marked for that alone. His life was always in danger. When he left PHQ, he had to ride in a motorcade of five cars, and his car would change position every few kilometres so they would never know where he was in the motorcade. That was the way he lived on a daily basis."

There were only eight female police officers working out of headquarters when Matiullah Qati became police chief. Most male officers considered them auxiliaries whose main jobs were to type up reports and search female suspects, but that is not how they viewed their own roles. They were under the command of a lieutenant colonel named Malalai Kakar, a remarkable woman who headed a unit called the Crimes Against Women Department. She saw her contingent as protectors of the female population of Kandahar, and she trained them for that job.

Malalai, not surprisingly, had not been on speaking terms with Sayed Saqib. Shortly before Saqib had been fired, he'd written her up for insubordination when he discovered she was conducting an independent investigation of a high-profile businessman alleged to have beaten his wife with a bicycle chain. When Matiullah Qati became chief he called Malalai into his office, tore up Saqib's reprimand and told her to conclude the investigation, make the arrest, and hire more female investigators. They then began talking about old times. They had known each other for twenty-five years.

Just five feet tall, Malalai was a striking woman of forty-one and a mother of six. She was known in the city as a kind of angelic reincarnation of her namesake, Malalai, the Joan of Arc of Afghanistan, a female Pashtun warrior who had rallied troops during the Second Afghan War and helped win a battle against the British in the 1880s. The daughter of a policeman, Malalai had in 1982 become the first woman to graduate from the Kandahar Police Academy—at the age of fifteen and under the direction of the Soviets. Those were the days when the Soviets had encouraged gender mixing on the force, and Malalai Kakar and Matiullah Qati had patrolled the city together.

A female officer named Magulla told me, "Malalai was a strong woman from a little girl. Even if there were no Russians to say it was okay, she would have lived as she liked." She refused to wear a burka and was a walking target for the mujahedin. A few years into her job, a group of radical Islamists ambushed her. To their surprise she drew her guns and fought back like a tiger, killing three of them in a shootout that went on long enough to have made a good scene in a movie. It certainly made a lasting impression in Kandahar.

When the Taliban took over, Malalai fled to Pakistan. She met her husband in a refugee camp and, after the Taliban were driven out, returned with him and their children to Kandahar. He took a job with the United Nations and she resumed her interrupted policing career, juggling the needs of her family with twelve hours a day of hunting wife-beaters, murderers and thieves. By 2008 she had become famous throughout Afghanistan for her achievements against overwhelming odds. She patrolled the city with a squad of female officers, gathering intelligence on women who might be held as slaves or beaten daily. She either rescued the women or, if a wife wanted to stay in the home, had a sit-down with the husband. She was known to wield her baton against the most outrageously abusive of them.

Matiullah Qati treated Malalai as an equal, despite the fact that, throughout Afghanistan, ANP provincial chiefs not only barely tolerated female officers but often sexually assaulted them. By contrast, as far back as when he had been a policy officer, Qati had advocated increasing the number of females on the force, and when he had become chief, had agreed with CivPol that twenty-four would be his short-term goal. In meetings with Malalai, he sought her advice on the feasibility of having these female recruits taught beside males at CNS's new Training Centre. That had not been done since the Russians were driven out.

They held their last meeting in the debris-littered city Police Headquarters, on September 15, 2008, just after the IED had exploded outside Qati's window. At least twice a week for years Malalai had received Taliban "night-letters" pinned to her door warning her to quit her job. To his lasting regret, Qati did not insist on supplying her with a full protection squad to supplement the single policeman he'd assigned to watch her house, because she had told him a protection squad of males would interfere with her work. Two weeks after Qati's meeting with Malalai, two gunmen on a motorcycle ambushed her in her car as her son drove her out of her compound. She died instantly from multiple gunshot wounds to the head.

Malalai's assassination made international headlines. Her bravery and life's work protecting women had been reported extensively in Western newspapers, magazines and TV documentaries. Front-page obituaries now appeared in all the outlets that had covered her life—*The Sunday Times*, *The Independent*, BBC, CBC, ABC, CNN, *Maclean's*, *Newsweek*, and *Marie Claire*—many written by female reporters who had risked their own lives going on ride-alongs with Malalai. In some ways, her assassination had effects as wide-ranging as the Sarposa Prison break-out in that it focused the Coalition's attention on the Afghan police.

A high-level meeting was convened in Kabul, attended by all the countries that contributed to the United Nations' Law and Order Trust Fund for Afghanistan (LOFTA), an overseeing body established in 2002 whose mandate was to collect funds from Coalition countries and distribute them in ways that helped the Afghans build a professional police force. All aspects of the ANP were discussed, from Malalai Kakar's murder to the ubiquitous corruption of officers in the field. Canada, LOFTA's third-largest contributor after the United States and Great Britain, made the point that posters in local stations preaching honour and ethics would not stop an average cop from taking bribes from civilians if his family's survival depended on it. Officers were convinced that they were less highly esteemed than the much better paid army, whose soldiers also received danger pay and double the ANP's food allowance. At the meeting, Canada successfully lobbied that the pay of ANP officers should equal that of Afghan soldiers, that policemen should receive risk pay and that their food allowance should be doubled. McAllister wrote home, "*Finally* we've got recognition of how dangerous their job actually is. We've got plans now to get the word out to the public."

In early December Matiullah Qati and McAllister were interviewed on Kandahar TV, on a show McAllister called the station's version of *Good Morning America*. As they had to speak through a translator to each other and to the audience, the conversation was stilted. The moderator asked McAllister a question about his mission in Pashto, the question was translated, McAllister answered in English, his response was translated into Pashto, Qati added his thoughts in Pashto, which were translated for McAllister, who then added his thoughts, which were translated for the moderator and Qati. "Matiullah was great," McAllister said, "but I'm not sure how much of what I said got through. Afterward the producer told me I had no career in TV. Pretty harsh, even if it was Afghan television."

McAllister's Christmas break was coming up and Matiullah Qati expressed his fear to Joe that he would not come back. "He called and said he wanted to see me before I went," McAllister told me. "So he came over to CNS and he dropped off some gifts. One was a nice big table cloth for my mom. This poorest guy in the world—he knows I'm fairly well off, and he brought me over some gifts. 'My friend, take this back to your family,' he said."

When McAllister returned in mid-January, he only had time to unload his pack in CNS before he had to hustle over to the Governor's Palace for the weekly security meeting with the new governor, Tooryalai Wesa, an Afghan-Canadian trusted by CivPol, and with the Canadian, Afghan and American brass. When McAllister got out of his SUV he saw about thirty high-ranking police and military officers socializing under the scalloped arcade outside the palace. Matiullah Qati broke from the group and ran to hug him. He held him tightly for a solid minute, saying in English, "My friend, my friend, you are back!" then drew him by the hand to the Afghan army commander and said with tears in his eyes, "Oh, my best friend has come back from Canada. I was worried he wouldn't come back. He helps me every day." As the officers filed in through the hardwood arching doors, Matiullah kept McAllister's hand tightly in his own, and did not let it go for the entire two-hour briefing as they stood over the topographical mock-up of the province while a U.S. intelligence officer lectured on Taliban threats and IEDs. "You seldom see Afghans holding hands with Westerners like that," McAllister told me. "It meant a lot to me. *He* meant a lot to me. We were really bonded."

Three weeks later another huge explosion went off near the Police Headquarters, this one in a wheelbarrow left at a construction site, and it was McAllister's turn to rush to his good friend's side and hug him good and hard. "I'm waiting for a ban on wheelbarrows in the city, as this is becoming way too common," McAllister wrote home afterward. "Two civilians killed and one police officer, but our chief lives on thankfully. This is the third attempt on his life and so far he has done well to avoid serious injury or death. The guy amazes me as he just shrugs it off as being another day on the job. I guess when you've lived through what he has this is just a way of life. Tough but true. That is why these people are so hard to defeat. Very little fazes them."

During his remaining months in Kandahar, McAllister devoted more and more of his time to developing the capacity of the police training centre at CNS and working with Matiullah Qati to write its curriculum. By the beginning of March there were about a dozen classrooms in a barracks-length portable in which CivPol officers ran classes all day long. Recruits were taught standards of behaviour in public, the role of police in a democracy, the concept of probable cause, the rights of the accused, how to interview witnesses and suspects, crime scene investigation, evidence collection, report writing (for those who were literate), the recruitment and handling of informants, international human rights law and community policing, among other topics. All personnel were required to qualify at the shooting range to use a 9mm Glock handgun (although, at this point, there were still not enough guns to issue to everyone). Another wing was added to the ANP dormitory, plus a gym, and a "chai" meeting room for trainees to socialize in the evenings. McAllister also submitted plans for a $3 million expansion that would double the capacity of the training facility over the next year.

As McAllister's two back-to-back tours came to an end, he took stock of his accomplishments in an e-mail home. Much of it expressed his admiration of Matiullah Qati Khan's accomplishments. "He has directly fired over 40 top guys in the past few months and upwards of a 100 others have been arrested, so the word is getting out. He is pushing for mandatory drug testing and has closed many illegal road tolls. Still a long ways to go but at least we know the top guy cares. And he is putting assets into dealing with the problem, whereas before dealing with the problem was mostly turning a blind eye."

He summed up his feelings about his time in Kandahar in a heartfelt paragraph:

> The mission itself has opened my eyes into a world I never thought I would experience 28 years ago when I joined the RCMP. Back then I was pretty happy just being a cop in a car running from call to

call. We didn't do International policing in this format back then and now that we are celebrating 20 Years of the International Peace Operations Branch it's hard to imagine that we will ever stop doing this. I think Canadian Police bring a very unique perspective to all the missions we are involved in around the world, cultural sensitivity being a key to our approach. The ability to understand others and look at the world through unprejudiced eyes, and to bring about positive change in small but meaningful ways, has always been a trait we have been proud of. And I do believe we bring home many abilities and ideas that help us in our duties back in Canada. Certainly my experience in Kosovo, East Timor and now here have helped my understanding of human nature in extreme circumstances and shown me a variety of ways to deal with conflict.

On a visit to CNS, RCMP Commissioner William Elliott and Deputy Commissioner Gary Bass offered McAllister a position as head of the Integrated Security Command Centre for the upcoming Vancouver 2010 Winter Olympics. He was due home in mid-May, shortly before I was to address him and his colleagues at the annual Senior Officers Conference in Chilliwack, B.C.

Just before he left Kandahar he attended his last security briefing with Matiullah Qati at the Governor's Palace. It was an emotional farewell. The slightly built police chief in his worn uniform looked up several inches into his mentor's eyes and uttered words McAllister would remember for the rest of his life: "Don't fear for me, my brother. They can neither kill my soul nor the soul of my country."

Matiullah Qati's new CivPol mentor was to be a fifty-eight-year-old retired RCMP superintendent named John White, a veteran of three missions in Haiti and the former director of the International Peace Operations Branch in Ottawa from 2006 to 2007. White arrived in Kandahar on June 26, 2009, a Friday. His first day of work was Sunday, and the first item of business was to arrange a meeting with the police chief.

The morning of the scheduled meeting, June 29, Matiullah Qati received a panicked call from Hafizullah Khaliqyar, the district attorney of Kandahar City. Hafizullah told Qati that about forty angry ANP were inside the compound of the attorney general's office demanding the release of one of their colleagues, who had just been arrested for forging documents. The officers all worked as security guards for an American Special Forces team in the city and felt they were elite enough to be above arrest. Rather than going the normal route of hiring a fixer to post bond for the arrested officer, the outraged cops had invaded the compound wearing their U.S.-issued combat gear and were now waving their M-16s around. Hafizullah asked if Qati could come down to the attorney general's compound and reason with them.

Matiullah Qati called Abdul Khaliq Hamdard, the head of the Criminal Investigation Department (CID), who had laid the charges against the ANP officer in custody. Then he, Abdul Khaliq and a police guard of about a dozen of Qati's most loyal officers drove in a convoy through the centre of the city and pulled up outside the white-plastered office of the attorney general. Through the wrought-iron gate they saw the mob of ANP officers loudly arguing with police at the entrance to the building. Both sides had their elbows up and their fingers around the trigger guards of their guns. Matiullah Qati led the way through the gate and ordered the outraged ANP to rank up and march out of the compound. There would be no discussion of the matter here, he said, but they could tell him their story back at Police Headquarters. The friends of the detainee began insulting Qati and the loyal officers with him.

When fifty or so armed Pashtun men square off in a compound and exchange insults, it is only a question of time before one member of a clan that is a historical enemy of another clan opens fire. No one knows who fired first, but in the ensuing shootout, the eleven dead police officers were all on Matiullah Qati's side. Qati and Abdul Khaliq, the CID chief, were among them. Qati had never drawn his Luger.

When John White received word of the shootout, he passed it on to Canada's representative in Kandahar, Elissa Golberg, who sent McAllister an e-mail. He opened it in his office in the Olympics Integrated Security Command Centre in Richmond, south of Vancouver, and began to weep.

Afterward, McAllister told me, "As a policeman you want to die a in a little more of a heroic fashion. For his own fucking corrupt people trying to get one of their own fucking nuts out of jail, to kill him—that was just too much! All the work we did went down the toilet."

Then six months later, on January 12, 2010, two of his Mountie CivPol colleagues, Chief Superintendent Doug Coates and Sgt. Mark Gallagher, were killed in the earthquake in Haiti. McAllister was turning fifty and facing a decision. He could spend another year as a Mountie working in peaceful British Columbia, then comfortably retire with a chestful of medals. Or, as soon as the Olympics were over, he could apply to the RCMP's International Peace Operations Branch for another tour in the heat, dust and war of Afghanistan. After such grave losses, it did not seem like a hard decision to make.

3

AN INTELLIGENCE TRAGEDY

SEVEN WEEKS AFTER THE MURDER of Matiullah Qati Kahn, a presidential election was held in Afghanistan. It was overseen by Afghanistan's Independent Elections Commission (IEC), a body staffed by seven supporters of President Hamid Karzai. Early results tabulated by the IEC suggested Karzai had been re-elected by a three-to-one margin over his main opponent, Abdullah Abdullah, who lodged a protest with the country's Electoral Complaints Commission (EEC), the majority of whose members were UN-appointed Westerners. The EEC, as well as Western and Afghan human rights groups, determined that the results were distorted by brazen ballot-stuffing, bribery and violent voter intimidation. Further investigation showed that much of the electoral fraud and intimidation had been orchestrated by warlords and other criminals who were running for provincial posts and wanted to ensure a Karzai win. The Western coalition pressured Karzai to change the makeup of the IEC and hold a second round of elections. Karzai agreed to the second round but refused to reconstitute the IEC. Abdullah Abdullah then announced that, with Karzai's cronies still packing the IEC, a transparent election was impossible. He refused to participate in the runoff, and the next day, November 2, 2009, Karzai was declared president for another five years.

The skewed election reinforced the view of journalists, scholars and diplomats that Afghanistan met the definition of a kleptocracy. The word derives from a Greek tribe named the Klephts that rebelled against the Ottoman Turks in the 1400s. Like many rebel groups that started out as freedom fighters—the Mafia in Italy, the Triads in China—the

Klephts robbed their oppressors to fund their rebellion and then devolved into clans of criminal syndicates, preying upon civilians in the areas they controlled. It was government literally run by thieves. Today, in the kleptocracies where CivPol serves, government thievery is so efficiently run that it resembles the businesslike mechanisms of organized crime.

Many of the CivPol cops I met in Afghanistan were experienced investigators of organized crime. They had arrived on mission aware that at its most fundamental level, organized crime is a licensing system. A gangster manoeuvres his way to the top and, to make sure he stays there, awards the right to engage in illegal activities in his territory to various subcontractors, expecting tribute in return and providing them protection from the law. CivPol cops observed this same mechanism at work in the Karzai government. It followed the quid pro quo of all politics—the rise to power is always accompanied by the return of favours—but with a kleptocratic twist. Wherever warlords, drug dealers and organized criminals help politicians achieve and maintain power, favours are returned in the currency of impunity. In the case of Afghanistan, government loyalists closest to Karzai were allowed to steal from the public treasury without restraint. They in turn cut similar deals with their supporters in the provinces, and so on down the line, until the circle of corruption embraced almost every hustling official in the country.

Afghanistan's official corruption followed another global pattern: the poorer the country, the more likely government theft will take place in the open, since constituents are powerless to do anything about it. A United Nations survey conducted the year of the election found that the average Afghan family, earning only $425 a year, had been forced to pay officials over a third of their income in bribes, adding up to an estimated $2.5 billion, or almost a quarter of the county's total economic output. Reporting this extortion to the police offered the public no relief. While the ANP did arrest small-time thieves and pickpockets, they left the licensed players alone—an omission for which the police themselves were rewarded with a licence to steal. Rather than

enforce the law and protect citizens, the police enforced crime and protected criminals. As Matiullah Qati and his ten murdered colleagues
had discovered, honest cops who attempted to defy this system often
died at the hands of police who worked within it.

After the fraudulent presidential election, the American-led coalition
finally recognized that a significant threat to their counter-insurgency
strategy was the public's perception that Afghanistan was more corrupt
under Karzai's democracy than it had been under the Taliban's theoc-
racy. The U.S. State Department therefore linked an increase in aid to
the establishment of an elite ANP task force that would investigate malfeasance at the topmost levels, where the example for the lower levels
was set. Karzai at first resisted, then realized the State Department
meant business and grudgingly agreed. The Major Crime Task Force
(MCTF) was launched and CivPol was enlisted to mentor the agents in
its most sensitive unit, the Intelligence Squad. Directing and analyzing
the agents' investigations, the chief of intelligence knew more about
what went on at the highest reaches of the Karzai government than
almost anyone in the country.

In the fall of 2010, the chief of intelligence was Colonel Yousef
Mohammad Ahmadzai, a man famous among CivPol officers for risking
death in order to bring justice to the kleptocrats closest to Karzai. Back
in 2007, heading a counter-narcotics investigation in Nimruz Province
on the Iranian border, Ahmadzai had organized a raid on a heroin store-
house that he believed was run by the Karzai-appointed governor. The
governor's brother—a senior ANP officer—arrived for the raid and shot
Ahmadzai as he was about to arrest the smuggler in charge of the load.
The smuggler fled, as did the governor's brother. Months later, after he
got out of hospital, Ahmadzai was awarded a medal for bravery in a
ceremony at the U.S. embassy. The ceremony also honoured him for the
seizure of over $4 billion worth of heroin that year. Ahmadzai refused
an award of $3,000—a year's salary—saying, "I am trying to rescue my
country, I don't want your money. Money is the cause of all our problems." When Coalition lobbying got Ahmadzai appointed as the MCTF's
intelligence chief, he publicly announced that his mission was to make

every corrupt official from Nimruz to Kabul "feel very worried I am still around to investigate your crimes."

To meet Colonel Ahmadzai I headed out to Camp Falcon, headquarters of the MCTF in Kabul, with Joe McAllister and Phil George, the OPP veteran who'd arrived with McAllister back in June 2010. We left the city via Airport Road, crossed through the last of the ANP's Ring of Steel checkpoints, and drove into the desert valley north of the airport. McAllister sat in the front of his armoured SUV beside his driver, and George sat in the back with me. He was mentoring the fifteen senior officers in the MCTF's intelligence section, spending much of his time with their boss, Colonel Ahmadzai. George was a slow-moving avuncular guy with a head of grey hair and a white walrus moustache. After thirty-seven years with the OPP he'd retired in January 2010, but within two weeks had seen an advertisement for a CivPol posting in Afghanistan and had applied under the organization's Retired Police Officer programme. At fifty-eight, he was getting close to the age limit for such duty but CivPol snapped him up, in part because of the reputation he had earned leading a high-profile investigation that broke up a criminal conspiracy between OPP officers, politicians and the Mafia boss Vito Rizzuto. "We've got it extraordinarily good in Canada," he told me as we drove between a derelict Russian military base and a cemetery with black flags flapping above the tombstones of martyred mujahedin. "I thought, before I hang her up I'd like to share some of what I've learned with the Afghans." His years as an investigator with the OPP's Professional Standards Bureau had convinced him that an elite corps of cops with unquestioned loyalty to the law could advance good government by ensuring honesty among officials. "I was really thrilled when they assigned me to the MCTF to work on that piece," he told me. "This place needs it. I told CivPol I'd like to stay for another tour when this one's up."

Just north of a U.S. military base called Camp Gibson, George leaned forward and pointed through the windshield. "We're turning left at the break up there," he told the driver, indicating a cross-armed gate that bridged a narrow gap in Camp Falcon's wall of towering blast barriers. Four Gurkha soldiers who manned the guard houses unshouldered their M-16s while two of their colleagues stepped forward with pole-mirrors to inspect the vehicle's underside. Because of the top-secret investigations that took place within its walls, Camp Falcon was off limits even to the general at Camp Gibson unless accompanied by a senior police mentor. To keep the base's investigations secure, all agents recruited to work within its walls, both foreign and Afghan, had to undergo regular polygraph tests. Their e-mails were monitored and their phone calls tapped. "If anyone crosses a line, we find out pretty quickly," George said. "As long as everyone knows that, we can do our jobs and feel relaxed." It didn't seem to matter to the grim-faced Gurkhas that George lived at Camp Falcon and that they'd seen him driving in and out for five months. After examining the car they made him show his ID, answer a few coded questions and then sign in. Only then did they break into smiles and wave us through to the parking lot.

As we crossed the gravel compound to the new MCTF building, George explained to me that Ahmadzai was at a crisis point in his long and dangerous career. Back in July his investigations had led to the arrest of the chief of administration for the National Security Council of Afghanistan, Mohammed Zia Salehi. The MCTF had wiretapped Salehi as he solicited a bribe to halt an investigation into a company that had allegedly sent $3 billion in undeclared money overseas on behalf of Afghan politicians, drug traffickers and the Taliban. As soon as Salehi saw his house surrounded by Afghan agents he phoned an ally in the National Directorate of Security, who had a direct pipeline to Karzai. After Salehi was carted off to jail, the president ordered his attorney general to release him and sent his presidential aides to take Salehi home. A couple of weeks later Karzai announced at a news conference that he was drafting rules to curtail the MCTF's operations, including limits on foreign funding for MCTF agents and the wiretapping of Afghan officials. Colonel Ahmadzai had immediately declared to Karzai's aides that he would oppose political restrictions on MCTF investigations.

Since then he had been on the receiving end of threats from what he termed "the Kabul mafia"—the politicians and businessmen who were closest to Karzai.

"The colonel's one of the bravest men I've ever met," George told me as he punched the codes on a hallway door in the MCTF building. "I've worked with him five months and have unalloyed respect for him. It's actually inspirational for me to be around him. I'm trying to get him to pass on his ethics, knowledge and skills to his underlings."

"Guys like him are few and far between," McAllister agreed.

The door's codebox light went from red to green and I followed the two cops into an open-plan squad room that held fifteen work stations for the intelligence crew. *"Salam aleykum! Haletan chetor hast?"* Ahmadzai shouted to George in Dari from behind his desk at the head of the room. "You have brought me your friends!" he added, through an interpreter. He shook McAllister's hand, then turned to me: "And greetings to you, my friend! I love journalists—they bravely investigate bad deeds!"

Ahmadzai, a big guy, was dressed all in black to match his dyed hair and a moustache as bushy as George's. CivPol cops called him "Tony Orlando," partly because of his resemblance to the singer but also because of what George called his "effervescence."

"Phil has been telling me about your own brave deeds," I said, shaking his logger's-size hand. "I'd like to talk with you about them."

"First tea, then business," he announced in English.

"Yeah, we never start business until tea," George said. "By the way, the colonel speaks several languages, including Russian, but he's just learning English. We'll be talking mostly through Balees."

The MCTF's interpreter was a lean and soft-spoken pediatrician in his late twenties who told me he'd taken this job to supplement the tiny salary he earned at the Indira Gandhi Children's Hospital. The entire hospital had a government operating budget of only $1,200 a month, and in some months he never got paid at all.

Ahmadzai took a call and I watched Dr. Balees pour hot water into a pot by the door, carefully set out cookies on a tray, and return to serve us. I mentioned to him that $18 billion in foreign aid had poured into his country since 2001. If a desperately needed pediatrician such as he had to moonlight as an interpreter to support his family, something was really wrong. Where had all that money gone? "Into people's pockets," he replied. "The work of Colonel Ahmadzai is to stop the thievery. As you say, it is a brave job for him to do." He poured Ahmadzai's tea, translating into Dari what he'd said to me.

"I have information about people who are trying to eliminate me, to kill me; always I'm assessing this information," Ahmadzai boomed at us. "The main problem is that all of the higher authorities have relationships with the criminals. When we arrest somebody, and present our evidence to the minister of interior, he says, 'You are going to get me fired, we should keep this matter secret and forget about it.' Every big criminal belongs to somebody in the government—it's the biggest problem we have here. We should have independence to arrest directly. But people we put in jail, like Mohammed Zia Salehi, Karzai releases. I am furious!"

"Karzai's people have been here twice to ask questions on how we [mentors] do business with these gentlemen," George said. "They've raised a lot of questions about the CivPol mission."

"The complaint from President Karzai," McAllister explained, "was that Salehi was not treated according to Afghan law, but was arrested because of foreign pressure. Karzai sent his people over here to make sure it was the Afghans who led the investigation and not the internationals who pushed it."

"Karzai is full of shit!" Ahmadzai shouted. "We arrested Mohammed Zia Salehi according to the constitution of Afghanistan, the law of Afghanistan, but the attorney general's office released him against the law of Afghanistan. Listen!" he said to me. "The mafia occupies Afghanistan. All of Afghanistan belongs to the mafia, from low officers up to President Karzai, all belong to the mafia. It's our good fortune we have Phil George to help with this situation. I told Karzai's flunkies, 'This Canadian helps me make right what's wrong. You want to make it wrong again, we will be watching you!'"

"Frankly, Colonel, in our country it's no different," McAllister said. "The bad guy always complains his rights are being violated and talks to a politician to see if he can get a favour. So we understand what you're up against."

"We have a saying," Ahmadzai declared. "'The water is dirty from the source.' From President Karzai, everything is bad. This is my advice. If we don't clean the source, we can't do anything. If the higher authorities are corrupt, it will affect all the government."

"How do you clean the government at the source?" I asked.

"We should put at the source those people who are honest, who don't have any nepotism, don't have any corruption, and are not partial to warlords and drug dealers! In my entire career I have not taken or given one Afghani! If you put honest people at the source, we won't have any problems! I need help bringing justice to the dirty ones!"

"We'll continue to work together so you can do your job," George reassured him. "Tiny steps will make a difference."

"I'm swearing on God!" Ahmadzai shouted, so loudly that every intelligence officer looked our way. "If I became president, I could solve all these problems in two days!"

Ahmadzai's cell phone rang, and he took the call. When he got off the phone, he shouted, "Mr. Terry! My younger son had an accident. He broke his leg yesterday. One fracture. He is okay but now I must take him to the doctor again." He turned to Balees. "Can you have a look at him also?" Balees told him that would be no problem. Ahmadzai looked back at me. "Can I meet with you on some other day?"

"Absolutely!" I said. "Whenever you're available."

I made an appointment to come back to interview Ahmadzai at length about his life. I told him I wanted to learn what had led him to his forceful convictions, and where he got the courage to stand up for those convictions in the face of mortal threats.

"I wouldn't refuse a reward of a year's salary if I got shot," I said to McAllister when I got back into the car. We'd left Phil George behind at his office in the fort.

"Yousef refused the reward because he thinks there's too much loose Western cash in Afghanistan," McAllister said. "I wouldn't doubt he lives by principles that probably exceed ours."

As we got into town McAllister pointed to a hundred carcasses hanging outside a block-long line of shops. "This is called Goat Street. They name the streets after what's for sale. Phil says there should be one called Politician Street."

McAllister's driver, Obai, cracked, "That street is by Karzai's palace."

"On the other hand," McAllister said, "you go shopping in village markets down south, they pick the change out of your palm so you pay exactly the right price. Our boots alone are worth more than their whole stall. They can ask for anything they want, but they don't."

"Because it is written," Obai said, as we approached the Gandamack. "We know how to behave from what is given from Allah to the Prophet. We read, we know."

He yanked the wheel to the right and we pulled up onto the sidewalk in front of the blank steel shutter that masked the entrance to the Gandamack Lodge. The hotel was a high-value target but unlike others favoured by Westerners, it had never been bombed. McAllister made a call and the shutter began clanking up. We drove into what security people call an "airlock," and the shutter descended behind us. We sat in the pitch dark until someone turned on an overhead bulb. A guard slid back a metal plate and had a look at us. Then the shutter ahead of us rose and we drove out into a mulberry garden with a gazebo in the middle. Beyond it, the ground-level hotel doors were fronted by a rustic patio.

The Gandamack was occupied almost exclusively by foreign journalists who reported on what was going on outside its walls. No one had yet written about Colonel Ahmadzai. There were just too many top officials vacuuming up astronomical amounts of money for them to notice the lone guy who was trying to stop them. I told McAllister I felt privileged to have met Ahmadzai.

"We all feel privileged," McAllister said. "See you tomorrow."

———

When I got to my room I searched an on-line concordance for the Koranic proscription against stealing. In a chapter called "The Dinner Table," the Prophet offers divine advice to his followers: "And as for the man who steals and the woman who steals, cut off their hands as a punishment for what they have earned, an exemplary punishment from Allah, who is Mighty and Wise."

I thought that if I had lived in an Islamic country where this law was strictly applied, I probably would not have made it into adulthood with both my hands. I had grown up in Brooklyn in the '50s and '60s, in an era when nobody thought twice about purchasing discount televisions that had fallen off the truck. When I went shopping for my first car, and I only had $600 scholarship money to spend, my dad told me, "Lemme call Johnny." (Everybody knew someone named Johnny.) Two days later I was driving a car with only 10,000 miles on the odometer. I suspected it had been stolen, but at eighteen, I didn't care. Later, when I drove a cab, I overcharged rubes left and right, taking the long way to the airport, following the example of all the other cabbies in my garage. At that time, most New Yorkers kept a five-dollar bill wrapped around their driver's licence. When cops pulled you over, they took the cash and let you go with a warning—or sometimes asked for more. All this despite the fact that I and my fellow Jews and Christians knew how to behave "from what was given"—in our case, from God to Moses. Don't steal. Don't lie. We read, we knew, we ignored.

I became honest when I left New York at twenty-one and started living among rural people who thought they would go to hell if they took something that didn't belong to them. There's some pretty rigorous research that explains why I went through my conversion to honesty. Our ethical fortitude depends on what we believe those around us are doing. Colonel Ahmadzai seemed all the more remarkable to me for living a life of death-defying honesty among totally corrupt officials who *expected* him to be corrupt.

In *The (Honest) Truth about Dishonesty*, Dan Ariely, a professor of behavioural economics at Duke University, describes a number of experiments he conducted with thirty thousand students at American universities that explained the psychology of corruption among ostensibly honest people. Ariely and his assistants distributed twenty simple math problems to groups of students and told them they would get one dollar for each correct answer. They were allotted five minutes to take the test, score their answers against a master sheet, then shred their answer sheets and report the number of their correct answers to the experiment monitor. What the subjects didn't know was that the shredder was disabled so that their answer sheets would remain intact. Ariely found that over half his subjects slightly exaggerated the number of their correct answers so that they received one or two dollars more than they knew they deserved.

Ariely then relates how he modified the experiment in several ways. In one modification, he had someone who was wearing a sweatshirt with the school logo stand up after only a couple of minutes and announce that he had answered all the questions correctly and then collect twenty dollars. The vast majority of students who went to the same school as the blatant cheater followed his lead, exaggerating the number of their correct answers to a far greater extent than had the subjects in the first experiment.

In another test modification, Ariely had the person overseeing the experiment receive a cell phone call from a pretend-friend in the middle of giving his instructions to his subjects. The overseer then rudely and selfishly ignored his subjects, talking on the phone as they awaited his instructions. After the overseer hung up he turned his attention back to the people in the room and completed his instructions, at which point the test began. The experiment's results showed that 86 percent of the test subjects collected almost twice the amount of money they knew they deserved.

In a third variation, the moderator had the students sign a statement before taking the test. For instance: "I understand that this experiment falls under the guidelines of the MIT/Yale honour code." None of these student subjects exaggerated the number of their correct answers.

Ariely concluded that the majority of people will behave a little corruptly if they think they can get away with it, but not so corruptly that it conflicts with their everyday notions of what society expects of them as basically honest people, and not corruptly at all if society expects them to be totally honest. But under two sets of circumstances, they'll behave in a far more corrupt fashion: if they actually witness people in their group cheating in a blatantly egregious way and getting away with it, or if they witness the authority figure who polices their behaviour behaving improperly.

Ariely believes that the social signals sent by other members of our own group and by society's authority figures are more important in governing our behaviour than our fear of getting caught. The majority of people believe that most people steal a little so it is all right for each individual to steal a little. They find it acceptable to steal more when others in their group steal more or when the authority figure who polices their behaviour demonstrates misconduct. But they will not steal at all if they are specifically told their moral souls are being tested. In the world at large, the solution to corrupt behaviour seems to require a clearly stated policy of zero tolerance and a reminder of expectations of honesty, announced and enforced by authority figures who follow the same rules they enforce.

In the nations that score worst on Transparency International's corruption index, citizens routinely witness the outrageous misconduct of the authority figures who police their behaviour, and they see people in their group behaving corruptly and getting away with it. In my own research in bribe-ridden nations, I found each country had an idiosyncratic metaphor for an acceptable level of corruption that had been in use for hundreds of years—one of the reasons the habit was so hard to break. In the Philippines, for instance, pre-colonial tribal chiefs attained their power based on a system known as *pasalubong-pabaon*—the giving of gifts in anticipation of receiving gifts. Today, aspiring Filipino politicians distribute wealth in order to gain power (*pasalubong*) and then accept even more wealth for slanting their exercise of power (*pabaon*). *Pasalubong-pabaon* eventually led to another saying that is used ubiquitously among the population: *Baka makalusot*, which essentially means, "Everybody does it, nobody gets caught, so I'll do it too." Across the Pacific in Colombia, the word *regalame* means "give it to me for nothing." *Regalame* once described the regal right of the conquistadors to take what they wanted from the indigenous peoples, and it evolved to signal a solicitation for a bribe. Today, if you want to ensure positive treatment from a Colombian bureaucrat, expect to hear *"regalame"* during negotiations. Across the Atlantic in Russia, the aristocracy once had the right to indenture tens of millions of serfs for life; the nobles' only responsibility was to supply their serfs with *krysha*—a roof. The communist revolution substituted party bosses for the aristocracy and *krysha* came to mean the purchase of protection from those who had the power to sell it. Today, gangsters routinely buy *krysha* from the police; students buy *krysha* from teachers; and safety inspectors sell *krysha* to airline companies, old age homes and nightclubs (accounting for why Russia has the worst accidental death rate in the world).

In Palestine, you advance your prospects less through merit than through *wasta*—who you know. In China, you get ahead through *guanxi*—who you know—and also through *cheng gui tua*, which is "the hidden rule" that governs under-the-table transactions. In both countries, favours are returned with favours, either in cash or in kind.

In Greece, the exchange of reciprocal favours is called *receti*. At the height of Greece's financial crisis in 2011, a CivPol cop I interviewed in Ottawa quipped that the word kleptocracy was "part Greek and part Greeks," meaning that since everyone in the country believed they were governed by thieves, citizens stole what they could, usually by paying a portion of their undeserved government bonuses to the officials who approved those bonuses. Wherever a population understands that they are oppressed by the ethic of "give it to me for nothing," they will try to get something for nothing themselves.

Across North Africa, the Middle East and South Asia, the euphemism for a payoff comes from the Farsi word for gift, *baksheesh*. In the 1600s, traders along the Silk Road in Persia received protection from marauders if they delivered *baksheesh* to the pashas who had influence over the marauders. The word travelled with the traders, eventually becoming synonymous with locally accepted norms of tribute. Today, from Casablanca to Calcutta, interactions with officials tend to begin or end with a negotiation over *baksheesh*—no more so than in Afghanistan, where officials boldly state fees for free government services up front, without any pretense of honesty.

The same year Ariely published *The (Honest) Truth about Dishonesty*, two economists published their own research on corruption and government, *Why Nations Fail*. Daron Acemoglu of MIT and James A. Robinson of Harvard concluded that the systemic corruption of a country's ruling classes, and the copycat behaviour of the population, is the handmaiden to nation failure. Nations face failure when they are "ruled by a narrow elite that have organized society for their own benefit at the expense of the vast mass of people." Nations prosper when they create societies where the government is "accountable and responsive to citizens, and where the great mass of people [can] take advantage of economic opportunities." The great difference between today's successful nations and failing nations, they say, is that successful nations at some point launched far-reaching democratic reforms "that transformed the politics and thus the economics of the nation. People fought for and won more political rights, and they used them to expand their economic opportunities. The result was a fundamentally different political and economic trajectory." Wherever people at the top play fair, and those who don't are prosecuted, the rest of society plays fair too.

I returned to the MCTF with Phil George a couple of days after my first visit. We walked up to the roof of the building so Yousef Ahmadzai could smoke as we talked. He said he was born in the Muslim year 1383, "also the thirty-first year of the reign of our beloved King Zahir Shah," he added, blowing smoke at the snowy Hindu Kush Mountains. "That's 1964 in your calendar."

Ahmadzai's father, Mohammad, was a non-religious academic who had been educated in Europe. He became a professor at the University of Kabul under the liberal King Zahir and wrote several scholarly books on quantum physics and mathematics. A member of the Kabul secular elite that King Zahir encouraged to run the country in the 1950s and '60s, he steered his children into the professions. Two of Yousef's brothers went into finance, his two sisters became university teachers and

Yousef, the youngest, entered a pre-med programme. Yousef said his father taught all his children a pattern of thinking geared to "solving mysteries." To a mathematician like Mohammad, the world was a quantifiable place and every problem could be "schematized" by assessing causation, deducing variables and then predicting outcomes according to the laws of probability. "Facts are holy," he taught Yousef, "and people who stick to facts are protected against dishonesty." While some believed the moral proscription against lying was given from God, Yousef's father believed it could be explained a different way. The mathematical facts were established at the beginning of time, and contradicting them violated those facts. With false facts that produced wrong answers, it was impossible to predict outcomes: systems did not work and there was chaos and suffering. That was why lying was immoral, not because God declared it immoral. "So Papa told me, whatever you do, remember this lesson from your father," Yousef Ahmadzai said. "Do not dishonour me by disregarding this lesson about facts and truth."

"You know what, I think that's where I got it too," George interjected. "My dad used to say to us: 'Whatever you're doing, wherever you're doing it, think that your father's standing there watching you.' It wasn't fear of my father that kept me honest. The worst thing for me was to bring dishonour on my father. I've only been offered a bribe twice in my life, and I just laughed it off. I think as a police officer you just send the right signals that you're not a player and they don't even attempt it."

I mentioned a Mountie liaison officer I had interviewed in Hong Kong in 1993 while he was investigating a Triad-run pay-for-visa scandal in the Canadian embassy. He told me that the difference between an honest cop and a corrupt cop was that the honest cop set his price so high nobody could afford it.

"I've heard that, too," George said. "But it's too simplistic." His experience investigating corruption led him to believe that sometimes a cop went dirty for reasons other than money. "He's pissed off about something, or he's taking revenge, or he's got psychological problems." George had heard of lots of cases of cops stealing drug money from an evidence locker. "For what? A few grand? You know they're going to count it and you'll probably get caught. Sometimes it doesn't make sense except to the guy who's doing it." In other words, the career-killing reason might seem irrational to everybody else, but it made emotional sense to the cop in the moment.

Ahmadzai smoked and listened to Dr. Balees summarize what we were saying. Then he laughed, and said, "Men with good fathers find it easy to be good. Men with bad fathers find it hard to be good. Am I correct or not?"

"I'll go along with that," George said.

"My father wanted me to be a physician, and at first I obeyed his ambition," Ahmadzai went on. "I was interested in diagnosing medical mysteries, too, but in my heart it was not exciting enough. A whole year memorizing anatomy and four years to go! My personal ambition was to be an analyst of mysteries that were the result of human actions." He quit medical school at twenty-one, joined the police and took the examination for the Criminal Investigation Department. "This was a disappointment to my family, but it was very thrilling for me. After my training and my year of probation I had my first big case—a horrible crime that showed the problems of our country."

He was a detective in Police District 10, in one of Kabul's outlying neighbourhoods. On patrol early one morning he inspected a derelict truck without licence plates. In the back was the decapitated torso of a young woman. He immediately suspected this was an honour killing. By then, the Soviets had been in Afghanistan seven years and, as part of their efforts to modernize the country, had ordered ANP officers to solve honour killings or be shipped to Kandahar to fight the mujahedin. To identify the girl, Ahmadzai had to find her head. Honour killings are generally perpetrated with the complicity of the entire family, although the mothers of the female victims are usually grief-stricken afterward and attempt to tend to the body. If the mother had known of this event, Ahmadzai reasoned, she would have taken the head for burial. He went to the closest cemetery and discovered the newly buried head in a plastic bag. He then rounded up some neighbours, one of whom identified the girl. Ahmadzai went to the girl's house and interrogated her mother, who told him her husband had arranged for his daughter to marry his cousin, but the girl had refused. The cousin was insulted, the father felt dishonoured and the family gave the cousin permission to kill the daughter. The cousin thought that by decapitating the girl he would get away with the murder. "He didn't think an Afghan policeman would take the crime seriously," Ahmadzai said. "But I take every crime seriously." He arrested the cousin, who was executed. For solving the case, the Ministry of Interior offered Ahmadzai 1,000 Afghanis, which he refused.

Three years later, in 1990, Ahmadzai led a raid on a gang-run heroin lab and seized a thousand kilograms of pure powder. Again, he was offered a reward, and again he refused. "Money is what all officials want—that is why they give it as reward," he said. "They think everyone wants money. I told them, you want to reward me, make me head of the Narcotics Bureau and I will get rid of this heroin poison in Kabul."

Like his father, Yousef was not a religious person. Neither was he a communist. But as a secular police official who had enforced the law under the communists and then under one or another faction of the mujahedin, he was considered a marked man when the Taliban won the civil war and assumed power in Kabul in 1996. Yousef Ahmadzai threw away his uniform and grew a beard. To earn a living he sold *shalwar kameez* in the street. "In one week, I went from the head of the Narcotics Bureau to a peddler who had to pretend he was a pious illiterate. Our whole country became a prison run by crazy people."

Five years later he followed the same post-Taliban path as Matiullah Qati Khan. When the ANP was reconstituted in 2003, Ahmadzai got his old job back as head of the Narcotics Bureau. He launched a four-year investigation of officials who facilitated the heroin trade to Iran from the poppy fields of Kandahar and Helmand provinces, which led him to the governor of Nimruz Province and then to his own boss in Kabul, the deputy interior minister for counter narcotics. "It turned out that the deputy minister was also involved in the smuggling. His name is General Mohammed Daud Daud."

Ahmadzai planned to raid the storage house of the head of the smuggling operation, seize the heroin and get the smuggler to turn and finger the governor and Daud Daud. The operation ended in the famous shooting incident that brought Ahmadzai to the attention of the American embassy. Despite the evidence Ahmadzai later presented to the ANP about the involvement of the Nimruz governor and Daud in the heroin trade, both remained in their positions. At the time we spoke on the MCTF roof, General Daud was still Ahmadzai's boss. (The Taliban assassinated Daud Daud on May 28, 2011.)

"You must be very frustrated in your job," I said. "It is very difficult for you to carry forward your investigations."

"It's frustrating because if I investigate somebody and he belongs to a mafia group and if it's a major case, they will kidnap all of my family. They can. They have the power from the top."

"They will kidnap his family and him too," Balees added.

"We have no security," Ahmadzai went on. "Just a guard with us, and that guard has sixteen bullets. The mafia are armed with RPGs! I will sacrifice my head, my body to the benefit of Afghanistan to bring the people safety from the narcotics gangs, from the corruption, from the traitors. I am going to sacrifice myself."

"It's worth dying for?" I asked.

"Yes! Because those people are trying to kill my people and addict them with their narcotics. We must sack their blades."

Sack their blades, Balees explained, was an Afghan expression that meant to disarm and neutralize opponents.

After our talk on the rooftop, Phil George and I went down to his quarters. He was packing up to leave for a week's holiday with his wife in Paris. I asked him for his assessment of his work so far at the MCTF. He said that Colonel Ahmadzai had taught him more than he had taught the colonel, and that he'd been very lucky when it came to the Afghans he'd put his trust in. "If I put any one of them in a room with millions of dollars, the cash would be sorted when I came back and there wouldn't be a dollar missing."

George left for his vacation and I left for Kandahar. A few weeks later, back in Canada, I received an e-mail from McAllister saying that

Ahmadzai had failed his regularly scheduled polygraph test and that an investigation was underway. "It looks like he may have taken a bribe recently and got caught on it," McAllister wrote. "Phil is absolutely devastated." I read the message three times, then wrote to Phil George. He waited until after the investigation into Ahmadzai's conduct had concluded before returning my e-mail, offering some doubly shocking information. "The day we spoke with him [on the roof] he got paid off to let a suspect go without charges." At the very moment Ahmadzai was explaining to us that he was willing to die to sack the blades of the drug trafficking mafia and the criminal politicians in league with them, he was planning to replicate their behaviour. "I'm a polygraph examiner and saw the results myself. I also know the rest of the [investigation]. I have no time for police officers that cross the line to the criminal element."

Dazed by the betrayal, George began work with a hastily appointed acting commander—work that was interrupted by a friendly call from Ahmadzai, who, in his primitive English, told him that he was okay and still wanted Phil's friendship and respect. George replied that he didn't want to speak with Ahmadzai again.

In the end, Ahmadzai was not charged by the Afghan government, merely reassigned to another bureau in Kabul. This did not surprise George: charging Ahmadzai would have also required charging the corrupt official who had bribed him. "Here I have to try to understand the culture," he wrote me. "I have my doubts that we can change it or they want to change. I have always been aware that my Canadian way tends to make me try to think the best of everyone until they prove me wrong. I have always thought that to lose that perspective would make me too cynical to be a police officer. I am very disappointed in Colonel Yousef. I liked the guy. I shall always remember the good times I had dealing with him, but I now carry a battle callous on my trust instinct."

Over the next several weeks I tried to understand why Ahmadzai had betrayed not only the Task Force but his father and everything he himself had sworn he believed in. Until the day he accepted the bribe he'd had a spotless record and an unshakable code of ethics, demonstrated publicly and at great risk time and again for twenty-five years. He'd been checked out and polygraphed dozens of times at MCTF. When he accepted the bribe he was fully aware that he was scheduled to take a polygraph, and that if he failed it, a citywide investigation by the sharpest cops in the world would ensue. He knew he would be found out if he conducted any untoward business. But that is exactly what he did.

I eventually heard several theories as to why Ahmadzai had betrayed the unit. The bribe he accepted was laughably small—less than the amount he had turned down as a reward from the Americans in 2007. This led the Western officers at MCTF to believe Ahmadzai had committed what they dubbed "law enforcement suicide": some things were going on that had caused him to lose his way.

Among them was the Salehi affair. Ahmadzai's outrage over the immunity given Salehi by Karzai had come to dominate his discussions not only with CivPol but with the FBI, the Australians and the French gendarmerie also serving as MCTF mentors. After a quarter century fighting corruption, Salehi appeared to be the last straw for Ahmadzai. Karzai had stymied Ahmadzai's case, which alleged that the president's chief of administration for the National Security Council was in league with drug traffickers, the Taliban and a whole coterie of corrupt politicians around the president. If Ahmadzai had been allowed to pursue the charges, he could have taken them all down. Instead, his work on the case had sparked threats to his life and to his family. If you follow Dan Ariely's logic, at some point Ahmadzai may have decided to join the people he had been trying to nail—with the curious twist that he had known he would get caught.

After pondering all this I wrote Phil George that Ahmadzai's betrayal didn't detract from his own idealistic mentoring. It just emphasized the heart-breaking difficulty of working with local officers who were surrounded by societal norms that repeatedly emphasized that honesty was an aberration punishable by death.

A few weeks later, George wrote back saying his mood had lifted.

"The new interim commander is doing well. He is eager to learn and make positive changes." But before he left Kabul in March, Phil George informed CivPol that he had changed his mind about re-upping for another tour. He did not want to return to Afghanistan.

4

WOMEN FOR WOMEN AND MEN

IN SEPTEMBER 2010, in the push to triple the ranks of the ANP, General Jonathan Vance, the Canadian commander of Joint Task Force Kandahar, helicoptered into Panjwai to welcome the first class to attend a new police-training compound. Before the ceremonies began, Vance and his entourage of American and Afghan generals gathered with the local ANP commander, Colonel Karimi, in the District Centre beside the compound. They took seats around a boardroom table, with Vance at one end and Karimi at the other. As tea was being served, an RCMP corporal in brown fatigues slipped into the room and quietly sat in a chair against the wall behind Karimi. Candice McMackin's junior rank kept her from a seat at the table, but her role as Karimi's CivPol mentor gained her access to the boardroom. She was a tall, lanky Manitoban of thirty-seven, with rosy cheeks, bright blue eyes and blond boy-cut hair—quite a contrast to her student Karimi, who was a foot shorter, built like a fireplug and, with his balding pate, grey beard and craggy features, appeared old enough to be her grandfather.

The officers went around the table introducing themselves in order of rank until it was Karimi's turn. "Before I speak about myself I would like to introduce someone the commanders in this room should especially honour," Karimi said in Pashto. He paused for his language assistant to interpret his words for the Westerners, then leaned around and dramatically extended his hand to McMackin, who sat bolt upright in surprise. The looks on the faces of the Afghan generals seemed to say, *The girl?*

"Here I have this police officer, this *female*," Karimi pronounced, with all the force and flourish he used to motivate cops on the parade ground. "She has chosen to leave her home and life in Canada to come to Afghanistan to make our policemen better people!" Placing his hand on his heart, Karimi described how McMackin taught investigation courses that he himself benefited from and that would form his curriculum for years to come. "At checkpoints, she teaches us the proper way to question suspects and gather information. In villages, she arranges meetings with elders so they disclose insurgent activity. Just last week a helicopter was shot down in front of her. It was she who led my men to defend their position until all were rescued by a Quick Response Force from Masum Ghar."

For his peroration, Karimi swivelled in his chair and faced his young teacher. "On behalf of myself and the Afghan National Police, we thank you, Candice McMackin, for teaching us to be a professional force!"

As the translation concluded, Vance and the other Western generals darted astonished glances at one another, aware something profound had taken place before their eyes. It was a rare thing for a Pashtun officer to publicly thank a noncom in front of his superiors. It was unheard of for a veteran colonel to admit to a group of generals that a female eight ranks his junior and decades younger had taught him how to do his job.

Two months later, when McMackin was about to be transferred to Camp Nathan Smith to teach Criminal Investigation, she and Karimi posed for a picture. There are thousands of photos of Canadian police posing with Afghan cops, but there is probably only one where a female corporal has her arm casually draped around the shoulders of an ANP commander.

Karimi was the third Afghan colonel that McMackin had mentored in her seven months in Afghanistan. At CNS, she began mentoring her fourth—the one who would be taking over teaching Criminal Investigation at the Training Centre when the Canadians left Kandahar.

"Every society creates certain expectations about what women and men can and should do or say or how they can or should act," reads the opening sentence to a section in the CivPol training manual on women's rights. "As Peace Operations personnel, it is your job to promote high standards of equality between men and women." Those standards, the manual continues, are set forth in the United Nations Universal Declaration of Human Rights and in international treaties signed by the countries that accept CivPol's aid. Women have equal rights to education and to freedom of movement; they are entitled to marry whom they want and possess equal rights within marriage and in divorce proceedings; and they have the right to be protected against domestic and sexual violence through the strict enforcement of local, national and international laws.

In Kandahar, every one of those rights was routinely violated by men who believed that female subservience to patriarchal rule was normal, natural and dictated by Islamic law. Kandahari women were expected to submit to corporal punishment; stay within the confines of the family compound; remain illiterate unless given permission to attend school; agree to being married off to old men when they were as young as ten; and acquiesce to *baad*—the ancient practice of offering female relatives as payment to resolve disputes between families. While sexual assault was a crime punishable by death in Islamic law, the Sharia courts in Kandahar that prosecuted rape cases usually found that the victim had provoked her assailant by behaving immodestly. Married rape victims were often jailed for adultery and single women were sometimes forced to marry their rapists—that is, if the victim wasn't murdered first by a relative who believed she had dishonoured the family.

Before she was assassinated in 2008, Malalai Kakar, the head of Kandahar's Crimes Against Women Department, had attempted to sidestep Sharia courts by using a secular Afghan law against assault to arrest wife-beaters, rapists and honour-killers, forcing them to defend themselves in civilian court. After her assassination, President Karzai eventually bowed to international pressure and issued a 2009 decree that categorized violence against women as a crime in Afghanistan's penal code, carrying a sixteen-year prison sentence. Other provisions of the decree guaranteed women the right to pursue an education, set sixteen as the legal age for marriage and gave a woman the right to leave her home without the permission of her husband. When Karzai submitted his decree to Parliament for approval, however, a majority of MPs refused to ratify it because, they stated, it violated Islamic law by nullifying the rights of husbands and fathers to "protect" their wives and daughters. A powerful mullah declared that "one of the most violent acts against a woman" was to allow her to sing or dance on television.

There were some in the U.S. military who felt that pressure from the West to break these deeply ingrained patterns of patriarchal domination would alienate tribal chiefs, religious leaders and other power brokers needed to fight the Taliban. In its training manual, CivPol phrased its opposition to this logic: "The comment is often heard that 'We are not here to change the culture.' That may be true, but a Peace Operation, by its very presence, contributes to cultural change. Culture is always in a state of change. It is not static. Conflict accelerates changes in culture. As Peace Operations personnel, your job is to uphold what is fair and just, supporting those changes which are bringing more equality between men and women."

To accomplish this cultural mission in Kandahar, CivPol mentors were ordered "to make sure that human rights principles are incorporated into the core training of the new police service, and are understood and applied by all police." Lawyers from Kandahar's Human Rights Organization were brought into Camp Nathan Smith's Police Training Centre to teach those principles; CivPol actively lobbied the ANP and the Afghan Ministry of Interior to hire more female cops to fill the classes being set up for women at CNS; and, beginning in 2010, CivPol for the first time posted its female officers outside the wire to train street cops and their commanders, offering a global lesson both to Kandahar's residents and to police that women were the equal of men in society and in law enforcement.

Candice McMackin had been working as watch-commander of the busy Thompson detachment in northern Manitoba when the International Peace Operations Branch phoned her in the fall of 2009 and informed her that her mission application had been accepted. Before she'd joined the Mounties at age twenty-two, McMackin had spent two years in the Canadian infantry and was confident she would feel right at home teaching cops amidst the gunfire and military hardware of Kandahar. She'd first begun applying for a mission in 2005 and had kept her name on the waiting list despite the facts that her husband's brother, Scott Cullen, a soldier based in Panjwai, had been badly wounded in a 2006 suicide bombing that had killed four of his colleagues, and that in August 2009, a CivPol Mountie named Brian Kelly had almost lost his legs in a bombing that had killed or wounded a hundred civilians.

"A mission was the last big thing I wanted to do before having children," she told me at CNS. "I'd talked to my brother-in-law, and he told me how desperately the Afghan police needed training so they could stand on their own. I really wanted to be a part of that, to teach what I'd learned to police who could possibly improve the future for their country." She had heard the stories about the attitudes of Afghan males toward women, but from the age of three her dad, Phillip, a Mountie corporal, had advised her how to get along in traditional male territory, whether it was playing baseball and hockey with boys in school, serving in the infantry in 1993 when there were very few female combat soldiers, or policing some of the roughest postings in Manitoba. "I was very close to my dad growing up, and I still am. He taught me if you just go up to people, shake their hands, introduce yourself and joke around with them a little bit, they'll become comfortable and forget the gender thing. If you give respect, you get respect back. Being respectful and showing you'd like to do a good job is just the right way to get along with people, whether you're male or female. It's what community policing is all about, and it's what teaching community policing is all about."

McMackin flew to Ottawa on January 9, 2010, and two days later began classes at the parklike campus of the Canadian Police College. Her roto of seventeen officers included two other junior-ranked females. One was "Sandy," an undercover constable with the Ottawa City Police (because of her work infiltrating organized crime, her real name cannot be used); the other was an RCMP corporal named Karen Holowaychuk, a police science instructor at Depot in Regina.

Holowaychuk, raised on a farm in Stoney Lake, Alberta, had been a high school English teacher in Saskatoon before she'd joined the Mounties at age twenty-five. Unlike McMackin and Sandy, she had spent her thirteen years as a policewoman in relatively quiet postings— six years patrolling rural Musquodoboit Harbour in Nova Scotia, three at the Toronto Airport, and her last five at Depot. Her sergeant at the airport had been Joe McAllister, who had just returned from his posting in Kosovo and who proselytized the good CivPol was doing around the world to every cop working for him. McAllister left for another mission in East Timor a year later, and Holowaychuk began considering a mission as an option for herself. She was teaching in Depot when McAllister began his 2007 tour in Kandahar and started sending e-mail updates to all his colleagues. Turning her mind to the possibility of an Afghan mission, she read *The Kite Runner, Descent into Chaos, Three Cups of Tea* and *A Thousand Splendid Suns*. "What stood out in my mind was the horrible treatment of women in Afghanistan," she told me. "I'd seen abuse in Canada and I felt, here's an area where I would like to be of some help. So I applied for a mission, and in the fall of 2009 I got released from Depot for a year."

On February 4 the roto mustered in the basement of the Department of Defence building to get "kitted out" for a combat zone. Their equipment included a tourniquet that allowed a badly wounded cop to tie off a mangled limb with one hand, and, for the females, a Freelax—an eight-inch shoe-horn–shaped device that enables a woman to pee while standing up. ("When you're walking down roads with IEDs, you can't go squatting in a ditch," one of the women told me. "That piece of plastic is almost as important as your body armour.")

The next day the roto travelled to Fort Irwin in the Mojave Desert for two weeks of scenario-based training with the military, then flew back to Ontario for another month of training at the Connaught Range in Ottawa, and finally, on March 24, commanded by Supt. Vic Park, flew off to Kandahar.

After two weeks of "in-clearance" training at CNS, McMackin, Holowaychuk, Sandy and fourteen CivPol males were deployed to Forward Operating Base Walton, named in honour of Joe McAllister's dead friend Jim Walton. Located in the desert twenty kilometres from CNS, FOB Walton was a primitive fort of Hesco barriers, watchtowers and small plywood huts that served as barracks. The women were shown to a shack whose walls were lined with wobbly metal bunk beds. Above Holowaychuk's bunk was a picture of a blown-up Humvee with the caption: "If it doesn't kill you, drive on."

The pin-up was an example of the gallows humour of the MPs in the U.S. 97th Battalion, who trained the ANP in even more primitive police substations that oversaw districts where Coalition vehicles were getting blown up all the time. Until the arrival of the CivPol officers, the ANP in those substations had received no training by civilian police. The women's assignment was to embed in separate substations and mentor local cops and their commanders as they patrolled their districts.

McMackin, the ex-soldier, hit it off with her district commander, Colonel Lali Momma, and began mentoring him and his men in the compound and on dismounted patrols. Sandy, accustomed to relating to gruff men in criminal gangs, had a similar fraternal experience at her police substation. Holowaychuk, however, never connected with her commander, nor with his officers or the U.S. MPs who accompanied them on patrol. She was a small, slightly built woman with a high voice that she self-consciously suspected made her look and sound out of place in a combat zone. After a week of walking IED-blasted roads, she became more and more depressed at how little civilian police training she was offering. From her point of view, the MPs were mainly training the ANP to set up fighting positions that could withstand frontal assault, and not how to police communities. "I was just a tag-along," she told me. "The Americans were nearing the end of their mission, they were tired, so there wasn't enough energy and time to do the work that I would have liked to have done. They were so close to going home, they'd taken so many casualties and they just wanted to stay alive."

Each evening she returned to face the shack she shared with the exhausted men. A small air conditioner kept the temperature at night just below thirty degrees, which did not help Holowaychuk's mood. She often wept in her bunk, overwhelmed by loneliness, fear and a sense that she was accomplishing nothing to justify her presence in Kandahar. She had signed up for a CivPol mission because of her three passions in life: policing, teaching policing and wanting to help women. She wrote an e-mail to Vic Park explaining that she was engaged in military training, not police training.

At the end of her first two weeks, Park rolled in from CNS. He asked Holowaychuk if she would like to accompany a Montreal city policewoman named Annie Lacroix to Kabul for a fortnight to observe a contingent of Norwegian policewomen as they taught security awareness to a class of female ANPs. Lacroix had been teaching female ANPs at CNS, and would be rotating home in July. Park wanted Holowaychuk to monitor the Kabul class and perhaps incorporate it into a full-curriculum course she could develop and then teach at CNS and in Kandahar Police Headquarters. Holowaychuk leapt at the chance.

Two days later, she walked into a classroom in Kabul's Police Headquarters. Until then the only Afghan women she'd seen had been shrouded in burkas as they walked silently behind men who put them out of reach of conversation with foreigners. In this classroom, all the women had slipped off their coverings. The first thing Holowaychuk noticed was how garrulous they were. Bursting with pride at being policewomen, they constantly expressed affection for one another and were among the most eager students Holowaychuk had ever met. *This is what I'm here for!* she thought. *This is what I'm meant to do! Teach policewomen!*

Holowaychuk returned to her posting in the middle of May and spent her evenings after patrols e-mailing back and forth with Lacroix, drawing up a curriculum for women. When she met Afghan CivPol Commander Dave Critchley upon his arrival at CNS in the middle of June, she was filled with optimism about the future of her deployment.

Two weeks later, when McMackin transferred from FOB Walton to Panjwai, Holowaychuk moved to CNS and began teaching ANP females full time. At the beginning of November, McMackin joined her at CNS, assigned to mentor the colonel who would take over teaching Criminal Investigation at the Training Centre.

McMackin and Holowaychuk were in the last two weeks of their deployment when I flew to Kandahar. For eight and a half months they had endured what some male Mounties had not been able to bear for two days. On the roto that had arrived in September, two middle-aged RCMP from the Prairies had been traumatized by the initial shock of the war. They had landed at Kandahar Airfield in the middle of a Taliban rocket attack and were ordered straight to the shelters. After another day of watching medevac helicopters landing with dead and wounded soldiers, the two cops had refused to join their colleagues aboard the chopper to CNS and had asked to be sent home. Critchley, their boss in Kabul, told me he didn't judge them: when he'd first arrived in June he too had experienced the panicky feeling that he'd made a big mistake.

However much they were trained for a deployment, Critchley said, a lot of CivPol cops had to hang on day to day and sometimes minute to minute until they accepted that for the next nine months they'd be in the middle of a war ten thousand miles from their families. Most of them were two to three times the age of the soldiers around them and had lost the elasticity that allowed twenty-year-olds to put up with just about anything. Even if, like McMackin, they'd been in the military as youngsters, he said, CivPol cops had spent their entire adult careers as *peace* officers. At home they possessed the non-negotiable use of force, but they used it rarely and only to enforce the law when criminals violated it. A CivPol mission in Kandahar, by contrast, meant training the ANP surrounded by thousands of Taliban who were determined to kill police. "The change I've seen in some of them in the six months I've been here bothers me," Critchley told me. "They're not the same people. I don't know how they're going to process the war in their heads when they go home."

Just getting to Camp Nathan Smith from Kandahar Airfield gave me a taste of what the CivPol cops had to process. There was heavy fighting west of the city when I landed, and the Blackhawk shuttle I was scheduled to fly on got diverted to take part in the battle. I spent the next several sleepless nights in one of the thousands of sandy Quonset tents across the road from the runway. The roar of military vehicles, helicopters, jets, transports and drones was constant, deafening and maddening. On my third morning at the airfield, sitting in a concrete shelter as the sirens wailed, I built a psychic wall an inch from my nose and pretended nothing could penetrate it.

Late that afternoon I was put aboard a big Chinook that was on a ninety-minute supply run that circumnavigated the surrounding districts on its way to CNS, giving me an overview of the forward operating bases where the women had served. We swept low over the barren flats and mountains, with three machine-gunners strapped to the fuselage so they could hang out the open hatches searching for Taliban who might be looking up the barrel of an RPG. To keep the enemy from getting an accurate bead, the Canadian pilot flew like a cowboy, banking the Chinook all the way to the left, then to the right, lifting the nose sharply as we climbed up over a peak, then plunging it down as we descended the other side. Every now and then we corkscrewed down to drop cargo, troops and cops into bleak compounds surrounded by Hesco barriers and guard towers. With each approach a front machine gunner held up a whiteboard on which he'd written "Walton" or "Arghandab," "Zhari" or "Panjwai." I had to reflect that the women had routinely flown on these stomach-churning flights, not to mention walking daily patrols along the IED-laden roads I was flying over in relative safety.

Opposite me, a beefy middle-aged bicycle cop with the Toronto Police gave me a thumbs-up as the Chinook pounded down in the Dand District Centre, which sat astride the main Taliban infiltration route into Kandahar City from the north. Back in Milton, Ontario, Sgt. Steve Moore lived on four verdant acres with his wife and two sons, aged eleven and fourteen, and did some hobby farming on his days off. Here, carrying a C-7 rifle, wearing forty pounds of body armour, a helmet, ballistic glasses, fire-retardant gloves and a Glock strapped to his thigh, he looked indistinguishable from the battle-ready young soldiers who followed him out the hatch. He'd arrived in September with the two Mounties who hadn't been able to endure the war, and was now kitted up to mentor the ANP in Dand's warren of streets. Eleven months earlier the Canadian journalist Michelle Lang and four soldiers had been killed in those streets when their armoured vehicle had struck a roadside bomb, about the same time that the Taliban had blown up the Dand District Centre. Canada had since rebuilt the centre, and CivPol considered it imperative that the ANP keep itself connected to the community through frequent patrols. As McMackin had done, Moore trained the local ANP commander and his men in community policing and intelligence gathering.

Before we'd put in our earplugs and entered the chopper, I'd heard a concussive boom in the mountains and asked Moore if he'd had any close calls. "I guess just being here's a close call," he said, laughing. "But it's risk versus value, eh? The value is the ANP really need our help and we're giving it to them. It breaks your heart how dedicated some of these young kids are. How many Canadians would join the police if last year twelve hundred cops had been killed for doing their jobs? And not just killed," he added, running his finger across his throat.

No policing job was more dangerous in Kandahar than the one done by the two dozen female ANP in the province. Each day they showed up in small groups for Karen Holowaychuk's classes at CNS, and over the next couple of weeks I learned some of their stories. On my second day there, I watched a military patrol bring them in an ambush-protected vehicle to the fort's front gate. They got out of the M-RAP, head scarves and dark cloaks blowing behind them in the desert wind, then threaded single-file through the maze of parked armoured vehicles, keeping their bearings by the minaret that towered above CivPol's fenced-in Training Centre. They turned the corner onto the wide road that fronted the compound, stepping onto ground that was gravelled over with fist-sized stones. Walking became difficult for the junior-ranked women in their thin street shoes, and the two senior women, their combat boots visible under their shawls, took their hands. They moved forward in a line beside the wire-topped fence, supporting each other.

The eldest among them was named Magulla, a seven-year veteran cop in her mid-thirties. She was born a few years before the Soviets rolled into Kandahar and attended school during the Russian occupation. At thirteen, with the Taliban in control, she'd been married off to a man in his fifties and had borne fifteen children, two of whom had died of disease by the age of three. In 2003, when her husband became too old to work, she followed in the footsteps of Malalai Kakar and joined the ANP. Magulla proved a crack shot during training, scoring the highest marks among her class of men and women at the old Kandahar police academy. As soon as she graduated, Malalai invited her to enlist in the Crimes Against Women Department. After Malalai was assassinated in 2008, Magulla began receiving night letters announcing that she too was on the death list. This past summer, her best friend and fellow squad member, Shoa Gul Bari, was shot dead in her home by the Taliban, leaving Shoa's seven children to be raised by their elderly father. Thinking of her own children, Magulla transferred to Police Headquarters.

Just behind Magulla in seniority and age was Ziagula, who'd also been married to a man triple her age when she was an adolescent. When her husband could no longer work, she and her eldest son had taken jobs in a textile factory, each earning only a few dollars a day. Two years ago they'd quit the factory and joined the ANP. Her son was now a literacy instructor in PHQ, where she worked mornings in the records department before going on patrol in the afternoons.

The other three women were named Murican, Gulsherin and Gulab, all in their late twenties. Murican had been with the force for a year. Her husband was in his seventies and she supported him and her eight children. Gulsherin had been with the force five months and her husband was also past working age. Gulab's husband had disappeared years ago, leaving her to raise three children on her own. She had joined the ANP only four months earlier.

Holowaychuk was waiting to greet the five policewomen at the door of the Training Centre. "Good morning, ladies," she said, leading her students down the fluorescent-lit corridor of the portable school and into a classroom. "How is everybody doing today?"

As they all took seats around a table, Gulab, looking anxious, said that something terrible had just happened to her. "I was on patrol. Suddenly I was surrounded by Taliban. They cursed and beat me. They took my baton, my duty belt, my holster and gun—I lost all my stuff. They told me if they caught me again they'd shoot me in the head."

All the women began speaking at once.

"We were telling her we don't wear our uniforms when we patrol alone," said Magulla.

"In our packs we keep a burka," said Ziagula. "When we know there are Taliban in the area, we put the burka on. Then we can do surveillance without them knowing."

"That's the way," Holowaychuk said.

"When I hear there are Taliban, I hide," said Murican.

"I'm still very nervous because of the incident," said Gulab. "But it doesn't matter. I am alive and can continue my work."

The women slipped out of their cloaks and loosened their scarves. Only four wore uniforms. "Gulsherin, do you still not have a uniform?" asked Holowaychuk.

"No. At PHQ they say 'tomorrow.' Every day they say 'tomorrow.' They do not take my request seriously."

"I will speak to PHQ logistics and get you a uniform," Holowaychuk said emphatically. "I'll fight for that, so we can get uniforms and boots for all of you lady officers. Anything else going on at PHQ?"

"Everything's good," said Magulla. "We are doing our jobs and that is all that matters." Like the other women, Magulla's hands were hennaed front and back, the burnt umber colour set off by golden rings on most of her fingers. She slipped one off, took Holowaychuk's right hand and put the ring on her middle finger. "Thank you for teaching us," she said.

Holowaychuk looked at the ring and her eyes brimmed with tears.

Magulla had buried her two best friends in two years and it rarely left Holowaychuk's mind that Magulla herself—or any of these women—might be killed between classes. "Thank you for serving your country," she said to Magulla, who leaned forward and wiped Holowaychuk's cheek. Holowaychuk steadied her emotions and then began the class. "Today we're going to talk about ethics and values."

"These are two very important concepts," the senior Magulla said to her colleagues.

Holowaychuk's method of teaching was collaborative. Rather than lecture, she asked a question, listened to the answers through her translator, then asked the students what they thought of their colleagues' opinions, encouraging discussion. Her intent was to simultaneously foster independent thinking and group decision-making. She knew that long after CivPol and she were gone, her students would have to apply universal policing principles in their own way and within a culture that had norms very different from hers.

She offered her first question of the training session: "What do you think the people of Afghanistan expect from women police?"

"First, greater security," Magulla said. "All Afghan citizens expect the police to bring security."

Holowaychuk looked at Murican. "Without security somebody can steal their things or harm them," Murican said.

"Then people will not trust the government to protect them," Ziagula offered. "They will seek protection from others outside the government."

"Is there anything else people expect from you when you interact with them in the community?" Holowaychuk asked Gulab.

"Certainly, to be a good and honest person," Gulab said, then looked to her supervisor, Magulla.

"Police should have good relationships with citizens and solve their problems with respectful attitudes so the gap between citizens and police will be closed," pronounced Magulla. "If police work with citizens in a respectful manner, they will be more eager to talk with us and give us information about the activities of bad people. And wherever police use force against bad people it should be done according to legal procedure. Our emotions should not be involved. At all times, we are respectful."

"Even toward the Taliban?" Holowaychuk asked.

"We were discussing how difficult that is," Gulsherin said. "When we have Taliban in our custody we treat them very good, but when the Taliban catch police, they treat us very badly." To illustrate her point, she put her hennaed hands behind her back. "They tie us like this. We found ANP like that. They shot them in the head."

"Some, they cut their throats," Ziagula said. "It is a terrible way to die. Because the body wants to breathe but the air cannot get in. The mind stays alive. The mind watches the body trying to breathe for a very long time. My son is very afraid for me. I am very afraid for him."

The language assistant looked at me. "Is it clear from my translation what she is telling you?" he asked.

"Yes, it's clear," I said.

"Some ANP, when they catch a Taliban who has just killed some of their colleagues, they do not think it is their job to show respect," Ziagula said to Holowaychuk. "If the Taliban is wounded, they do not give medical care."

"But we give medical care," Magulla said. "Even though they are trying to do terrorism. Because they will see, the police have good hearts. They will think, 'They have hearts that are better than mine. So perhaps their heart is right and mine is wrong.'"

"Here are my feelings," Holowaychuk said. "As police officers, we always have to do what's right. We can only know we are doing right by following the laws we've been given. As professionals we act according to the law, not what we feel at the moment. We may not like someone, but we must treat them with respect and fairness when dealing with them. Does anyone here have a different opinion about what I just expressed?"

"The insurgents who abused me," Gulab replied, "they told me, 'The people who teach you at CNS, they are foreigners. They will leave you. They do not care about you. They work for foreigners and their minds are foreign. What they teach is for their foreign country, not for Afghanistan.'"

"It's true I'm a foreigner," Holowaychuk replied, "but it's also true I work for you. We are not the same, but as police officers we are similar. I uphold the law in my country and I am here to share with you ways of upholding the law that you might find work here. When people ask you who you work for, what do you tell them?"

"We work for the country, Afghanistan," Magulla said, "according to the laws of Afghanistan."

"Not for one person in the country," Gulsherin added. "For all the people of Afghanistan."

"There is an important point I would like to say to that," Ziagula declared. "In Afghanistan, most rich people get special consideration, because they pay bribes to police."

"And you have all seen this happen?" Holowaychuk asked.

The five women talked among themselves. "Yes, we all have," Magulla said. "Poor people do not get treated the same as rich people."

"Well, it happens in my country, too," Holowaychuk said.

"We have to be sure we show it's wrong to take bribes," Murican said.

"Yes, but we have to remember that it's impossible for us to control what the high-ranking officers do," Magulla said. "All we can do is control what we do and what the lower-ranking officers do. I cannot go to the chief of police and report my superior for corruption."

"What would happen if you did that?" I asked.

The interpreter translated the question into Pashto. Magulla looked at me, then looked back at the interpreter. *"Na,"* she said.

"She doesn't want to answer," the interpreter said, "which is your answer."

The women were in the middle of discussing their next class—learning how to assemble and disassemble an AK-47—when Candice McMackin stuck her head in the door and waved at me. Earlier that morning she'd asked me if I'd like to volunteer to be the victim in a scenario-based training session for her Criminal Investigation course. "You're a new face, so it'll be more realistic for them," she'd said. The class was to be held in a wood frame building outside the portable schoolhouse. The students were to be taught tag-team style by McMackin, a CivPol colleague and Colonel Rahim, Kandahar's chief of the Criminal Investigation Department, who had served under Chief Matiullah Qati Khan and CID chief Abdul Khaliq until both were murdered. "This is the third course I've run with Colonel Rahim since I got here," McMackin told me as she led me outside. "The idea is train-the-trainers. Repetition is the big thing. Rahim's taught the course with us so many times that hopefully he can instruct it himself after Canada leaves. We want him not only to have a grip on teaching Afghans but to be able to identify others who are potential teachers of the courses too."

When she finished this explanation she took a bite of chewing tobacco, a habit she'd picked up working with the U.S. MPs in FOB Walton. It had helped distract her from the tension and unbearable heat on patrols, but it was one of the accommodations to the war zone that Critchley had told me worried him, since in his entire life he'd never seen a woman chew tobacco, not even among the sociopathic gang molls he'd dealt with, much less a straight-arrow Mountie like McMackin. I'd suggested to McMackin that instead of chomping carcinogenic Red Man she should try one of mine. I gave her a 4 mg Nicorette—about two cigarettes' worth of nicotine. "Bite it in half," I'd warned. She'd chomped it whole, waiting for it to hit. "It's just gum," she'd said after a minute, feeling nothing.

In the parade yard McMackin introduced me to CNS's senior translator, who was leaning on two aluminum canes. Because of the threats to his life living outside the base, the cops at the Training Centre had given him the code name Junior. He was a cosmopolitan-looking twenty-five-year-old, dressed in a black sports jacket over his white silk *shalwar kameez*. He was something of a legend on the base. A one-time ANP officer, he'd quit the force in 2003 because of its ubiquitous corruption and hired on with the American military as a translator, then moved over to the Canadians when they took over CNS in the fall of 2005. On May 24, 2006, while he was travelling with Canadian Forces in

Panjwai, a rocket-propelled grenade fired by the Taliban blasted away both of Junior's legs below his knees. A medic named Cpl. Andrew Eykelenboom applied six tourniquets under heavy fire and saved Junior's life. Ten weeks later, Eykelenboom was killed in a suicide car bombing near the Pakistan border. When Junior got out of the hospital, he was moved to Camp Nathan Smith and entered a rehabilitation pro-gramme. By the time he met Joe McAllister in November 2007, he'd been fitted with plastic legs and was out of his wheelchair. He'd been CivPol's chief language assistant ever since.

With Junior translating, McMackin introduced me to Colonel Rahim, a stout and snowy-bearded gent in his sixties. McMackin then began taking Rahim through the morning's lesson. She talked to him straight, looking directly at him, not at Junior. "Terry's going to play a drug dealer who your men find on the couch taped up and strangled," she said. "They enter the scene and get instructed on the proper inves-tigative procedure that you yourself practice. Officer safety. Preservation of scene. Don't disturb the evidence. Who are the potential witnesses and what are the questions to ask those witnesses."

Rahim, who had fought in four wars and seen hundreds of dead bod-ies, hadn't lost his sense of humor. "Thank you for being killed," he said to me. "My men will solve your case. You can rest in peace."

When McMackin left to set things up in the scenario building, Rahim invited me to share a chai at the picnic tables where two dozen trainees were seated. About half of them were rumple-haired and wear-ing man-jammies and sandals. They looked as if they'd just rolled out of their bunks, and were sharing a brunch of Frito-Lays, sweetcakes and cigarettes. The others wore ill-fitting blue uniforms but at least they had new combat boots. They all had grim expressions on their faces but as soon as Rahim introduced me they cracked wide smiles. They were from towns all over central Kandahar, and after the two-week course they would be returning to their jobs manning the province's most blasted checkpoints and police substations. Given the rate police were being killed, there was a good chance at least a few of them would not live through the next fighting season. "Canadians very good," a uniformed officer with a maple leaf pin on his pocket said to me in English, giving me a thumbs-up. "We like to have them for teachers. Candice McMackin is very brave to come to Kandahar to teach us."

"She is *exceptionally* brave," Rahim told his students. "A fighter and a warrior, like Malalai. She stands and fights the Taliban."

"She thinks you and your men are very brave, too," I said.

"We are defending our country!" one of them announced, and at that the grim expressions returned to all of their faces.

In the classroom, McMackin had overturned chairs and tables, tossed an ice chest on its side and littered the floor with water bottles and crumpled up cigarette packs. As she set me up on the couch as a bound and strangled drug dealer she explained how important these scenarios were to her teaching, partly to break the old habits of the officers who had policing experience. "We have to repeat these things like ten times before they learn new habits—if they ever do," she said. "Hopefully they shouldn't be trying to take anything off you. You don't want any tampering with forensic evidence, right? But that's North American policing. In Afghanistan they do things differently with their evidence—they do things differently with just about everything."

She said her experience in substations and Panjwai had been that no matter how often she had reinforced a lesson, the ANP had always reverted to their habitual ways of policing. For instance, she had taught them to stand well back from a car at a checkpoint, ask the driver to step out, make sure they could see his hands, and then order the driver to open the trunk himself. They would practise the scenario repeatedly, tell her they understood the lesson, and then the first car they stopped at a real checkpoint they would immediately open the doors, pop the trunk and stick their head inside examining its contents. "I found they were very reckless in really dangerous situations," she said. "They grew up with this kind of threat around them all the time. I don't think danger is a big deal to them. They always seem to want to just get the search done and go on to the next."

"Like they haven't seen guys die doing it that way?" I asked.

"Oh, they have! They have! That's why we're trying to get them to change."

She left me alone on the couch and went out to organize the class's entrance to the building. It took more time than I expected, and I began to feel claustrophobic. I'd anticipated I wouldn't be able to take notes, so before entering the room I'd started a tape recorder in my pocket. I occupied myself by describing the room. "Above me there's a white-board," I said aloud. "Written on it are the words, 'What happened?'" More minutes ticked by. "This is good practice if God forbid I ever get kidnapped," I said to my recorder. "I'm waiting for the Afghans to come for me." But the rope around my neck felt real and I frightened the wits out of myself. I turned to thinking about riding my bicycle in Vancouver. "Breathe normally," I said.

Finally, Colonel Rahim led his men into the room, accompanied by McMackin and a Mountie on her roto named Lorant Hegedus, a tall constable with a military brushcut whose last posting before Afghanistan had been in the beachside town of Parksville, B.C.— Canada's Fort Lauderdale. "Okay," Hegedus said, "so we enter and see the victim. Now, when you come onto a crime scene like this and see the victim strangled like that, the first thing you wanna check is safety risks for the officer. Then you wanna see if he's still alive by putting a finger on his neck, feeling for a pulse, but what you *don't* want to do is touch any evidence."

Rahim then did exactly what Hegedus had told his students not to do. He went straight to me, unwound the rope around my neck and began stripping the tape off of my wrists as he felt my neck for a pulse.

"Um, what's good to do is leave those items like they are and take photographs of them first," Hegedus advised politely. "Then use gloves. Because there could be the bad guy's fingerprints on the inside of the tape where the criminal pulled it. But if, um, you unwind it barehanded, then your—then the investigator's prints are going to contaminate the crime scene."

"What other evidence can be found on the tape?" Rahim asked his men.

"Hair!" a cop said.

"Yes, hair will stay on the tape and we can examine it to see if it matches the suspect." Rahim instructed.

"Anything else?" McMackin asked, aware that most hair on the tape would belong to the victim, not to the suspect. Rahim looked at his trainees and his trainees looked at each other and then back at Rahim.

"Remember what I mentioned about tape in class?" McMackin prompted.

Rahim studied the balled up tape on the floor and scratched his beard. McMackin finally broke the silence by lifting the intact roll of tape from beside the couch. "You can forensically match the tear on the tape to the roll used," she said. "If you have a suspect and he kept the roll on him, then you have evidence that could connect him to the crime."

"We came in with a large amount of people with the colonel," Hegedus said. "Once you see that the scene is secure, how many people would you keep in here now?"

"Keep all to search for evidence," one said.

"Remember our lesson?" Hegedus prompted again.

Mumbled answers were offered by the officers. Rahim contemplated them with a pleasant smile.

"This is kind of a big thing," Hegedus said. "Once you know that the scene is secure, you try to get everyone out so other people have room to work."

"Now I like what this officer is doing here," McMackin said, trying a bit of positive reinforcement by pointing out a young cop who was assiduously taking notes. "You need to have someone as your documenter for your report writing: date and time of entry; what they found; the scene as described. This would be your initial report that you would use to do a follow-up report. So someone needs to be documenting everything on the scene as it unfolds. It's very important that everything gets documented."

The lesson went on for another fifteen minutes, touching on identification of the victim, searching out potential witnesses, moving the body by means of a blanket, not by officers carrying it—all of it dancing delicately around what had happened at the lesson's start. Rahim, Kandahar's chief of the Criminal Investigation Department, had violated the everyday procedures that McMackin had taught and assumed that he practised.

"I know! I know!" she said to me outside the scenario room later. "This class graduates in only a week! That's why we have to keep refreshing them on stuff like that, because they just fall back into their old routine. I don't know if it's a cultural thing or something they've been doing for so long that they're just going to go back to what they were doing before. To tell you the truth, I just have to hope they eventually learn. It's all we can do here, is hope they learn."

Midway through their Criminal Investigation course, McMackin's students sat through a full day's seminar called Human Rights and the Rule of Law. The course was taught by a lawyer named Zaman Raofi, the head of the Canadian-funded Kandahar Human Rights Organization. Every Wednesday morning Raofi left his office south of the Governor's Palace and made the dangerous four-kilometre drive to CNS to teach the course. Though he was marked for death by the Taliban, he was determined to carry forward the three goals of his organization: training the province's police in human rights law; eliminating violence against women; and disseminating free legal aid to Kandahar's population.

Raofi was in his young forties, spoke four languages (Dari, Pashto, English and Urdu), held several university degrees, including one in business management, and could have easily joined the government gravy train or gone into some lucrative business in his hometown of Kabul. Instead, he'd chosen to live in the most dangerous city in his country, supporting his wife and two children on a few hundred dollars a month and driving the streets in a rattletrap Corolla. He passionately believed life could be improved here if only a system of honest justice were put in place that held everyone accountable to the law and upheld individual rights. "We face a lot of problems in Kandahar, particularly with the police," he told me before the class. "They abuse the rights of the accused person. They don't know the proper procedure for questioning a suspect. Also, they think a husband has the right to beat his wife or daughter and do not lay charges when we file complaints. They are uneducated in all these things because no one has taught them different. I am emphatic this be taught! This is the biggest need in Kandahar."

Raofi made an impression on the students when he strode into the classroom. In contrast to their baggy ANP uniforms or *shalwar kameez*, he wore sharp Western dress—black loafers, khaki pants and a brown bomber jacket over his grey vest and khaki shirt. He also towered over the young cops milling about the room. He was six-foot-three, with coal-black wavy hair, intense blue eyes, and rugged features that bore a startling resemblance to those of Amitabh Bachchan, Bollywood's most famous film star, which everyone in the room immediately noticed and commented on.

Raofi casually dropped his teaching folder on the front desk and, sitting side-saddle on the desk like a Western college teacher, asked each student to state his education—information he'd told me would help him gauge his teaching of concepts that were culturally foreign to Kandahar. "Teaching adults is different than teaching children," he'd explained. "I must reach each one at his level of education." Quite a task in this classroom, since the educational attainment of the ANP before him ranged from grade seven to a high school certificate.

Raofi announced that he would be dividing the day into three components. The first was the lawful way to arrest, treat and interrogate prisoners. The second was criminal procedure, including the roles played by police investigators, prosecutors, defence attorneys and judges in criminal trials. And the third involved how to investigate sexual and domestic assault, as well as human rights abuses committed by government officials.

He wrote the words "reasonable grounds" in Dari on the blackboard and asked if anybody knew what they meant. While he waited for an answer, a cop beside me took my pen from my pocket and pointed to himself, asking, I at first assumed, if he could borrow it. Then he said,

"Gift for me," turned his back on me and began writing in his notebook.

"Say goodbye to pen," said the interpreter I'd hired to sit through the morning's lesson with me.

"'Reasonable grounds' is the first concept of human rights between police and civilians," Raofi explained, after no one had answered. "It means you cannot arrest someone unless there is a reason that you can explain. The person has the right to be free. His freedom cannot be taken away unless there is reason you think he has broken the law. What is a reason you could give to a judge?"

Various replies erupted from the class. "Taliban!" "Criminal!" "Thief!"

"That is who he *may* be, but you must have a reason for thinking that before you make an arrest. You must be able to explain, 'I arrested that man because I saw him steal a motorcycle.' 'I arrested that man because his friend told me he threatened him with a knife.' A reason is an explanation for your arrest that you can tell to the authorities, so they can say, 'I accept that reason as lawful.' You cannot just *think* a man should be arrested. You must be able to explain your reason for thinking it." Raofi then asked the class to write down a number of reasons that might give them justification for arresting someone.

"He is a good teacher," my translator said. "He is trying to show them they can't just throw in jail someone they hate or their boss hates or that the politician hates. There must be a law they have broken because without law we have nothing."

After about half an hour of the students reciting what they thought might be reasonable grounds for an arrest, Raofi turned to the subject of questioning detained suspects in the police station. "Is it permitted to slap a prisoner if he will not talk to you?" he asked.

"Not so hard that you hurt him badly," said one of the cops.

"You are not allowed to make him bleed," said another. "But he is not allowed to threaten you with violence from his Taliban friends. If he does so, you are permitted to teach him a lesson."

"Who told you that?" Raofi asked.

"My commanding officer in Maiwand. It is very dangerous in Maiwand and we cannot be threatened or we will be afraid. So we must stop these threats."

"Let me explain something," Raofi said. "If you give a prisoner food and talk nicely with him, he will probably talk to you about something that has nothing to do with the crime you arrested him for. Slowly, slowly, as you talk with him friendly, you can move to the subject of why you arrested him and he might explain what he did. It is against the law to slap a prisoner. You can be arrested yourself for doing so. Also, those methods don't work if you are trying to get information. It is better for a policeman to stay within the law because it works better for getting information."

"It is the criminals and Taliban who break the laws of Afghanistan," said the cop who had taken my pen. "The police do not break the laws of Afghanistan."

A half hour later my translator left to do his official job in Holowaychuk's class next door. I sat through the next hour without understanding a word until, mercifully, Raofi announced a forty-five-minute break for lunch. I sat down with him to share a meal of bananas and flat bread. He said he had nine lawyers working under him at the Human Rights Organization. He and his colleagues were responsible for human rights education in twenty of Afghanistan's thirty-four provinces, but Kandahar was his biggest challenge. "The big problem is that they are so un*educated!*" he said, with a brooding expression on his handsome face that made him seem personally burdened by the province's endless tragedies. "They don't know what is good for them from what is not good for them! They cannot compare the things that are good for them with the things that are bad for them because they don't know!"

I asked if there was less corruption among the ANP than in previous years.

"I cannot say it is better for all the ANP because in every district in Afghanistan there is huge corruption," he said. "But in the police here it is better than it used to be, because now at least the new ones are being trained by Canadians. They are good trainers. For example, the last six-month class: when we saw the police before the training and when we saw them after the training, we witnessed a lot of change in them on the street. We wish they should continue these programmes in the future."

"You know the Canadians are leaving here and moving to Kabul in July," I said.

His eyes widened. "This is for sure?" he asked. "They will transfer the trainers to Kabul? They will leave Kandahar permanently?"

"Yes, that's the policy of the government," I said. I explained that a week earlier Canada had announced it would be bringing its Kandahar combat soldiers home, leaving a few hundred military trainers to operate from a safer base in Kabul. Since the soldiers protected CivPol, the police trainers would be based out of Kabul, too. "They didn't tell you that?"

"No, no," he said. "I didn't get any information. In July! So after seven months they will be gone. That is so sad." He looked at the gravelled ground and folded his hands in his lap. "They will leave us to continue on our own."

"The Americans will still be here," I said. "They're taking over the base."

"But they are different. They don't teach with efficiency. Oh, I did not know this." He rubbed his long face with his palm. "Maybe what you will write will persuade your government to send back their trainers?"

"I doubt it, Raofi." I told him Joe McAllister in Kabul and Vic Park down here wanted to keep the police trainers in Kandahar, but they'd been overruled. I stood up and shook Raofi's hand. "I will write with honour and respect about your work. I think you're a brave person who's making a difference."

"Well, thank you for coming to Kandahar," he said, then shrugged and headed back to his class, a tall man now stooped with the knowl-edge that he would soon be abandoned. At the door to the portable he turned to me, his hand scribbling in air words I should write in my notebook. "Please say we are educating them. Please say we are hopeful."

———

Many of the CivPol cops at CNS were in a frazzled and emotional state in the last days of their tour. They'd lived through a lot and they showed it. As I went from cop to cop to get their assessments of their mission, one of them slammed a door in my face. A couple of days before flying home, Contingent Commander Vic Park walked over to the Training Centre barracks to talk with the students in McMackin's class. He came away with tears in his eyes. "Just given the attrition rate and the stories they were telling me, I knew the percentage of how many of them could be killed over the coming year," he told me later in his office. He showed me a picture of a young ANP whom McMackin had trained in Panjwai. "Look at the way he's turned out in his uniform, he's impeccable. And look at his index finger, it's not on the trigger, it's outside, like it should be. That's amazing. That kid was blown up two days after I took that picture. A suicide bomber drove up to the checkpoint where he was working."

Park believed, however, that the young man had not died in vain. Public trust in the ANP now stood at 53 percent, the highest it had ever been, according to a survey conducted by the Canadian military, which had hired Afghan civilians to interview people throughout the province. "The public said the police looked more professional, they treated people better than they ever had, they were more approachable, and they were improving all the time," he said. "But there's a price." Park's face was deeply creased from exhaustion, and it became more creased as he considered that price. "Community policing also happens to be the most dangerous kind of policing." He paused, then added, "My team was willing to die on the cross to train them, but our government's made its decision to move to Kabul and there's nothing we can do about it." He leaned back in his chair, inhaled and exhaled deeply as he gazed at the roster board that showed the work to be done by his team's replacements between now and July. "After we push everyone up north, the ANP will still be here. What these kids are facing . . ." His voice trailed off and his gaze returned to the photo of the dead officer. "At the end here, I'm thinking about that all the time."

Karen Holowaychuk also spoke emotionally about the end of her mission, but for a different reason than she'd shown in her class. She was concerned about something that CivPol had never trained its officers to deal with in a war zone. The tensions, she said, had been building between some CivPol members in CNS. For so long they had handled the war procedurally, showing exemplary behaviour while working together as they instructed their students on the street. But as they'd been pulled in from the field to work in the tight quarters at CNS, some of them had begun flying off the handle at one another, in the same way parents or spouses will take out their frustrations on those closest to them. They were all decent people, and the incidents Holowaychuk witnessed had deeply upset her. "Being a police officer, you come into this with the skills to work with people you may not get along with," she told me in a trailer beside CivPol headquarters. "There's a job to do and you put your personal feelings aside and you get the job done. It requires focus." She paused, and then the tears came. "The goal isn't to freaking pound the shit out of each other. I mean there's been times where there's been conflict where guys have almost gone at it. For what?" she said. "For what?"

She seemed overwhelmed by this final impression of her mission, so I asked, "Do you have any kind of way of dealing with what you're feeling?"

"No, I don't," she said. "I don't."

It was an unanticipated aspect of the mission she would have to work through at home, as would those who had fought with their own.

December 9 was graduation day for McMackin's Criminal Investigation course.

"Good morning everyone," Vic Park said to the class from the front of the room. At their desks, the thirty students in their man-jammies and uniforms called "*Salam.*" It was a cool morning in southern Afghanistan and Park wore his gun in a shoulder holster outside a blue Mountie jacket. To Park's right was Junior, shifting his weight from one prosthetic leg to the other. Behind Junior, leaning against a lectern, was McMackin. Beside McMackin was Colonel Rahim.

"As CivPol's contingent commander here at Kandahar," Park said, "I want to congratulate each and every one of you for putting a lot of time and effort into practising the skills that you have learned over the last two weeks. We really appreciate that you came here so that you can assist and help out other people on the job and to make things better for the Afghan National Police."

The cops at their tables called their replies, summed up by Junior: "Thank you, sir. Thank you for commanding. Thank you for the school."

Rahim stepped forward. "Officers," he began, "it is a grave time for our country. Criminals and insurgents attack our province and do much harm to our people. You have joined the ANP to stop them and protect the people. No one can ask more from you than to be policemen in this dangerous time. The skills you have learned here from our friends the Canadians will help make our people more secure by stopping those evil-doers who do great harm against the law. We have the law, and as policemen our duty is to enforce the law so that the people can live their lives in some secure fashion. The law is written. You have learned it here and how to investigate those who violate it. I know you will do a good job. Long live the Islamic Republic of Afghanistan!"

"Long live the Islamic Republic of Afghanistan!" the students shouted back. Rahim then turned, and with a bow of deference, extended his hand to McMackin at the lectern.

McMackin congratulated her class, recapped the areas they had covered during their sessions, and thanked them all for sharing their stories with her. "I found that a very moving experience for me." She paused a moment, swallowed, and brushed the fingers of each hand below her eyes. She cleared her throat. "I learned a lot from you—" She cleared her throat again. "I want to thank you for giving me experiences that I will take back to Canada with me."

The officers called out their replies in English. "Thank you, Candice McMackin!" "We enjoy your course!" "We learn so much!" "We will follow the techniques you teach!"

"Today is actually my last day in Afghanistan," McMackin said, then looked down at her lectern. She took a deep breath and looked up.

"After a nine-month mission, it's been a pleasure that I have had the opportunity to end my tour on such a positive note. . . . I will take back many lifelong memories from this course and my tour." She again looked down at her lectern. She seemed to be trying to add something to her remarks, but emotion overcame her. She turned to Rahim.

Rahim moved to the front of the room and stood at attention. "Officers!" he shouted. "Rise!"

As one, the ANP stood to attention and shouted "Yaw!" Rahim turned smartly right and saluted McMackin.

One by one, McMackin called the names of the officers standing behind their desks. British-style, each cop high-stepped a march to the front of the room. They stamped their feet in place and saluted McMackin, palm outward. She handed each of them a framed certificate, their mugshot in the middle flanked by the arrowhead logo of Task Force Kandahar and the mosque-and-minaret Seal of Afghanistan. Each of the cops turned to the class, held the diploma high up above his head and shouted, "Long live the Islamic Republic of Afghanistan!"

When the ceremony was concluded, some of the students proudly insisted I take a picture of them holding their certificates. In the late afternoon I watched them climb into the open backs of ANP pickups and head out the front gate, back to their embattled stations and substations. I still have the collection of those photos, and I've often looked at them as the death toll of Afghan cops has risen, from 1,400 in 2011 to 2,200 in 2012. So many police were killed in 2013 and the first quarter of 2014 that the Afghan government fell behind in its record keeping, and, at this writing, has not announced the casualty figures for the period. The Ministry of Interior does not publish the names of the dead, and I can only guess at how many of McMackin's students have survived the almost four years since their hopeful day of graduation.

Joe McAllister receiving a medal from RCMP Commissioner William Elliott at Camp Nathan Smith.

McAllister surveys defensive positions in Panjwai with a team of Afghan National Police, including the police chief who was later murdered by his own men, Matiullah Qati Khan. Qati is on the right side of the table at the far end.

A lonely Afghan National Police checkpoint.

Colonel Yousef Ahmadzai, then chief of the ANP's Intelligence Unit, Major Crime Task Force, and OPP Inspector Phil George. Ahmadzai, a gifted police officer, was later transferred for allegedly accepting a bribe.

McAllister in full battle gear.

Corporal Candice McMackin teaching gunnery.

The Kandahar substation where McMackin was posted.

McMackin with her student, an ANP commander, Colonel Karimi. There are thousands of photos of Canadian police posing with Afghan cops, but there is probably only one where a female corporal has her arm casually draped around the shoulders of an ANP commander.

McMackin with her students.

RCMP Corporal Karen Holowaychuk asks her class of five Afghan policewomen, "What do you think the people of Afghanistan expect from women police?"

Holowaychuk and RCMP Superintendent Vic Park, CivPol's Kandahar contingent commander.

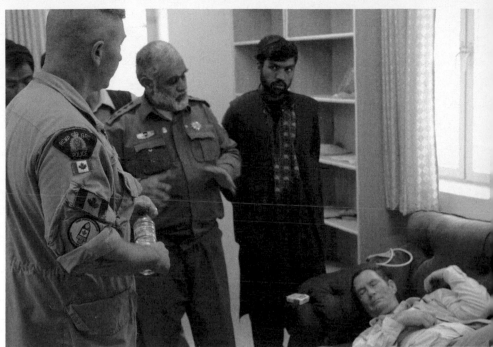

The author plays a murder victim for McMackin's class on best practices in criminal investigation.

The author with ANP officers in training at Camp Nathan Smith.

Kandahar City.

PART TWO

PALESTINE

Borders without Borders

5

HA-MATZAV
המצב

EVERY MORNING CIVPOL OFFICERS Serge Robitaille and John Copeland awoke in their East Jerusalem apartment and beheld the first ground God created on earth. Called Mount Moriah in the Bible, its limestone peak was now sheltered by the golden Dome of the Rock, which straddled the border between the Muslim and Jewish quarters of the Old City. The six-hectare plateau surrounding the Dome, captured by Israel along with the rest of the West Bank in the 1967 war, was the cosmic centre of what Israelis called *ha-matzav*—"the situation"—the unsolvable conflict between themselves and Palestinians. From Moriah's sacred stone God had fashioned Adam, upon it Abraham had offered his son for sacrifice, atop it ancient Jews had built their twice-destroyed temple, off it Mohammad had launched himself to heaven, and above its summit Muslims had raised the coruscating dome that since the seventh century has been a beacon to Islam.

After Mecca and Medina, the entire plateau was Islam's third-holiest site, but it was Judaism's first—there was no second. All day and every day, throngs of Israelis gathered below the plateau to press their faces against the foundation of their vanished temple, weeping over the millions of Jews slaughtered in exile since the Romans expelled their tribe two thousand years ago. It was a measure of how high the stakes were in the neighbourhood that God's Last Judgment was prophesied to occur from Mount Moriah after an apocalyptic war. Both sides wanted the mount within the boundaries of their national capital in Jerusalem. Neither side would yield sovereignty over it as part of a two-state solution. The Palestinian Authority (PA) had made its non-negotiable demand absolutely clear by placing an image of the Dome of the Rock at the apex of the seal of the Palestinian Civil Police (PCP), whose officers Robitaille and Copeland trained every day in the West Bank.

First thing in the morning, on March 17, 2011, Robitaille and Copeland set out on their daily commute to Ramallah, the administrative centre of the West Bank, fifteen kilometres north of the Old City. Copeland, a fifty-three-year-old inspector with the Ottawa City Police, drove the five-ton armoured SUV, while Robitaille, a forty-one-year-old Mountie staff sergeant, sat beside him tapping out drafts of a training curriculum he and Copeland were developing with the Palestinian police. Had Robitaille and Copeland had their way, they would have lived in Ramallah but they, like all foreign officials working in the West Bank, were overseen by Israel's Coordinator of Government Activities in the Territories. COGAT had determined that the threat of an uprising was high and that a nighttime evacuation from Ramallah would be too dangerous to pull off. It was safer, COGAT ordered, for Copeland and Robitaille to sleep in Jerusalem.

All along Route 60 the Canadians' view of the West Bank was blocked by the grey concrete wall Israel had built to halt the infiltration of suicide bombers during the Second Intifada, the Palestinian revolt that had erupted after the failure of the 2000 Camp David Summit. The intifada had been suspended by the inauguration of the 2003 "Road Map to Peace," whose markers included the training of the Palestinian Civil Police, which led to CivPol's first mission to Palestine in 2008. In Road Map theory, if the Palestinian Authority could demonstrate its ability to prevent attacks on Israel from Area "A" (the one-fifth of the West Bank the PCP patrolled on their own), Israel would consider withdrawing its occupation troops from Areas "B" and "C" (the other four-fifths, split between shared patrols and sole Israeli control). Road Map negotiations between the PA and Israel collapsed in 2010 over the expansion of Israeli settlements in all three areas, but the PA had appealed to Canada to continue its mission, declaring that, whatever the parameters of a final peace deal, a professionalized Palestinian civil police force would be critical to the territory's evolution into an independent state.

To help that process along, Copeland, a forensics expert, was design-
ing a $40-million forensics school and laboratory in Ramallah, and
Robitaille, a former police science instructor at Mountie Depot, was
supervising a multi-million-dollar Canadian effort to help rebuild the
Palestine College for Police Sciences in Jericho. The original college,
and almost all other PCP facilities on the West Bank, had been bombed
to rubble by Israel in retaliation for the participation of the PCP in the
Second Intifada. For the six months they had been on mission,
Robitaille and Copeland had lived with the possibility that the facilities they were developing would be among the first Israel targeted if a
third intifada exploded and the PCP joined the struggle.

Just after the exit from Route 60 toward Tel Aviv the Canadians
came to a break in the wall that marked the crossing from the cypress-
lined suburbs of northern Jerusalem to the ramshackle streets of southern Ramallah. Even during lulls in the conflict, Qalandiya Checkpoint
was a high-security zone of gun towers and razor wire manned by soldiers dressed for battle, but on the Ramallah side this morning security
was even tighter than usual. Hundreds of Palestinians were crammed
into a fenced-in pedestrian chute and thousands more sat in a line of
idling vehicles that stretched for three kilometres back to Ramallah's
al-Manarah Square. Most of the Palestinians were waiting to show
their permits in order to travel to their construction jobs in Israel or
their olive groves alienated by the wall where it dog-legged into the
West Bank to encompass Israeli settlements. Even elderly farmers who
made this crossing every day were forced to submit to hands-up pat-
downs, their exhausted eyes rolling skyward at their fate.

The increased stricture at Qalandiya was a response to two events
making international headlines. A week earlier, Palestinian militants
had infiltrated the West Bank Israeli settlement of Itamar, near Nablus,
murdering a couple and their three children, decapitating the youngest
child in her crib. Four days later, March 15, the two-month-old Arab
Spring had bloomed in Ramallah, with thousands of demonstrators
filling al-Manarah Square, shouting their own version of the "dignity
chant" heard in Tunisia, Egypt, Libya and, most recently, Syria: "Raise

your head high—you are Palestinian!" Posters strung across the square's surrounding buildings listed the three main demands of the demonstrators: an end to the schism between the West Bank's PA and the militant group Hamas, which controlled Gaza; free elections that would democratize President Mahmoud Abbas's rule-by-decree government; and a more forceful stand by the PA against the Israeli occupation. When several dozen teenage demonstrators broke from the square and headed south for Qalandiya, they were intercepted by a phalanx of Palestinian Civil Police firing tear gas canisters and swinging truncheons. The PCP had been ordered by President Abbas to keep the demonstrators from giving the Israelis an excuse to close the border or, worse, reoccupy Ramallah to restore order. The rock throwers who made it through the PCP lines only succeeded in choking on Israeli tear gas and increasing the wait time for those trying to cross.

As usual, the traffic jam headed into Israel this morning contrasted with the smooth flow of vehicles going the other way, since the Israeli soldiers didn't care who entered the West Bank, as long as they had a hard time getting back out. Locals were waved through with barely a glance from the single soldier in her booth, and Robitaille and Copeland proceeded through the canopied plaza at ten kilometres an hour.

Ten minutes later they were climbing a steep hill to a low-slung sandstone office building at the crest of Tokyo Road. Beside a high-security double door was a tiny blue plaque that read, in white letters, EUPOL COPPS, with the "O" in the word COPPS formed by the European Union's signature circle of twelve yellow stars. Throughout the world, CivPol served under various overseeing bodies. In Afghanistan it was NATO. In Haiti it was the United Nations. In Palestine it was the European Union. EUPOL COPPS was the euphonious acronym for the European Union Police Co-ordinating Office for Palestinian Police Support. Its headquarters was purposely designed to be inconspicuous in the neighbourhood, but also purposely situated for strategic vistas. From their desks, officers from nineteen countries had unobstructed views of the hilly white city of forty thousand around them and, to the east, the highest hill in Ramallah, Jabbal Tawil, atop which sat the square-kilometre Israeli settlement of P'sagot, blocking Ramallah's expansion into the West Bank. The red-tile-roofed settlement watched over Ramallah like a Mediterranean-style condo development that served double duty as a fort.

Just past one, Robitaille and Copeland left their desks to meet me at my hotel in the suburban valley between EUPOL COPPS and the P'sagot settlement. I'd arrived in Ramallah with two questions uppermost on my mind. How did they mentor a police force of a partly formed state that was occupied by a hostile power? How did they deal with two peoples whose arguments for ownership of the same land rested on stories that, like warring armies, attempted to outflank one another as they marched forever backward into the preliterate past?

Opposite the front desk in my hotel was a green and black needlepoint map titled "Palestine," the squiggly black thread marking the country's eastern border with Jordan and Syria, its northern border with Lebanon and its western border with Egypt. The names of cities such as Jaffa and Jerusalem were stitched onto the fabric, but not Tel Aviv and Netanya. There was no black thread indicating the borders of an Israeli state within Palestine. Israel was absent.

I took a picture of the map, then asked the general manager, Burhan Bani Odeh, if the map was an antique embroidery from British Mandate days seventy years ago. He replied that it was a modern map, sewn by locals. He'd purchased it in 2006 after the reconstruction of his hotel, the City Inn Palace, which had been taken over as a military command post by the Israelis during the Second Intifada and left a shambles by the time the Road Map to Peace had been launched. It had taken three years to rebuild the hotel, and the needlepoint was his message to any Israeli soldier who happened to walk through the door again.

"We are supposed to forget this is our land, but it's not forgotten," he said, holding his hands out to the map. "You are a journalist, so you know. It is all our land, from Jaffa to the Jordan. *They* took it." He leaned over his desk and pointed through the hotel's east entrance to the P'sagot settlement across the valley. "Now they sit on our heads to remind us,

'Stop dreaming of a state. . . .' There will be no peace until they get out of the West Bank and our capital, East Jerusalem, and accept our right of return to the cities they took from us. Then we can begin negotiations on the rest of the issues."

And there the conflict was stuck, in the same place it had been stuck when I was here thirty years ago during the first Israeli invasion of Lebanon, aimed at driving the Palestine Liberation Organization out of its sanctuaries. All the peace plans Israelis and Palestinians had signed in foreign capitals since then—Madrid in 1991, Oslo in 1993, Cairo in 1994, Oslo II in 1995—had been torn to shreds by the passionate winds of the Holy Land, and few Israelis and Palestinians thought the Road Map would end any differently.

As I waited for the CivPol cops outside the City Inn Palace I looked up at P'sagot. At the peak was a water tower I had climbed in 1982, and the view had left a lasting impression on me. In the mind's eye Israel and Palestine loom as large as a continent, but from Jabbal Tawil you can take in three-quarters of Palestine and almost half of Israel, which is partly why the fight between the two sides is so fierce. There is hardly any land to fight over. The West Bank, that kidney-shaped area of Palestine between the Jordan River and Israel, is smaller than Prince Edward Island. If it had a freeway system you could drive its width in half an hour and its full length, north to south, in ninety minutes. Israel, that imagined national behemoth next door, is a little bigger—about the size of Massachusetts—but 92 percent of Israelis live north of the Negev Desert in an area about the size of the West Bank and only twenty kilometres wide at its vulnerable neck. These two tiny entities have dominated world politics for seventy years because they have dominated the world's imagination for four millennia. The United Nations has passed approximately five hundred resolutions sparked by the deadlock over this minuscule parcel of land—more resolutions than for any other place on earth.

Before they arrive on a mission in Palestine, CivPol officers are given the short-form history of the Palestinian situation, beginning with the first

UN resolution, passed in November 1947. Great Britain, which had wrested control of Palestine from the Ottoman Turks at the end of World War I, was scheduled to withdraw its colonial troops by the summer of 1948. The United Nations interceded to prevent an impending civil war between the resident Palestinians and the Jews who had been settling in the Holy Land by the thousands since the 1920s, and by the tens of thousands in the aftermath of the Holocaust, which had exterminated half the Jews of Europe. General Assembly Resolution 181 created the new nations of Israel and Palestine by partitioning the Holy Land equally— the first two-state solution. Jerusalem was given the status of *corpus separatum*—an international city administered by the United Nations.

The Jews accepted the resolution, but, as the saying goes, they had jumped out of a burning building and landed on Arabs. Outraged at having a Jewish nation imposed on Arab land, Palestinians and the surrounding Arab League countries attacked the new state from all sides. During that war, Israel seized twice the territory the United Nations had allotted to it. Six hundred thousand Palestinians were either forcibly driven from their homes or fled—some into the Gaza Strip, others into the West Bank and East Jerusalem, at whose borders Jordan halted the Israeli advance and took military control of what was left of Palestine. Palestinians called the lost war and its accompanying mass exodus the *nakba*, "the catastrophe." Israelis called it the War of Independence. There was no reconciling the two memories of the war.

Two decades later, in the weeks before the 1967 Six-Day War, Egypt declared a blockade of Israel's Red Sea port of Elat and it appeared to the Israeli government that every Arab state around them was mobilizing for another attack. Israel struck first at Egypt and Syria, and won a massive victory. It was a war, Israelis said, they had not sought, and if they'd conquered East Jerusalem and the West Bank it was only because Jordan had joined its Arab allies and attacked Israel too. Two weeks after the war, Israel annexed East Jerusalem as part of its capital and began its decades-long defiance of UN resolutions that urged an end to the occupation and condemned the building of hundreds of Jewish settlements on Palestinian land.

My hotelkeeper shared the views of almost all Palestinians, both within the territory and in the diaspora: Israel must evacuate all the land it had conquered in 1967 and the five million descendants of the Palestinians who had fled Israel during the *nakba* had the right to return to their ancestral homeland. The Israelis would yield on some of their settlements but never give up half their capital in East Jerusalem, and adamantly refused to allow an influx of Palestinians into Israel that eventually would swamp their Jewish majority. Since terrorist missiles could fly over even the tallest West Bank security barrier, the Israeli position was that the occupation would stay in place until a final peace deal was reached. That was the *ha-matzav* that Robitaille and Copeland found themselves in the middle of when they arrived on mission in September 2011.

Robitaille and Copeland climbed out of their tank-sized SUV in front of the hotel to welcome me to their complex mission. At six-foot-one, Copeland was almost half a head taller than Robitaille, with snow-white hair and a lugubrious face that seemed to show every day of his three decades as a city cop and every minute spent on mission in one of the world's most disputed regions. By contrast, Robitaille, a veteran of the Ivory Coast mission, had an easy smile that was set in a face as rosily fresh as the cadets he'd taught in Depot. A physical fitness enthusiast and the unofficial personal trainer at EUPOL COPPS, Robitaille looked years younger than his age, while Copeland, who'd trained for two months to pass CivPol's fitness test, looked pale and somber. I thought to myself: "Moses and Joshua."

As Copeland drove us past the ongoing demonstration in al-Manarah Square, he lifted his hand from the wheel to indicate the Judean Hills north of the chanting crowds. "These killings in Itamar are a bad thing," he said, in a basso profundo voice. "It happened in Area C, but Nablus is right there, in Area A"—that is, in one of the eleven urban ink blots where the Palestinians were allowed self-rule. "The Israeli Defence Force [IDF] entered Nablus and told the PCP they were in charge of the investigation, like they always do with settler issues. Being a PCP under the occupation has to be one of the most challenging jobs on earth."

"It's a new force, so the Israelis won't rely on them to find the perpetrators," Robitaille said, his English inflected with a slight Québécois accent. "Of course it goes beyond that. We live in Israel and work in Palestine, so we hear both sides. But we're here for only a year. Our clients are the PCP, we have friendships, we listen to their grievances, but our job is to stay completely focused on helping them build a new force, a college, a curriculum, a forensics centre—all on a very tight deadline. They understand we can't participate in the debate about who did what to who first and who did what to who last."

"Both sides say good policing is going to be part of the two-state solution," Copeland added. "They both want us here. There's a hope that if we can get these facilities and the training programme running before there's another war, it may in fact prevent another war." He thought on that for a moment, watching an Israeli helicopter fly by just outside the Area A limits. "*May* is the operative word."

Copeland parked on a narrow street, across from an upscale restaurant within earshot of the demonstrators in al-Manarah Square. The downtown neighbourhood, the most picturesque in Ramallah, was a popular stroll for middle-class Palestinians trying to live according to their culture in the midst of a foreign occupation. It was lined with shops selling prayer carpets, beads for doorways, song birds and giant lacquered hookahs. Wandering among the lunchtime crowd were young men in Ottoman-era scarlet pantaloons and black fez hats, golden coffee urns with fluted spouts strapped to their backs. When a man in a business suit wanted a coffee, the vendor whipped out a glass, leaned forward and poured a shot. Unlike in Kandahar, where you never saw a woman in public unshrouded, here cosmopolitan ladies with perfect posture strolled arm-in-arm, wearing long, snug coats fitted at the waist, their hair piled high underneath stylish scarves. "They're a very proud people," Copeland said. "They'll be eager to tell you the outrage they feel when they visit a relative in the West Bank and are interrogated three different times at Israeli checkpoints."

As we crossed the street two PCP cops on patrol noticed the maple leaf CivPol patches on Robitaille's and Copeland's grey shirts. They called "Canada!" and came up to us and saluted smartly, looking sharp in their EUPOL-issued blue vests, pressed slacks and black berets. They spoke a little English, and Robitaille, who spoke no Arabic, managed to communicate that I was writing about CivPol's training. "Welcome, thank you for coming to Palestine, *thank* you!" the senior of the two cops said to me, appearing sincerely grateful. Turning to Robitaille, he asked, "You take him to our data-entry school?"

"Absolutely I will," Robitaille promised, then explained to me that Canada was responsible for developing the entire communications system for the PCP. He'd just started up a keyboarding class for dispatchers run out of a computer school in Ramallah's new commercial area that President Abbas's modernizing prime minister, Salam Fayyad, had been instrumental in developing. Before Robitaille had started the class, he said, PCP officers had never entered data in an accessible information bank—crucial to modern policing. "We're training over a hundred police dispatchers to take calls, enter the info and focus on the emergency and not the keyboard."

"For this there is no substitute," the senior PCP officer told me. "We can get the information and go to the scene knowing what we will find." The two of them each grasped Copeland's and Robitaille's hands in both of theirs, saluted smartly again and returned to their patrol.

"The police treat us great here," Robitaille said, as we mounted the stairs to the second floor of the restaurant. "They are the most welcoming, friendly people I've ever met. They're under a lot of pressure now but they're very optimistic—which is remarkable considering all they've been through and the complex obstacles they face getting their own state."

I asked what the Palestinian officers thought of their role in containing the crowds in al-Manarah Square.

"They say they just want training in how to do it," Robitaille replied, adding that much of the protest was against Abbas's one-man rule— the very reason the cops themselves had no option when Abbas ordered them to keep the demonstrators from leaving the square. "They've never dealt with a civil protest movement before, so they *desperately* just want training in how to control a crowd."

"We're preparing nineteen training modules with them, broken into lesson plans—including crowd control, respect for human rights, respect for the rule of law," Copeland said. "But things move pretty slowly here, when they move at all. We're mentoring them on democratic policing when they don't live in a democracy. That about sums things up on this side of the fence."

Over a long meal of lamb, fish, hummus and pita bread, washed down by thick Arabic coffee, I learned that CivPol's Palestine mission was not Copeland's first official visit to this side of the fence. As a senior officer with decades of experience in community policing and criminal investigations, he'd been sent here in the spring of 2008, three months before CivPol's first deployment, to research the state of the Palestinian police. He'd landed in Tel Aviv on April 27, 2008, met with members of the Israeli National Police (INP) who liaised with the PCP, and then travelled to the West Bank.

The PCP had originally been created in 1993 by the now-yellowing first Oslo peace accord. Although PLO Chairman Yasser Arafat had supported the idea, a civilian police force had been a low priority for an Arab strongman who preferred to rule through local militia commanders to whom he could dispense patronage and impunity in return for loyalty. In addition to these armed irregulars, Arafat maintained twelve separate security services that kept official power in Palestine spread out among commanders competing with each other for the Chairman's favour. After Arafat's death in 2004 and the election of the more moderate Mahmoud Abbas in 2005, the PA, with support from Israel, invited in the international community to professionalize the PCP so it could serve as the pre-eminent law-enforcement arm of Palestine. EUPOL COPPS had started up in 2006 in Gaza and the West Bank, and then immediately suspended operations when Hamas, pledging to drive the Jews out of both Israel and Palestine, handily won an election that gave it control of the Palestinian Legislative Council. Economically isolated as a terrorist organization by the European Union and the United

States, Hamas was forcibly ejected from the West Bank by the PA in 2007. That was the end of democracy in the West Bank. Hamas's seats in the parliament were left empty, future elections were put on hold indefinitely, and Abbas began to rule by decree. EUPOL then resumed its mission in the West Bank, though not in Gaza, where Hamas won a civil war against the PA and retained control.

At the time Copeland took his inspection tour in 2008, rubble from Israeli shelling during the Second Intifada still littered PCP compounds. Of the thirty-one police stations in the West Bank, only half had a patrol car that had survived the assault, and these were rattletraps from the early 1990s, with no garages left standing to make repairs. Half the stations had no jail cells or radios, and each station had only one pair of handcuffs. There were only ten traffic cones in the entire West Bank, no narcotics testing kits or Breathalyzers, and just twenty computers and a dozen printers for the entire seven-thousand-man force. Eighty PCP had been killed in the fighting during the Second Intifada and three hundred still sat in Israel's jails.

And yet the individual officers Copeland interviewed demonstrated an esprit de corps that matched the best-equipped forces in the world. They patrolled Area A cities like Ramallah, Jericho and Nablus on foot, practising community policing naturally, since they were neighbourhood boys who knew everybody in their districts personally. On the other hand, in the Area B suburban zones that comprised 20 percent of the West Bank, the PCP had to patrol at the side of Israeli soldiers, earning the disdain of the locals, who could not accept that collaboration was a necessary step to getting rid of their oppressors. While the police could not say so publicly, they resented the collaborative modus operandi as much as the residents, and were only waiting—and waiting—for the end of such humiliating concepts as Areas A, B and C, the last of which (amounting to three-fifths of the West Bank) the PCP were not allowed to enter at all.

Copeland was so moved by what the rank-and-file PCP faced from all sides that, after he returned home and submitted his report, he decided he'd like to return on a CivPol mission. "I came back here precisely because the situation is so complex," he said. "In the last year of my career I wanted to help accomplish something significant in the international world of law enforcement."

Attempting to achieve that "something significant," however, frequently made Copeland and Robitaille feel they were being squeezed by a Palestinian olive press. "Our dealings with the PCP chain of command, such as it is, have been very challenging," Copeland said. "Everything has to go through the chief. There isn't one person among the seven thousand under him that can make a decision on his behalf. There's no delegation of authority whatsoever."

"In this region, one person has control, and that control means power," Robitaille added. "To delegate authority means sharing power, and that poses a threat to the man at the top."

Every time they wanted to invite a PCP officer to their headquarters they had to apply in writing to Chief Hazem Attallah, regardless of whether that officer had been to EUPOL a dozen times before. Each of those PCP officers had to get the written approval of Chief Attallah for the most minor equipment requests, from buttons to bullets, ensuring that the officers making the requests knew exactly to whom they were beholden. Naturally those requests piled up on Attallah's desk by the hundreds, and nothing got done. "You can imagine the difficulties that causes for running a large police organization," Robitaille said, "never mind developing a new training programme and a college."

"You can add to that the competing security forces," Copeland said, rubbing his weary face.

Abbas had disbanded four of Arafat's security brigades, but seven remained: the PCP, the National Security Force, the Presidential Guard, the Civil Defence Protection Force, the Preventive Security Force, the General Intelligence Service, and the Military Intelligence Service. An eighth, the Central Training Administration (CTA), had been added by Abbas in 2010 to "standardize" training across the services, although several of its nine officers owed their appointments to patronage and its short tenure had been marked more by conflict with the other services than by coordination. All were vying with one another over law enforcement jurisdiction, and no formal document had yet been signed allotting lines of demarcation between these forces. Disputes over resources and bureaucratic and physical territory erupted all the time, exacerbated by continual tensions with the Israelis, who were ultimately the ones who controlled the West Bank's two and a half million Palestinians.

Despite their experiences with the exercise of power in Palestine— military force on one side; autocracy, subterfuge and back-biting on the other—Robitaille and Copeland clung to CivPol's hope that good civilian policing makes for good societal outcomes, whatever the geopolitical craziness afflicting a society. They set aside the irresolvables inherent to the Israeli-Palestinian conflict (and the conflicts between the Palestinians themselves) and concentrated on the long-term effects of short-term achievements. "We structure our approach around mentoring one police trainer at a time," Copeland said.

Robitaille echoed his partner's confidence in small steps leading to big outcomes. "It may sound like we're thinking small," he said, "but between now and our return date in September, if we're able to assist them in developing a human-rights-oriented training package, taught in international-standard facilities, that will be a major milestone for them and we will consider our mission to have been successful."

Over the next couple of weeks I would learn that the psychological sources of that shared belief came from opposite upbringings. Copeland had been the only child of a manic depressive mother who gambled, drank and constantly ran him into the ground, telling him he was a failure in everything he did. Ten years after he became an Ottawa policeman, his mom's behaviour became extreme and he had a bout of depression himself while taking care of her. He saw a psychologist and, during many months of treatment, he learned to practise cognitive therapy, disciplining his thoughts so they did not repeat the tormenting judgments of childhood. Overriding bad old memories with new good scripts was now his daily discipline, helping him both as a community policeman in Canada and as a CivPol officer here. His life's code was: "If you're a good person and you treat people well, good things will happen to you and good things will happen to them." It was a therapeutic mantra he believed the Middle East could benefit from repeating daily.

Robitaille's source of positive inspiration was the same as Copeland's source of negative inspiration: his mom. When Robitaille was a little boy in Maniwaki, Quebec, his mother was diagnosed with crippling rheumatoid arthritis and hospitalized for what the doctors told her would be a bedridden year. A month later, by sheer willpower, and against medical orders, she left her hospital bed and returned home to do the laundry and cooking for her four kids. No matter the pain, she persisted. She inspired her son to believe that impossible odds could be overcome by positive thinking. She taught him to live in the present, which she said lessened her pain because she had trained her mind to not anticipate more pain. Taking each moment as it came made the unendurable endurable and got her through each task, one at a time. That was the mindset Robitaille had brought to his first CivPol mission in the war-ravaged Ivory Coast in 2008, and to his mission in Palestine today.

"I'll tell you a story," Copeland said. "When I was a junior cop I had a father-figure mentor who always offered pearls of wisdom regarding policing. One of the things he said to me specifically related to how I dealt with the worst of the bad guys: 'Always treat them with respect, always give them the benefit of the doubt, and when you go to court and testify against them, always be fair to them.' That was something that stuck with me because it was counterintuitive to the high-crime environment I was patrolling. The police I worked with mostly displayed an us-versus-them attitude. I adopted my mentor's fairness procedure, though, and it works." He recalled an incident that took place after he'd been on the job a year. As he approached a drug dealer's back door, the fellow inside got the drop on him, put a shotgun to his forehead and racked the slide. Copeland's first sentence could have been his last, but what he said saved his life: "I'm here to help you." It turned out there was a contract on the drug dealer's life, and help was exactly what he needed. Copeland persuaded him to lower the shotgun and then took him into protective custody. Ever since, he'd been attempting to bridge the gap between himself and desperadoes by pulling on the threads that connect criminals to the rest of the world. Safety and respect are universal needs, and when he was eventually put in charge of the unit negotiating with hostage takers, he taught his officers techniques for addressing those needs. The approach saved lives, and also solved crimes, since cops get far more cooperation from criminals on the street by cultivating relationships than by acting threatening.

"I believe that as a police officer you need to develop relationships even with people who've done terrible things," Copeland said. "You need to treat them with respect, treat them like human beings, understand where they come from and treat them the way you would like to be treated."

Copeland steepled his palms and rested his jaw on his thumbs for a thoughtful moment. Then he folded his hands on the table and looked toward al-Manarah Square and beyond it, to Jerusalem. "That's all I say to them in terms of advice about the conflict. I let it lie there, because there's nobody who disagrees with the premise that people deserve respect. They all accept it—at least at first. Then of course they launch into their 'Yeah but' stories."

Galaxy Information Systems was on a block within a new strip-development that would not have looked out of place in suburban Toronto. Six-storey tinted-glass buildings lined the street, right to the edge of where the decrepit rest of the city began. Prime Minister Salam Fayyad had built the development with foreign financing and with considerable cooperation from the Israelis, who believed that tech-based businesses offering employment to hundreds of Palestinians would make them feel the occupation was a boon, not a burden. Fayyad disagreed with the Israeli premise but the unemployment rate in the West Bank was 24 percent, and he preferred to see Palestinians working in skilled jobs in poverty-plagued Ramallah rather than pounding nails in booming Tel Aviv.

On the sixth floor, in a computer lab, several dispatchers-in-training sat at their desks with headphones on, recording radio reports that were scripted and read from another room. Robitaille went up to a student officer named Abad and looked over his shoulder. The transcription was in Arabic, but the computer lab's owner, Majeed Bakeer, summarized. "He is getting a radio call about a murder," Bakeer described the scenario training. "So he is entering the name of the victim and all the information on his identity card. Now the victim's details are in the system for investigators to access from their computers when they go to the scene."

Robitaille put his hand on Abad's shoulder and the corporal took off his headphones.

"How are you finding it?" Robitaille asked.

"Now I am quicker," Abad said. "Last week, I had to look at the keyboard, it was very slow, I could not keep up."

"You're looking at the screen now," Robitaille said. "You're doing fine."

To meet their deadlines on the PCP's curriculum, Robitaille and Copeland had to sit down every other day with police trainers in Jericho, guiding them through the writing of lesson plans for each of their nineteen modules. Their schedule, however, was now thrown off by the Middle East's tectonic shifts. On March 19, in an effort to prevent a mass slaughter of civilians in Libya, NATO had commenced its bombing campaign against Muammar Gaddafi's forces closing in on an uprising in Benghazi. Gaddafi had always been a staunch supporter of Palestine, and some of the demonstrators in al-Manarah Square brandished hand-painted placards that railed against EU-American-Israeli imperialism (even though Israel had nothing to do with the air campaign). After a day of intra-Palestinian arguing about pan-Arab nationalism versus democracy, fifty pro-Gaddafi demonstrators took their rage out on Qalandiya Checkpoint, where they again battled PCP officers who were backed by Israeli tear gas. The next morning the checkpoint was shut down for several hours and the CivPol cops had to cancel their trip to Jericho. Two days later a bomb went off in Jerusalem's Central Bus Station, killing a fifty-nine-year-old woman and wounding another forty civilians. Qalandiya Checkpoint was closed for much of the next day, trapping Robitaille and Copeland in Jerusalem.

I too was stuck in place, but for a different reason: no one in the PCP's chain of command—the one that drove Robitaille and Copeland batty—would give me permission to cover CivPol's work at the Jericho college. I'd filed my application via e-mail three months earlier, when I was still in Afghanistan, and had heard nothing back. I'd refiled the application when I first arrived in Ramallah. Since then I'd been through a series of meetings with PCP majors and colonels but my request still sat on Chief Attallah's desk. EUPOL's media person, Julio De La Guardia, told me there was a reason for that. "For reporters like you, usually it's one official after another until it's time for you to fly home. The security forces have so many internal conflicts they don't want a foreign reporter to witness them. Everybody is afraid to give approval before the chief gives his, and that approval may never come."

Then, early on the morning of March 24, De La Guardia phoned to tell me an important PCP general had just returned from an international conference in Greece and I should get right over to PCP headquarters to meet with him. De La Guardia thought General Yousef Ozreil might be able to grease the skids and get me my letter of permission. Ozreil, one of the liaison officers between the PCP and EUPOL COPPS, had been chief of police in Nablus in 2007, Ramallah in 2008, and Jenin in 2009 and 2010. As a young man he had gone to school in the United States, spoke English fluently and had an American-born son. He had played a critical part in the struggles of his homeland from the 1980s to the present, and had borne witness to the difficulties in developing the PCP. Chief Attallah had recently made him head of the force's media relations department. "I told him about your project and he likes it, so just go up and talk to him—he's close to the chief," De La Guardia said.

PCP headquarters was three blocks downhill from EUPOL COPPS in a pre–World War II sandstone building that had once served as a mission post for British Mandate officials. Across the street was a rubble-strewn lot where a newer headquarters had once stood, until it was bombed in 2000.

Ozreil greeted me in his cramped third-floor office dressed casually in a civilian parka, sweater and loafers, which set me at ease, given what I'd heard about the officiousness of Palestinian generals. He was forty-nine years old, with soft brown eyes, a moustache, and short greying hair. Behind him were pictures of Arafat and an avuncular President Abbas. On his desk was a shot of a blue-uniformed Ozreil saluting Chief Attallah, who was dressed completely in black.

After offering me a seat on his couch, Ozreil sat down beside me and launched into a paean of praise for Canada that I found surprising. With an overtly pro-Israel government in Ottawa, Canadians didn't often hear themselves described by Palestinian generals in such glowing terms. "I hope you will thank the Canadian people for helping Palestine," he said. "The work your police are doing for us is of enormous value. John and Serge are true fighters. To leave your family and your kids and your country to serve another country is something special. They are serious men. When you talk to them about a cultural issue, they take it into consideration. They try to understand and analyze and then to formulate plans for us. Without them and all the other EUPOL members, we would have no forward direction."

He went on for some length about his gratitude for the forensics lab. Back in 2001 the PCP had just laid the foundation for a fingerprint lab when the Israelis employed their F-16s to bomb the site. Now, thanks to the support of the Canadian government, he would have a lab in Ramallah that was built and outfitted according to Canadian standards—a development that amazed him. "Can you imagine? DNA, fingerprints, biometrics—like it is in Canada? Everything? That's a huge step forward!"

If the forensics lab seemed like a gift, the Jericho police college struck him as divine intervention. "Ramallah will train forensics experts from the college; the college will make the experts into professional police," he said.

At that, he lifted his hands to encompass the world beyond his office door. "I would say all these facilities would make a difference, but under occupation there can be no difference. They can barge through that door any time for any reason. Suppose we have the region's best police force, do you think they would be more willing to trust us and leave? No, because they are playing a game. 'You make a police force so the settlements we are building on your land will be safer.'"

I asked him how he was treated when he left Area A, whether his rank and position earned him some deference at checkpoints.

"Deference?" he asked, amazed I'd used such a word. "When I drive out of here, the IDF stops me, finds out I am a PCP general and makes up a reason to give me a ticket. I got two tickets last week. I get tickets every week from these kids that speak maybe a few words of Arabic and a few words of English. Here is a ticket for driving too slowly, or swerving your car. Sit down there. Wait, we'll call you. Raise your arms, spread your legs." Ozreil rubbed a rough hand along his stubbly face. "What we put up with no one else would take."

Ozreil held conventional Palestinian ideas about the immutable claim of his people to all of Palestine, but he was willing to settle for East Jerusalem, the West Bank and some kind of negotiated cap on the millions entitled to "return home" to Israel. His journey to moderation had been a long one, he said, influenced by many factors. He was born in the Judean Hills between Nablus and Ramallah, in the West Bank town of Salfit, to parents who had fled Jaffa during the *nakba*. They were educated business people and raised their son as a secular bourgeois whose destiny would be fulfilled through a professional career. He was a brilliant math student and when he graduated from high school his father sent him to the United States to become a civil engineer. After spending eighteen years among the olive groves and goats of highland Palestine, Ozreil landed in the booming oil town of Houston, Texas, home to NASA, a month-long rodeo, four swinger clubs, an out-of-control drug trade and the mass murderer Dean "Candy Man" Corll, who in the 1970s had kidnapped and killed at least twenty-eight boys. Ozreil withstood the culture shock that was undergraduate life in the crazy Gulf Coast town but after a year he'd had enough.

In 1981 he transferred to the more soothing environment of the University of Oregon, taking courses in hydrology. He married an

American woman in Portland, then moved to Tennessee to finish his graduate civil engineering degree. Tennessee was home to the Tennessee Valley Authority, and he became a specialist in municipal water management.

When he returned to Salfit in 1985, he hoped to solve his hometown's water problems by laying pipes that would tap into the large number of springs outside the city. The Israelis put a stop to his plans by diverting half the city's total water supply, including the springs, to the huge Ariel settlement north of Salfit. In 1987 Ozreil became one of the main organizers of what we now call the First Intifada. It was only in part an uprising, he said. A good deal of the intifada involved the organization of a civil society, and Ozreil put together a local police force that practised community policing. At the time he thought he was just following a time-honoured tradition in Palestine, not inventing a new concept of law enforcement for his people.

"We helped the poor people, we visited hospitals, arranged funerals," he said. "We practised all the things that a community Palestinian force has to do. We solved so many problems between neighbours and between those who were fighting with each other." Indeed, when the Canadians eventually showed up with their modules for community policing, he told them, "This is no problem for us. We do it already. We only have to change the name." He leaned back on the couch and added, "We are a very simple people. We are trusting of each other. The West Bank is a big family. We all know each other. When you talk about two and a half million people, it's not a big deal."

Ozreil was arrested by the Israelis during a violent demonstration in 1988, released after a few months and arrested again in 1991, serving the next eight years in jails Israel had built in the blistering Negev. His wife, still in the United States, divorced him while he was in prison and when he got out he married a Palestinian woman. Because of his advanced degree in engineering, Arafat appointed him to the Ministry of Planning in Ramallah. When the Second Intifada erupted and waves of suicide bombers began killing hundreds of Israeli civilians in cafés and pizza parlours, the IDF bulldozed his house in Salfit, as they did to the houses of many of Arafat's officials. With the arrival of the Road Map ceasefire, Arafat recruited Ozreil into the Ministry of Interior as a Palestinian Civil Police colonel in charge of the security department. "But I didn't want to be in Ramallah fighting with everybody for the Chairman's attention," he said. "It was not for me to be an apparatchik. I wanted to be a policeman in cities around the West Bank, where the people were facing so many problems." In 2007, three years after Arafat's death, he began his tenure as PCP chief in Nablus, then Ramallah and Jenin—the first and third being the most difficult postings in the West Bank.

In those two cities, Arafat's old clan and militia chiefs, backed by Islamists, made up their own laws, enforcing them through their independent armed wings and spy networks. Extortion backed by terror, often linked to disputes between warring factions, was frequent, and in 2007 EUPOL encouraged President Abbas to disband the militias. Abbas then appointed the reformist Salam Fayyad as prime minister, and with international and Israeli support, the PCP and other PA security forces swept the areas under their control, arresting the most violent of the militia leaders in Nablus and Jenin.

The sweep marked a turning point in Ozreil's attitude toward a possible peace deal with Israel. For the first time as a policeman, he faced the worst elements of his own people in a showdown that could only be resolved by force. The clan and militia chiefs combined their patronage networks, corruption, criminal activities and infighting with Islamic piety, calling themselves a liberation movement. "This was how the Israelis saw us—narrow-minded, fanatical people who acted like Mafia. But I knew this was not who we were. After Nablus, when I became police chief of Ramallah, I began working directly with EUPOL COPPS and with your first two Canadian RCMP officers. They all lived in Jerusalem and heard the Israeli side. 'They tell us security is number one. If you can provide it, maybe they will be reassured,' they said. I had trouble seeing that side—maybe I still do—but reality is reality. I believed in EUPOL's Rule of Law Section, what it could teach us—the improvement of safety and security, reforms to our structure, investigations training, human rights, hiring of policewomen, equal treatment of men and women—all these things are promoted and taught by your people.

"When I became chief of Jenin in 2009 and 2010, I saw the progress," he went on. "Those bad groups are still there, they are underground, but we have radicals on the Israeli side too. The question is: How can we bring the moderate parties from both sides together to solve the problem? In my life I have had enough with radicals on both sides telling us there is no way it can be done. Maybe I was radical too once, but now I want peace for my children, not another 500,000 years of bloodshed."

I asked him about a 2010 poll that showed that while more than half of Palestinians felt the police ensured a safe environment, less than a third felt they could criticize the government without retaliation. It was illegal to call for Abbas's ouster.

"The feelings may be true or not, but if they are, look at our problems," he said. "I would like democracy too—but do you want Hamas back? That was a civil war. There are many people who want democracy so they can end it. Ask EUPOL COPPS: we have controlled many demonstrations without deaths. When we have to control the rock throwing at Qalandiya, that is a whole other issue. Probably our police would like to throw rocks at Qalandiya themselves, but they know what we live with all around us. We are trying to fulfill our side of the peace plan, but those Israelis—even God couldn't do anything with them. You want *us* to do something with them? That's the meaning of our situation exactly."

I finally got around to mentioning that the "command structure" of the PCP was holding up my application to visit the Jericho academy. Ozreil said, "Just go. You have my permission." He picked up the phone and talked for a couple of minutes in Arabic, then hung up. "It's done. Everything is arranged."

"That's all I need?" I said. "No letter of permission saying I can do my reporting on the PCP?"

"That's all you need. I will take care of everything. We are not afraid of you seeing anything in the way our police operate."

To demonstrate he had nothing to hide, he summoned two cops to drive me through al-Manarah Square and Al-Am'ary refugee camp on the way back to my hotel. He introduced me to the driver, Mohammad, who spoke some English. In the square Mohammad pulled to the side and engaged in a tête-à-tête with a group of protestors. The back and forth was at first friendly but then became emotional. The demonstrators pointed their fingers at Mohammad, then down Palestine Road toward Qalandiya. Mohammad insisted on finishing off the discussion by shaking each of their hands, a rapprochement they agreed to, their smiles returning.

As I drove off, he filled me in: "So I asked them how are things. They said 'Abu Mazen [President Abbas] rules by decree, he's a collaborator and he should go.' I could have arrested them for that but I am taking your Canadian courses, ha ha ha!"

The Al-Am'ary refugee camp was a steep block down from my hotel. The grade got even steeper at the entrance and the car flew up in the back as we bounced through the archway into the camp. Atop the arch was a picture of Yasser Arafat beside the seal of the PLO: two Kalashnikovs above a hand grenade in front of a map of Palestine, *sans* Israel. The "camp," established in 1950 and now with eight thousand permanent residents, was indistinguishable from the rest of the city, with five-storey stone buildings, paved sidewalks and electric wires strung on modern metal stanchions. Sixty percent of the Palestinians in refugee camps were under the age of twenty-four, a statistic evident from the crowds of kids idling their time on the sidewalks and entrances to apartment blocks. Mohammad again had a through-the-window repartee with the locals, this time encountering less willingness to engage in conversation. As we drove back up out of the camp he said, "I ask them how things are going. They say, like you hear in the movies: 'A policeman is never around when you need him and always around when you don't,' ha ha ha!"

The next day, Friday, was the Muslim Sabbath. Ramallans with free time swelled the ranks of the demonstrators in the square. The number of rock throwers at Qalandiya also increased. It looked like it would take until Monday before all the checkpoints were open and I could cover the work of CivPol in Jericho.

As always when "the situation" seemed likely to spin out of control, Robitaille and Copeland spent their evenings in Jerusalem fielding Skype calls and e-mails from relatives at home worriedly following the violence on the Internet. The Itamar murders, the demonstrations in Damascus and Ramallah, the bombing campaign against Libya and the bombing in downtown Jerusalem were all reported as part of the same story in the Western press. Robitaille's wife of twenty-one years was a Mountie, so she had the training and discipline to absorb unsettling news. But his mother saw an arc of flames from Libya to Syria, with her son in the middle of it all. He'd spent an hour on Skype every night since the Itamar murders, assuring her he was okay, that Palestine was not Afghanistan.

Copeland's wife, Isabelle, a manager at a human resources company, was as worried as Robitaille's mother, and showed it. During their last reunion three months earlier, she had confided to John that she was afraid he would come under fire or be killed in a bombing. John and his wife had been married twenty-eight years and were extremely attached to one another; after the Jerusalem bombing Copeland forwarded to me an e-mail Isabelle had written him. Before they'd last parted, she'd promised she wouldn't mention her worst fears again, but she did, indirectly.

"Thank God I have Pat when I get home or I think I would go crazy," she wrote, referring to her youngest son. "I dread the time he leaves the house and I am all alone. I shouldn't say that. . . . I have no regrets encouraging you to do what you wanted to do. This is important, you need to do something to help society and some people just don't care. I am extremely happy that you do care. I hope this assignment strengthens our relationship and that we can live our old age in peace and happiness."

"That last line is what's on her mind," Copeland told me in EUPOL COPPS headquarters that Sunday, as he worked on plans for the forensics centre and Robitaille worked on the Jericho college curriculum. "I told her we're not being shot at, but there's no hiding we're in turbulent times. This mission has an effect on our families back home that I'd like you to mention in your book."

I asked him if he himself was feeling the effect too.

"For me my lowest moments on mission are being really homesick, on a couple of occasions, *really homesick*," he said. "When I said goodbye to Isabelle in January I knew I wouldn't see her for another six months. We've never been apart this long. On the other hand, whenever I feel the need for human contact, Serge is always close by. I'm fortunate because I live with Serge and we get along great. We both seem to have fallen into a role; he does the cooking and I do the cleaning."

From across the office a Czech officer cracked, "Their food is awful and their house is filthy."

"Actually," Robitaille said, "we're amazed how well it's gone. We work in the office side by side, drive in the car side by side, but we have our own rooms and purposely spend time away from each other." He took a call, then turned to me. "Charlie One Checkpoint is open near the Ofra settlement, so we're going tomorrow. It'll be just you and me." John, he said, would be meeting "with our PCP partners" about the forensics centre.

"They're a group of people who have a common good purpose," Copeland said, looking on the bright side. "Of course, everything we agree on will be passed up to the chief." He made his hands into two birds taking wing, following them with his raised eyes as they disappeared into the clouds.

6

INSECURITY
انعـدام الأمـن

THE HALF-FINISHED CAMPUS of the Palestine College for Police
Sciences sat in the blinding sun on the northern edge of Jericho, the
oldest continuously inhabited city on earth and, at 258 metres below
sea level, also the lowest. Looming behind the campus was the Mount
of Temptation, where Jesus had fasted for forty days. It was the last
promontory of the Judean Hills, which Robitaille and I had just passed
through, switch-backing in low gear among desolate badlands on the
thirteen-hundred-metre descent from Ramallah. Below the site of the
college lay a shimmering plain through which the Jordan River flowed
and beyond that the escarpment in Jordan that Moses had climbed to
behold the Promised Land. The escarpment ran beside the West Bank's
entire border with Jordan, visible in one sweep from the Dead Sea to
the southern Galilee.

Robitaille pulled into the parking lot of the college's new administration building and radioed EUPOL that he had just arrived. Between
us and the view, red dust clouds swirled behind bulldozers flattening
the parade ground in the middle of the ten-hectare campus. Forklifts
roared down a service road carrying pallets of roofing tiles for the
three dorms that would be home to 550 cadets. "They'll be studying
our curriculum in those learning centre buildings we're funding," he
said with some pride, pointing to three beige buildings to our right.
"That big curved-roofed structure is our gym where they'll muster for
drill, fitness and defensive tactics. Down at the bottom, those three
buildings that look like homes are our scenario training houses." In all,
he said, six countries were funding fourteen buildings that were being

constructed by the United Nations' Office for Project Services. The $20-million institution was scheduled to open for a full complement of cadets in about a year.

"Hello my friend, hello!" shouted a PCP officer as he came toward us out of the administration building. Khalid Arar Shawabke wore the three stars of a captain on his epaulettes, and was a one-time tourist cop who now served as the college's translator. After we were introduced, Shawabke told Robitaille he had some bad news. That morning Major Omar Bari Munir, the deputy commander of the college, had received word that his brother, exiled in Yemen since the First Intifada, had suffered a heart attack and passed away. Major Omar had just contacted the Israeli authorities and asked to bury his brother in Palestine. "They say it will not be possible," Shawabke said. "He was born in the West Bank but his papers are not recognized." He turned to me: "Such is what we live with every day. Even the dead cannot come home."

He looked around at the view. "Anything you would like to know about the area's history before we go in?" he asked me, falling into his old role as a tourist cop. "I myself trained here when I joined the PCP in 1996. You could write your whole book about what has gone on."

The college was situated a hundred metres above the Jordan River, on a gravel bench washed down from the mountains. The Turks, the British, the Jordanians and finally the Israelis had all used this high ground as a military post. In May 1994, in the lead-up to the second Oslo peace accord, 350 PCP had proudly marched over the Allenby Bridge and crossed the nine-kilometre swath of Area C into Jericho's Area A, and for the first time in five hundred years the city passed to Palestinian control. The choice of this site for the original PCP college had been Yasser Arafat's idea, based partly on his desire to plant the flag on ground visible from the Allenby Bridge and partly on a belief that Jericho had been home to the world's first police force. This cop creation-story was more than a patriotic myth: it was grounded in the wondrous geological and archaeological history of the Jordan Valley.

The fifteen kilometres between the Judean Hills and the escarpment across the river marked the dividing line between the African and

Arabian tectonic plates. The deep depression, called a "pull-apart valley," lay at the northern end of the Great Rift Valley that stretched south to Ethiopia and Kenya, where our hominid ancestors had evolved into modern humans. About fifty thousand years ago our forebears had used the Rift Valley as a path out of Africa, skirting the Red Sea to reach Palestine before spreading out to the rest of the world. Some of those émigrés took advantage of the perennial springs burbling from the Judean Hills and settled a few hundred metres south of the college, at Tell es-Sultan, now an archaeological dig that the Palestinian Authority had nominated as a UNESCO World Heritage Site. The dig had unearthed streets, staircases, towers and city walls that were constructed at least ten thousand years ago. For the first time in history, hundreds of humans had found themselves living permanently within a walled urban area. Writing had yet to be invented in the Neolithic era, but burial plots discovered at Tell es-Sultan pointed to a hierarchical social order that had organized the city's architectural planning, defence and crafts. Obedience to rules governing the day-to-day lives of the inhabitants had almost certainly been enforced by agents of the city's hierarchy. In other words, there had probably been some form of policing in Jericho five thousand years before the Israelites under Joshua had besieged the walls—an ancient lineage of law enforcement that Yasser Arafat had referred to when he had inaugurated the college in 1995. "We don't know for sure, but we like to think the PCP has this heritage," Shawabke said. "When I trained here they told us, 'We guarded *Tal Assultan*; now we are back.'"

By the time of the Second Intifada in 2000, about 150 PCP cadets were living and training in the college's old military buildings. When the Israelis suspected that some members of the Jericho detachment had collaborated in the burning of a Jericho synagogue (or at least that they had looked the other way), helicopter gunships, reprising Joshua's attack, reduced much of the college to rubble. Eight years later, EUPOL and CivPol officers visiting the cratered campus found its cadets sleeping in tents and attending classes under tarps in the forty-five-degree summer. Wind storms were frequent in the valley, and every few months the tents and tarps were swept toward the Dead Sea. The conditions were a direct challenge to EUPOL's mandate to establish "sustainable and effective policing under Palestinian ownership in accordance with the best international standards." Without a modern academy you could not have a sustainable police force. And so, in 2009, Canada and EUPOL began constructing the new facility "to provide state-of-the art police training." Today's 150 cadets were quartered in the town and attending classes in the new administration building, but once the campus was completed, the Jericho academy would be graduating about a thousand male and female police a year.

The construction seemed to be going according to plan, although a question remained. Would the Israelis ever trust the state-of-the-art-trained PCP to patrol the Jordan Valley on their own? Shawabke had his doubts. Israeli prime minister Benjamin Netanyahu had laid down a condition for a two-state solution: Israel's twenty military bases in Area C of the valley would be permanent fixtures after an independent Palestine was established. "We don't want to see rockets and missiles streaming into a Palestinian state and placed on the hills encircling Jerusalem," Netanyahu had declared. "If Israel does not maintain a credible military and security presence in the Jordan Valley for the foreseeable future, this is exactly what could happen." A continuation of the status quo seemed probable: Palestinian police would be forbidden to drive on most roads and have to submit to Israeli inspections on others. "They want us to police a Swiss cheese country," Shawabke said, shaking his head at the absurdity as he led us into the administration building.

In a classroom, beside a whiteboard, stood a broadly built mustachioed cop in his early thirties. Major Rami Ahmad Mahmoud Hussein, in charge of the training programme at the school, was dressed in a blue and white camouflage uniform and black combat boots. Several PCP trainers listened as he pointed to Arabic bullet points on the white board. When he turned around and saw Robitaille he broke into a broad smile and extended his hand. He greeted us in Arabic, then, through Shawabke, explained to Robitaille what he had on the board. Thus far, of the nineteen modules Robitaille and Copeland had outlined for the training manual, he and his staff had adapted eight for the PCP and were breaking them down into individual lesson plans for each module. The modules they had completed were on hand-to-hand self-defence, fire-arms training, community policing, human rights, ceremonial drill, vehicle searches, note taking and basic Hebrew language skills. The modules that still had to be written included the most technical: crime scene investigation, police administration, anti-narcotics, scenario-based training, crowd control, police driving, and report writing, among others. "We are trying to make as much progress as possible," he said. "We understand the time limit is very short but, as you know, the CTA is causing us problems."

Rami was referring to the Central Training Administration, the new branch of the Ministry of Interior that was stacked with some of Abbas's clique of old-guard officers, who were attempting to usurp control of training from the PCP, installing their own satraps. Their interference was a particular headache for Rami,* as well as for Robitaille and the dean of the academy, Lt. Col. Zahir Sabbah.

Upstairs in his second-floor office, Sabbah sat behind a desk flanked by PCP flags. Crossed scimitars embraced the Dome of the Rock, tempered by the olive branches that bordered the flags, as if to say: the Dome is ours, we will fight to defend it, but we want peace. He was a handsome man of forty-four, wearing a dashing black beret and black sweater over his camouflage shirt. On the lacquered table beside him was the usual array of photos I'd seen in the office of every senior cop I'd visited in Ramallah. There was a picture of Arafat, this one with a black mourning ribbon in the upper right of the frame. Beside Arafat was a photo of President Abbas, and beside that a photo of Sabbah with Chief Attallah—an action shot of the two inspecting a line of PCP officers on parade, with Attallah in front and Sabbah behind, smiling as he looked at the back of his boss's head.

---

* At the academy, Major Rami went by his first name.

"I want to welcome you on a personal level," Sabbah said to me. "I am sure you have followed all proper procedure to arrange your visit."

"Terry met with General Ozreil last week," Robitaille said. "He was given unrestricted access to the PCP for the purposes of writing a book that will not be published for at least two years."

Sabbah held up a finger and smiled. "But Ozreil is not Chief Attallah. I have received nothing in writing."

"We are following the chain of command," Robitaille said. "Ozreil is arranging everything with Chief Attallah."

"In our system 'arranging' is not 'arranged,'" Sabah reminded him. "If we start deciding by ourselves about who to bring here, we might provoke the chief." He seemed to weigh his own words for a moment, then came to a decision. "In any case," Sabbah said to me, "I trust the proper procedure will certify your visit, and I again extend my welcome.

"What I would like you to communicate is this," he went on. "We are very happy with our relations with Serge and John. The cooperation between us is based more on our policing ideals and friendship than on any assignment from superiors." He said the Canadians had worked tirelessly on the curriculum, as well as on providing their specialists' advice to him and his men. "I am referring to the whole project—the buildings, our needs for the training, choosing the trainers and adapting the best practices of policing for our very special situation, which as you know is unique, to say the least." He turned to Robitaille. "You have heard the news about Major Omar's brother?"

"Within seconds of our arriving," Robitaille replied. "And of course, we would like to offer our condolences to him, to his family and to his PCP family. The situation is very sad."

"Particularly for his mother," Sabbah said. "She has not seen her son for many years and now she won't even be able to see him buried. You see, this is how we live our lives," he said to me. "We are walking on unsure ground since we were born. Even here amidst this construction, one incident could imperil everything."

Sabbah had become commander of the academy just before the

Israeli gunship attack, an experience of war that had replicated the time of his birth in 1967. His hometown of Tulkarm sat along the 1949 ceasefire line, at Israel's narrowest point. On the second day of the Six-Day War the Jordanians defending the city found themselves completely surrounded, and surrendered. The ten thousand residents of Tulkarm's refugee camp hung white sheets out their windows, terrified of the Israelis they had fled nineteen years before. Sabbah's father, who worked for the Jordanian government, was suddenly unemployed. "Parents always try to protect their children from feeling insecure," Sabbah said, "but maybe from the age of three or four, my first memories are of this insecurity. My father told me to lower our eyes when the soldiers passed. When you feel your father is insecure, you grow up feeling insecure."

There were no Palestinian police at the time, but local "self-help units" performed the same function as police, albeit clandestinely. Watching those volunteer units at work convinced Sabbah that he wanted to become a Palestinian policeman. "I thought of it every day, because the units helped the people all the time; they gave us a sense of security and everything we needed."

When Sabbah was a teenager, his father, unable to endure the humiliations of occupation any longer, moved his family to Syria, where Sabbah entered Damascus University, studying law, he said, "because there is a direct relationship between civilian law and civilian police." He was about to begin his practice when the Oslo peace accords were signed and the PCP was founded. He applied to the PLO to be sent for advanced officer training in Sudan, where he met the nineteen-year-old Rami Hussein. Sabbah returned to the West Bank in 1999 and moved up quickly in the PCP to become commander of the Jericho college, whereupon he appointed the young Rami to the training programme. "Some day, *inshallah*," he said, "the work Major Rami, Serge, John, EUPOL COPPS and I are doing will all come together and Jericho will be a world-renowned academy."

"On that very positive note," Robitaille said, "we just met with Major Rami downstairs. And he gave us a brief update on his very promising progress. According to my calculations, we're at least 40 percent complete."

"I've read his reports and am really looking forward to seeing all the modules completed," Sabbah said. "But Serge, there is a big problem, and you are in the middle of it. I don't want you to listen to the CTA anymore. They do not understand the difference between a civilian police curriculum and a militia training course."

"Yes, I know," Robitaille said, and I could see a cloud of distress pass across his face; he was caught in a Palestinian power struggle he was kicking himself for not avoiding. Back in late January, the CTA had met with EUPOL COPPS and informed the organization that they were interested in participating in the PCP training programme that Robitaille and Copeland had worked out with Sabbah, Rami and Attallah. The Ministry of Interior certified to EUPOL COPPS the CTA's law enforcement expertise, and Robitaille had agreed to meet with CTA officers and pass on their ideas. In reality, the Central Training Administration was composed in part of ex-militia members loyal to Abbas who spent much of their time devising ways to put their particular stamp on the training of Palestine's competing security forces. A couple of days after their meeting with Robitaille, about half a dozen CTA officers had shown up at the college and begun their own training programme, displacing the one that was already running, handing out material that, when Robitaille finally got it translated, made his heart sink. It was a paramilitary training programme, with the CTA's name at the top, not the PCP's, and it was designed to turn out enforcers of government rule rather than civilian upholders of the law.

"I'm the one who told Major Rami to stop participating in the CTA programme because their programme is different from what we should be doing," Sabbah pronounced. "Worst of all, their participation has delayed the work. As soon as possible we're supposed to finish the basic training materials. After I'm done with our work I'll look at their programme, but not until our work is done because it's not reasonable that I start building for others before I start building for myself. We wasted a whole month because of that training course they started with their own people. One hour is important not to waste, never mind a whole month."

"The material that I just saw downstairs is exactly what we wanted," Robitaille said, a little sheepishly. "So that would be more than an appropriate format for the rest of the material."

"Those people at the CTA don't know what they are doing!" Sabbah said, raising his voice. "I don't want you working with them any longer. We are so far along, yet they are coming in here with their own ideas and doing a different thing entirely. Police are not militia, we are an entirely different discipline. I have told you before, I am really happy with my team and I know their capability and their willingness. The CTA cannot be allowed to supplant my team with their team!"

"Understood and agreed," Robitaille said. "And lesson learned in terms of the CTA. It did not deliver as expected. You know of course it is not my doing or my wish to—"

"The CTA and I are on two different tracks, we cannot meet together anywhere!" Sabbah said.

"That's why we want to clear this up," Robitaille said. He explained he had been totally unaware he was being used to advance a programme that would cause such trouble for the college and for himself. "And believe me, Colonel, I am trying to undo that. I will follow up with the CTA and I will report back to you on what I uncover. I will see what, if anything, I can do to put this issue to rest so we can move on and make progress."

"Their use-of-force course is a disaster, Serge. A disaster!"

"Absolutely agreed on that," Robitaille said, "and thankfully we have someone of Major Rami's calibre standing up for that module. Major Rami is the one who should be teaching it, not only to his own students but to the trainers of the CTA."

That seemed to be exactly what Sabbah wanted to hear. "Thank you, Serge," he said, and stood up to shake Robitaille's hand across the desk. "I am putting my faith in you to help me against these people." Then Sabbah looked at me. "I am embarrassed you are exposed to their intrusions. It is a complex situation. I know it is not Serge's fault."

On his way out to attend to other duties, Sabbah gave Robitaille a brief hug and said quietly, "My friend, it's a long path for us."

Robitaille looked as if he had aged five years. After we'd settled to talk in one of the building's computer rooms, he said, wearily, "There's supposed to be a security reform process in place. Unfortunately, it's a process-in-progress." He booted up his laptop, opened a document and then just stared at it. "I know Major Rami has had it up to here with his work being undermined." He sat back from the computer without typing anything, then turned to me. "You know, at the end of the day we don't go on mission to fix bureaucracies. Our greatest satisfaction is working with officers like Rami. Thus far, I have learned more from him than he has from me. He's an amazing individual. I'll ask him if he'll sit down with you. Rami is why I'm not overly worried about this. He's a big man, Terry, in all senses. When he tells the CTA to back off, they back off."

Downstairs, the six-foot-three Rami stood on a judo mat in a classroom, offering a lesson to a dozen cadets in "graduated response"—the opposite of the force-and-submission training the CTA was teaching the cadets. After a few minutes observing him I realized I could have been watching a class taught according to the Peelian principle: *Police use physical force . . . only when the exercise of persuasion, advice, and warning is found to be insufficient.*

"In a situation where the suspect is threatening to you, everything you do to deal with that threat is done according to step-by-step procedure," Rami told the class. "The first steps we use are all related to human psychology—negotiations first. You protect yourself and those around you but you analyze the problems in non-violent ways, solve the problems in non-violent ways. You can't use violence first to get your way, you must first use communications to achieve conflict resolution."

He invited a volunteer onto the mat, handed him a wooden dowel and had him assume a threatening posture by raising the dowel over his head. "This man has just committed a crime. He is telling me to stay away or else he will attack me. I do stay away, far from his lunging distance. What is my first action according to the graduated response procedure?"

"Talk to him," one of the students said.

"Correct. This is my brother and he has gotten himself in a bad situation. So I tell him, 'My brother, things look bad now but I'm here to help you work things out.' I ask him what happened, to get the communication going. Whatever he says is good, because we are talking and not fighting."

If the criminal refuses to talk, Rami explained, the officer should address the problem of the weapon, both from the suspect's point of view and the officer's point of view. "Be honest and be firm. You say: 'It would be easier for me to help you if you put the pipe down so I do not feel threatened.'"

"What if he doesn't listen and attacks you?" one of the students asked.

"We will be training you to use your hands to protect yourself and control the suspect. People who are watching will see that the police think of the safety of others. You have your own weapon, but as a last resort."

"Now lunge at me in attack," he said to the student in front of him. "Really try to hit me."

"No," said the student.

"Yes!" Rami ordered.

The student leapt forward with the dowel raised. Rami's right hand went smoothly under the wrist of the attacker while his left hand grabbed his elbow. He used the locked arm as a lever to turn the cadet's hips so he toppled over on the mat. The student was now flat on his stomach facing in the opposite direction of his original attack posture. Rami pinned the student's shoulder to the mat, pulling backwards lightly on his arm. The whole procedure had taken half a second.

"If I wanted, this would be a painful pin immobilizing the suspect," Rami told the class. "From here you can handcuff him."

The students applauded and the attacker stood up. Rami bowed and shook his hand. "This is a very simple aikido technique you will all learn here so you will not even have to think about it twice. It will come naturally."

When I sat down with Rami in a nearby room I discovered that, as well as having a black belt in aikido, he possessed degrees in management and counselling and was about to graduate from the U.K.'s Open University with yet another degree in sociology—all of them earned by the age of thirty-four while working his way up to the rank of police major in the midst of war, displacement, and occupation. He said he had chosen his fields of academic study because they were directly connected to his role as a Palestinian policeman and as a police trainer. From his studies and his own life he had come to understand that the basis of a functioning society was the government's ability to provide its citizens with a minimum amount of security. Palestine, by contrast, suffered from a total lack of physical, social and economic security, all due to the occupation. "The institutions that make up the normal protective structures of a government are absent in Palestine. They are absent for me at this moment."

He told me he hadn't seen his parents and siblings in Gaza for fifteen years because they weren't allowed to travel the forty kilometres across Israel to the West Bank and he wasn't allowed to travel to Gaza. He'd only seen his wife and children six times in six years because his wife was a Palestinian refugee in Jordan and the Israelis wouldn't allow her into the West Bank. Most times when he tried to visit his wife and kids the Israelis would turn him back at the border or tell him there was a problem with his papers, and if he went to Jordan, he wouldn't be allowed back into Jericho. Then there were the insults at the checkpoints—the searches, the pat-downs, the hours of delay on what should have been one-hour trips to meet with officials in Ramallah.

"The Palestinian people are in emergency need of techniques to psychologically survive the insecurities they feel," he said. "It is my belief that the police are in the best position to teach them those techniques, by example."

To that end, he had developed a sophisticated approach that everyday

policemen could use with a traumatized public. Rather than teach policing disciplines to be used in the service of government power, he would
teach public service principles that would reassure Palestinians their
government was represented in the community by respectful cops
engaged in cooperative problem solving. He was now incorporating
that approach into the basic curriculum he was developing with
Robitaille and Copeland. His ultimate goal was to foster a strong community even as it lived under the indignities of occupation. He felt that
every police officer should be schooled in a distilled form of the knowledge he had learned in his studies, and graduate equipped with skills in
counselling, conflict resolution and social awareness, as well as with
expert training in self-defence.

Martial arts training, he said, imparted "procedural preparedness"—
the ability to take instant action without resorting to lethal force, even
when totally surprised. Instilling a sense of professional pride in the
role the police played in protecting their "brothers and sisters" helped
engender a positive self-image—both for the police themselves and for
the population. Community policing—constantly consulting with the
people in a neighbourhood to find out their concerns—helped convey
positive messages about the (hoped for) future of the government, of
which the police were compassionate examples.

"Different disciplines, different skills must come together in each
trained officer, so that they go out on the streets both as defenders and
teachers—teachers of skills like how to deal with the opposite side in a
strong but non-violent way—with Hamas, with radicals and criminals.
I need to bring all these elements together so that each officer understands the themes and goals of being a Palestinian policeman. I believe
with all my heart that each element of police training should strive to
impart these institutional goals. At their best, the police goals would be
related to the government's goals, which should be to replace our acute
insecurity with a sense of safety, worth and identity." He paused a
moment and smiled. "I am trying to explain what is in my professional
mind. Do I sound like a dreamer to you?"

"On the contrary," I said.

"I have lived as an exile in so many countries, I have no alternative but to keep trying to establish psychological safety in my homeland. We are an oppressed people, our rights have been stolen, armed resistance hasn't worked, so I am interested in teaching my people how to attain inner security until some other means frees us. Because without a sense of inner security we cannot survive in this impossible situation."

Rami was born in Beirut, Lebanon, in 1977, and the history of his family is the history of the insecurity that has marked successive Palestinian diasporas. His grandparents were from a town near Beit Guvrin, in central Israel, midway between Hebron and Gaza. During the 1948 *nakba* they had fled to Jericho and then to Jordan, where Rami's father, Ahmad Mahmoud Hussein, was born in 1955. By the time Ahmad turned sixteen, half the population of Jordan was Palestinian and PLO leader Arafat decided it was time to overthrow the Hashemite king, Hussein bin Talal, whose grandfather, Abdullah I, had been assassinated by a Palestinian who had feared Abdullah would make peace with the new state of Israel. Arafat held similar suspicions about King Hussein, and Ahmad joined the PLO in the fight, the aim of which was to turn the entire state of Jordan into a war machine against Israel. King Hussein trounced the PLO and drove Arafat, his followers and all their families into Syria, from where they were driven into the fractious state of Lebanon. By the time Rami was born, Ahmad was a PLO colonel, coordinating cross-border attacks against Israel—a position that made him a marked man when Israel invaded Lebanon in 1982. Beirut soon came under air, artillery and rocket attack. At the outset of the bombardment the six-year-old Rami had an experience that convinced him that protecting others against harm would be his mission in life.

Ahmad had been driving Rami and his brothers home from school when he saw a Cobra helicopter bank steeply and lock on him. He swung the car onto a downward-sloping parking ramp just as the street exploded in heavy-calibre machine-gun fire. He continued into the underground garage, threw his three boys out of their seats, then screeched back up the ramp into a narrow lane and jumped out of the car two blocks later. "God gave me a great example to live by even when I was a small boy," Rami explained to me. "My father told me the helicopter had been looking for his car and would have destroyed the building above the garage to kill him. So he drove out from the garage to lead them away, ready to die to keep the helicopter from killing us and other civilians."

The PLO was to endure a third diaspora when the Israelis expelled them from Lebanon. Rami's family wound up in Tunisia, where Rami spent the next twelve years. In 1995, with the Second Oslo Accord in effect, Rami's father moved them all to Gaza, the area of Palestine closest to his ancestral hometown. "I approached the Arafat party in Gaza," Rami told me, referring to al-Fatah. "Through them, I applied for police training here in Jericho, but was mysteriously told by Fatah officials that I should apply instead for training abroad."

Rami's application was accepted at a police college in Turkey—at least that was what the Fatah officials told him, assuring him he would graduate with a police captain's rank. A week before he was to fly to Ankara, one of the officials asked him for $2,000 to cover his "travel expenses." When he said there was no way he could raise that vast sum, he was informed that another candidate who could pay the fee would take his place. But not to worry: there was an opening in France for him to train as a pilot. The "travel expense" fee for the trip to France was "negotiable." Again he applied through Fatah; again he was accepted. A week before he was to leave, the "negotiable travel expenses" were opened up for bidding, and Rami found himself bumped off the list of candidates.

"In my entire career, I have never paid *rashwah*," he said, using the Arabic word that means an openly expected bribe that no one gets around paying. "Nor have I ever used *wasta*," he added, referring to the who-you-know mechanism of advancement in the Arab job market. "I never mentioned my father was a lieutenant general in the army and therefore I was entitled to rewards. My sense of integrity led to all these previous problems and now to future problems."

Those problems became so legion that I was amazed he had survived them.

A Fatah official offered to make up for the aborted training in Turkey and France if Rami enlisted in the PLO Security Services and enrolled for training at the Egyptian police academy. "He told me I would graduate as a lieutenant," Rami recollected. "I devoted a whole month to preparing myself for the tests. I scored top marks and signed the papers for my enlistment. But when I arrived at the PLO embassy in Cairo, I encountered the old business again." The PLO embassy officials separated the recruits into two groups: those who could afford to pay processing fees and those who could not. The first group was bused to the police academy and began training; Rami's group was put on a waiting list. After a couple of weeks of sitting idle in a barracks, the group was told by Palestinian officials that they were being sent to Sudan for a year to be trained as military officers. "It was very strange," Rami said. "I didn't know why I was being sent to become an army officer when I wanted to become a policeman." But he followed orders and was shipped fifteen-hundred kilometres south to the Sudan Military Academy, in the Bayuda Desert outside Omdurman, one of the hottest places on earth. He ranked up in fifty-degree heat with twelve hundred newly arrived recruits from countries such as Chad and Niger. The recruits were informed they had enlisted in the academy for three years (not one), and there would be no days off or leaves of absence until they graduated. "I tried to quit, but they told me they would not let me leave the base," he said. "There were twelve Palestinians from my group with me. The Sudan officer told us there was some kind of special agreement with the PLO for our services." As part of their basic training, they would spend their first year labouring around the base. Rami and his fellow recruits were given picks and shovels and told to get to work in a quarry. It was then he realized he had been indentured to the Sudanese academy for his first year of training. "It was like slavery," he said.

Toward the end of Rami's year of "basic training," Zahir Sabbah arrived at the nearby police academy from Palestine. Sabbah, who had entered the PCP as a lieutenant, visted the military academy and saw the Palestinians digging foundation holes and enquired of them whether they were on punishment detail. When Sabbah heard Rami's story he went to the Sudanese commanding officer and succeeded in getting Rami and the other Palestinians enrolled in proper training. "The good aspect of this painful adventure was that I was assigned to an elite special forces training programme, where I excelled," Rami said. "In 1998 I graduated with a lieutenant's rank in Arafat's security forces, qualified to be a member of the presidential guard. Of the twelve hundred men in my class, only 312 graduated."

The PLO official to whom Rami reported back in Gaza told him his records showed that he had only been assigned to a year of training in Sudan and therefore was entitled to no more than a military diploma. Rami explained to him that in Sudan he had been told of an arrangement whereby the PLO would give him a Bachelor of Arts degree for his three years of training. The PLO functionary said that would require making an alteration to the records, and, therefore, a processing fee. "This was unjust—they were not fulfilling their arrangement, and I protested," Rami related. The Fatah official told Rami he was insolent. He handed him his military diploma and instead of posting him to the presidential guard in Ramallah, assigned him to a tiny outpost in the middle of the Gaza Desert. "Even the Bedouin weren't there," Rami told me. "There were no tents for us. The PLO director of the base didn't explain what we were doing there. He told us to go sleep in the sand and that was it."

Rami complained to the director that he was a special forces officer who should be on active assignment at a place of strategic significance, not living in the middle of nowhere on a post that nobody cared about. The director slapped him and then began beating him for his insubordination. When Rami defended himself by pinning the director to the sand, his commanding officer's aides drew their guns. Rami was locked up and told he would be brought before a chief of police and charged with assaulting an officer.

"I sat in a box in the middle of the post, asking myself: How has this happened to me? All I wanted to do was serve my country as a policeman but because I didn't adhere to normalities, I was kept from three training opportunities, then put to work like a slave, and now, even though I overcame obstacles to become a special forces officer, I was facing jail."

He spent a suffering day in the box pondering the situation faced by a million poor people in Gaza who could not afford to pay bribes to bureaucrats. The system was a hole that swallowed up the hopes of Palestinians without means. He decided that if he ever got out of this situation he would educate himself in ways to achieve "social reform."

He was saved from being charged with assault by the chief of police, who read Rami's record of elite special forces training in Sudan, listened to his side of the story and deduced that he had justifiably defended himself against an unprovoked attack. After the exoneration, he took Rami aside: Why, with his stellar qualifications, had he been sent to this desert post to begin with? When the chief heard the explanation, he asked Rami what his goal had been when he had first approached Fatah. Rami replied that he had started out on his journey over three years ago in order to get police training, and that was all he ever wanted. The police chief said he would contact Yasser Arafat directly and have his case looked into.

At last, at the end of 1998, Rami was put under the wing of an honest major general named Abu Sawali, who, like the chief of police, recognized that Rami's integrity, talents and accomplishments had been nearly sacrificed to the greed and cruelty of self-interested officials. Sawali enrolled Rami in Gaza's regional police school that, six months later, qualified him as PCP officer—a step he could have taken in 1995. Without having to pay any travel expenses or other processing fees, Rami was bused across Israel and the West Bank to the Jericho academy, where Zahir Sabbah assigned him to training young cadets in the skills he had learned in Sudan. "In addition, I patrolled Jericho as a community policeman, teaching cadets and trainers the proper friendly relations PCP officers should have with the public."

Most of the problematic people Rami dealt with on the street were in their teens, as were the cadets he trained, and they all suffered from the acute lack of security he'd mentioned to me. "They had problems at home, problems with the government, problems with the occupation.

To be a policeman and a trainer I needed a scientific knowledge of all their social problems and the problems of our governmental structures. That was when I applied for my academic training, and from then until the present I have been in long-distance learning." He was now completing his thesis, "Social Reform through Civilian Policing," integrating that thesis into the modules he was developing with Robitaille and Copeland. Conflict resolution and counselling techniques were two key elements of his community policing module. "In Palestine we do not have what I call a 'social guarantee.' We do not know where to turn to find security when we feel we are being treated unfairly. Young people are in distress because of their grievances. They can act in self-destructive ways. In my counselling component, I am including ways of carrying on conversations in such a way that people consider the difference between manners of behaviour that will benefit them and those that will cause them harm. The police at the academy are learning to practise the techniques that provide one part of the social guarantee, so that the public can look to the government for help in their problems."

I asked if the other part of the social guarantee provided by the PCP was keeping officials honest, investigating them for corruption. At that Rami inhaled deeply and lowered his eyes to the table. He then turned his enormous palms up on the table, as if to say, *It's complicated.* "We are trying to adopt the European model. Until quite recently the PA had no such model. We are moving in the right direction, but like everything else, it is taking time."

At the moment, there was no special unit within the Palestinian Civil Police that dealt with corruption, and so Robitaille and Copeland had not included a course module that trained officers in conducting specialized investigations of bureaucrats on the take. Eighteen months ago, at EUPOL's urging, the PA had established an institution called the Anti-Corruption Commission, but that was a high-level board separate from the PCP, beyond Rami's purview. Members of the Anti-Corruption Commission were now being sent to Scandinavia to learn how corruption investigations were conducted in a region that had managed to keep itself the cleanest on earth. The PA had also established a Corruption Crimes Court and had hired prosecutors and judges to staff it, but the process was still in its infant stages. "As you know, these kinds of investigations can be misused for political purposes," he pointed out. "It is a technical field that requires oversight to prevent it being used as a tool by people in power to charge opponents."

On the other hand, in his own unofficial way, the giant cop was not averse to dealing with complaints about avaricious bureaucrats from the Jericho public by offering officials personalized counselling sessions in civilized behaviour. Close to where we were sitting, he'd recently been trying to deal with what he viewed as harmful interference with the running of the academy by a self-interested outside body—the CTA. "Last week I arranged a training demonstration between my people and the CTA's people," he told me, and, as he proceeded to explain his "demonstration," I began to see why Robitaille had said that with Rami around, he wasn't overly worried about the CTA.

"I took seven of my trainees and put them in a room with four of the CTA trainers and invited the foreign trainers, one from Greece and two from Britain, to observe a lesson in use-of-force. I set up a self-defence scenario for the CTA to teach them. In five minutes the Greek and the British witnessed with their own eyes that my trainees were teaching the CTA's trainers. When the CTA trainers told them to take out their batons, my trainees said, 'We don't need that force-and-submission technique. We use our hands to protect the suspects against injury.' The worst of my students were more proficient than the best of the CTAs. They knew aikido and the CTA trainers felt embarrassed they didn't. Those CTA trainers have not come back. There are only a few remaining, and we will deal with them too."

Robitaille came into the room then to retrieve me. I couldn't help but offer him my assessment of his student. I told him that I'd just listened to a ninety-minute disquisition on humanist policing offered by a man with a trained body and a trained mind who was totally dedicated to sharing with cadets and trainers what he'd learned in life and school. "He's a superior kind of person," I told Robitaille, "and it's very impressive to listen to him." I turned to Rami. "I am honoured to meet you," I said, offering my hand.

We shook, but then Rami said he had something important to tell me before I left. He stroked his moustache, seeming to gather his thoughts. His cell phone rang and he shut it off. "It's good that people like you meet with the Palestinian police and learn about their personal backgrounds, the problems they have been facing in their lives, the problems they face as policemen," he said. "Our mental and educational levels are advanced compared to other Arab countries. I'm sure that you are surprised while talking to all the officers here. After Afghanistan, maybe you thought you were coming to profile a very primitive people with limited levels of knowledge, education and awareness. The media plays a role in portraying us as only interested in running after the Jews, wanting to kill them. What I hope is that the media in your country conducts an awareness campaign, studying and researching Palestinians to describe their true and genuine situation. We have the motivation to work, we have all the ways to solve our problems, to face any problem. I hope your book will explain the factors that make life so difficult for Palestinians, and why making our country independent is so important to ending our social and psychological suffering."

Before we returned to Ramallah, Robitaille and I sat down for a meal in a restaurant that fronted Jericho's town square, a manicured turnabout ringed by date palms and storefronts selling roasted meat and household wares, all overlooked by an ivory minaret. A block east of the turnabout was a huge sycamore tree that arborists had estimated to be over two thousand years old—the Biblical "Tree of Zacchaeus," named after a corrupt publican who had climbed it in order to catch a glimpse of Jesus as he came into town, whereupon the publican became instantly converted to a life of honesty and charity. Further east of the tree was a late addition to the scene: the remains of a police station the Israelis had destroyed with tanks and bulldozers in March 2006, part of an operation to arrest the assassin of an Israeli cabinet minister whom the PCP would not give up.

Midway through the meal I looked around at the walls of the restaurant, covered with heavy red damask curtains. Maybe I'd had too much of the amphetamine-like black coffee, or the red curtains excited synchronous neural activity in my brain, but I suddenly felt a surge of historical euphoria. Jesus had been right here, Moses had been up there in the hills, the beginning of civilization was over my shoulder, and I was sitting opposite a Mountie doing whatever he could to resolve a conflict whose seeds had almost certainly been sown somewhere in Kenya, where we had evolved into predatory beings driven by territorial imperatives and spiritual awareness.

"Serge," I said, glowing with a high as crimson as the curtains.

"Hmmm?" he asked, his mouth around a pita sandwich.

"You're Catholic, right?"

"Raised Roman Catholic, but I'm not a practising Catholic," he said with his mouth full.

"But there are certain precepts of the church that stayed with you?"

"Oh yes. Now that I'm in this area, obviously I remember my schooling. It seems all very fresh in my memory."

"Do your memories ever make you think you're in the middle of something profound?"

He literally chewed on that for a moment. "Interesting question," he replied, putting his pita bread down. "You mean in a religious sense?"

"Religious, political, historical—you're a mission operative at the centre of current events, at the centre of historical and religious events. Even geological events. We're sitting on the tectonic line between continents. And you're on a mission here, trying to prevent the Battle of Armageddon."

He held up a finger, as if to say, *I see what you're getting at.*

"That's an interesting way of putting it—a writer's way of putting it, if you will. But I don't see myself like that at all. If I did, I couldn't get my job done. As a professional, I try not to think in those terms."

"Impassioned terms," I said.

"Yes, we're trained *not* to think in passionate terms while we do our jobs. Of course as a policeman you always want to help and protect vulnerable people, it drives you. But I'm not much of a dreamer. I get satisfaction from even the most minor achievement. That's why policing was a fit for me. I didn't become a policeman to necessarily go after the world's most dangerous criminal or the smartest organized crime boss and I don't go on missions to solve the world's problems. I always think I am here to simply go to work and make a small difference in somebody's situation on that day. And that has always been the most appealing aspect of policing to me. The opportunities to make small differences on a daily basis."

"You know I'm Jewish, Serge," I said.

"It had occurred to me from your last name," he replied neutrally. "What perspective does being Jewish give you on writing about this situation?"

"Like you, I'm non-practising. It's a tribe, though, so I have an awareness. I know Canada wouldn't take the Jews when they tried to flee the Holocaust. Neither would the United States. One full ship was turned back in 1939. The Germans killed a lot of them. The Jews of Europe were kicked out of everywhere until they were almost all killed. My grandparents left long before World War II, but everyone who stayed behind was killed, on both sides of my family. There were a few European Jews who survived, and they came here because there was nowhere else for them. They think Palestinians see a state as just a first step to getting Israel back. Israelis may give up some of the West Bank—I think they should give up all of it—but they'll die to the last man before they give up Israel. They think Israel is the last stand of the Jewish people."

He kept his eyes on the table as I spoke these words, then contrasted his core procedural mission with my own. "As a writer, of course, you have to think in those terms as you assess and perhaps try to feel the various passions of Palestinians and Israelis in conflict. But my job is much more practical."

After dinner, as we made the long climb out of the valley, we passed the first of many Bedouin encampments set at the bottom of bald clay valleys, without a blade of grass for miles. "Interesting how they choose this life," he said. "You couldn't pay them to live in the towns. In fact, on the Israeli side, they do pay them to live in the towns, but most of them like it better out in the desert."

I took a picture of one encampment. Camels were tied in a line beside a corrugated iron enclosure, with goats inside it. "Abraham came in from the north," I said. "You wonder why he didn't stop in the Galilee where it was green." Then I answered my own question. "Somebody else was probably there and he had to move on."

7

THE BEAR TRAP

ONE AFTERNOON WHEN Robitaille and Copeland attended classified meetings at EUPOL COPPS, I followed the advice of my *Lonely Planet* guidebook and hired a taxi to take me north to the Jenin refugee camp, sixty kilometres as the crow flies from Ramallah. I wanted to see members of a Palestinian acting school called Freedom Theatre perform an adaptation of *Alice in Wonderland*. Jenin is in the heart of the West Bank's most Islamically conservative district yet in this production a Palestinian Alice refuses her arranged marriage and is transported to Wonderland, where she encounters personifications of her inner desires and the leering rulers of her repressive culture. "The performance shines a different spotlight on today's Palestinian society," the theatre's website said. "It is a subversive, radical, humorous, extravagant, larger-than-life production . . . questioning many of the social restrictions that limit the roles available to both women and men."

I estimated that the trip would take an hour, yet long past that my driver was still negotiating hairpin turns through rocky olive groves. At the turn-off to the Itamar settlement we got stalled at an IDF checkpoint and sat staring at the Kabir Hills above Nablus while the drivers of the vehicles ahead of us were interrogated one by one. When we at last pulled abreast of the armoured Jeeps, a young soldier asked me where I was headed. I told him Jenin.

"The city is safe for tourists," he said, "but don't go in the camp."

"That's where I'm going," I said.

"To each his fate," he replied, then waved the next car forward.

Two and a half hours after we left Ramallah, my driver finally descended to Jenin, a city of forty thousand that filled the valley bottom with densely packed, three-storey block houses. On the city's west side the refugee camp covered a hill like a midden of shells. I asked Fatheem, the driver, if he was allowed to enter the camp and he told me that was no problem: all the tourists he took this way were headed to the theatre. "It's an Israeli who runs it," he said, referring to Juliano Mer-Khamis, the actor and director who had been staging plays and musicals in the camp for five years, garnering a lot of attention in the international press.

The camp entrance was marked by a five-metre-tall sculpture of a horse made out of scrap metal. "From the intifada," Fatheem said, pancaking his hands to demonstrate how pieces of cars destroyed by tanks had been flattened and shaped into this defiant work of art, which was called "War Horse." He skirted a traffic tie-up by turning into a bullet-pocked alley, with the shreds of old posters commemorating suicide bombers still pasted to the walls. After negotiating a couple of mould-blackened lanes that never saw the sun he entered a street that ended in a T-intersection. At the top of the T was a block-long terracotta wall featuring Freedom Theatre's bilingual marquee above a stone archway that framed a yellow door playfully graffitied with the words "Alice Home." Along the wall to the left were two billboard cases displaying composites from the play, with one showing a red-masked denizen of Wonderland entertaining an upside-down Alice and the other a crimson-dressed Red Queen screaming her part from a raised platform. At the end of the long wall, shaded by silvery trees, was a gated courtyard with a relief sculpture of the comedy and tragedy masks. Beside the masks was a glass door to the lobby.

I paid Fatheem my hundred shekels and got out. Two years ago, someone had firebombed the theatre during its run of *Animal Farm,* in which Palestinian politicians were portrayed as pigs collaborating with the IDF. Theatre staff had extinguished the fire, although that same night a Western-oriented music centre in Jenin, Al-Kamandjâti, had been burned to the ground. Some locals told reporters that Freedom

Theatre had been attacked because the play insulted Islam by having Muslims dress as pigs; others said that it was targeted because boys and girls were appearing on stage together. Whatever the motives, anonymous leaflets were soon distributed in the camp condemning the theatre as the work of a Jew who was staining the memories of the intifada's *shaheeds*—that is, martyrs to the resistance.

Mer-Khamis was actually half Jewish, the son of an Arab-Israeli father and a Jewish-Israeli mother, both Communist Party stalwarts. He had been an ardent opponent of Zionism for two decades. Seven years earlier he had won a Tribeca Film Festival award for a documentary about the young fighters of Jenin during the Second Intifada, which he had filmed from behind the boys' shoulders as they planted bombs and waited for Israeli patrols to pass. In 2006 he had partnered with one of those fighters, Zakaria Zabeidi, the leader of the Al-Aqsa Martyrs' Brigades, to found Freedom Theatre as a lifeline to the traumatized children of the camp ("our cultural intifada," he dubbed the enterprise). After the firebombing, Mer-Khamis held a press conference in the theatre to counter the allegations of the leaflets, declaring that he was opposed to a two-state solution: "I'm in favour of a single Palestinian state from the river to the sea. If the Jews want to live with us, welcome." Then on Israeli Radio, he pronounced paradoxically: "I'm 100-percent Palestinian and 100-percent Jewish." A year later, reflecting on the firebombing, he told a reporter: "Many people didn't like that we criticized our own society. But this is the policy of the Freedom Theatre. As well as criticizing the occupation in all its atrocities, we should also be able to look at ourselves."

The metal gate to the theatre courtyard was locked and the neon welcome sign in the lobby was unlit. I called "Hello?" but no one answered. I walked back along the wall and knocked on the "Alice Home" door, then knocked on the two metal stage doors to its right. Fatheem was still parked in the lane so I went over to him. "Closed?" I asked. He looked at the building, puzzled. "Wait," he said, and got out, leaving his door open as he approached the building. A driver in a hurry almost crashed into his door and that got him side-tracked in an argument that went on for some minutes, drawing the attention of a group of young men in hooded sweatshirts and jeans. I walked up to the corner and looked left down the length of the building. The renovated structure was immense; it had originally been built by the Ottomans to accommodate steam engines. I walked back to Fatheem, who looked at me apologetically. "They say finish," he said, indicating the boys. "Show no more. Two-seven," he added, tracing the number on his palm, meaning the last show had been performed days ago. "They say maybe somebody inside but"—he glanced at his watch—"closed at five. Back to Ramallah?"

I couldn't stand the thought of another two hours in a car after a failed expedition so I told him I would get something to eat in the camp and find my own way home. I pointed toward Jenin city, where we had passed the Direct Service Taxi Garage, whose signs advertised half-hourly van transport to Ramallah. He looked at me doubtfully, then indicated a minaret between buildings. "You hear call, you go garage. I wait for you. No good you walk at night by yourself. Problem here."

"What's the problem?"

"These boys say a new play. No good. Men with men. No good."

A play about gays? In Jenin? "When?" I asked. He shrugged. The boys in hoodies looked at us without expression.

The muezzin call would come at sunset so I had about twenty minutes. I walked up the block and then in the opposite direction from the theatre until I stood across from a courtyard of pink and yellow apartment blocks. Sounds of family life descended from the open windows, predominantly the voices of women and young children intermingling with clashing kitchen utensils, all amplified ten times by the stone walls. The exterior of the buildings were newly plastered, with shiny black water tanks and satellite dishes on the roofs—something of a miracle, considering the neighbourhood's war-ravaged history. During the Second Intifada the camp had come to be known as Martyrs' Capital for the thirty suicide bombers it had dispatched to Israel to detonate their backpacks in crowded buses, cafés and pizza parlours. On April 2, 2002, the IDF had entered the half-square-kilometre camp, closed it to outside observers, and ordered the sixteen thousand residents to stay in their homes while they went house to house searching for the organizers of the insurgency. The fighting was most ferocious around the spot where the theatre now stood; fifty-two Palestinians and twenty-three Israeli soldiers had died and more than a third of the camp was destroyed. Thanks to money from the international community, this section of the camp had been rebuilt in 2006, the year Mer-Khamis had decided to make his theatre the neighbourhood's centrepiece.

At the far end of the apartment courtyard several teen males were kicking a soccer ball around. One of the boy's eyes held mine, concentrating an energy that pinged my amygdala and made me feel I wasn't welcome. I had experienced that look frequently in places like Iraq and Afghanistan, but only once so far in Palestine, while walking through Ramallah's Al-Am'ary camp. As a boy in Brooklyn I had been the object of gazes like that in neighbourhoods just three blocks from my own—but that was gang stuff. This was something different.

I walked back to the theatre and knocked on a different entrance, then circumnavigated the block. A group of men in dashikis and black skull caps approached. Checking my driver's information, I asked them if the theatre was really closed. They were friendly enough, but didn't speak English. Probably thinking I was lost, one pointed to the theatre and said its name, "*Masrah il Hurriyah*," and another pointed east to the city, saying "Jenin."

I headed up a heavily trafficked thoroughfare on the bottom edge of the camp for a couple of blocks, then came to a street that went uphill to my right. There was an Arabic sign on the corner, below which someone had spray-painted the words "Shaheed Sematry." I walked up the hill through poor neighbourhoods crowded with locals selling wares from stalls or going about their stoop-side business—chatting with neighbours, calling to children down the block, repairing a toaster or a carburetor. People glanced my way as I approached but no one would meet my gaze. On one corner I passed an oversize poster, featuring twenty heroic portraits of young men. (I later found out they weren't martyrs, but protestors held in Israeli jails.) The poster partially concealed a double track of pits made by heavy-calibre machine gun fire. I smiled at children running in the street, but didn't even get hostile stares in return. When they looked at all, they looked through me. At the top of the hill I came to another modern neighbourhood of brilliantly painted red and yellow apartment buildings that surrounded the cemetery. Protected by a graffiti-adorned ochre wall were about thirty graves, with round stone bolsters at the tops and bottoms, as if making a bed for the dead. About all the Arabic script I could make out were numbers: most of the graves gave the same year of death—1423, the Muslim calendar year for 2002.

From the cemetery I had a view of the camp and the city below. Beyond them the surrounding hills were turning gold-green in the setting sun, the smooth pastureland rising to the Israeli security barrier that noosed the district on three sides. The evening muezzin called *God is Great*. In my hotel room when I heard the call I would sometimes put a blanket down, bow, rinse my face with air and bow again. I had no idea if Muslims would consider it blasphemy for a Jew to pray as a Muslim, but I had been sincerely asking for divine help in writing about Palestine. I took my jacket off now, faced the eastern hills and knelt as the muezzin continued his beautiful chant.

When I stood up I scanned Jenin and found the Direct Service Taxi Garage near where my driver had turned off Route 60. I walked downhill through the camp and onto the main drag, where I stopped at a kiosk and pointed to a dish of hummus and pickles. I sat down with my paper plate beside three old men in keffiyehs who were drinking tea and sharing a hookah. I watched the evening crowd of bearded men in dashikis and skull caps and women in floor-length dresses and headscarves crossing the street through the clog of motor bikes and beat-up cars. A couple of PCP carrying old rifles left the sidewalk and leaned down to speak to the driver of a Toyota. The driver was trying to make a left, and they seemed to advise him to go straight ahead and make his turn somewhere else. He flipped the backs of his hands at them, shouted something, rolled up his window and inched his car forward. The cops let the situation go and went back to the curb. The men smoking their hookahs had a chuckle over that. "No ticket?" I asked, writing one out on my palm to make myself understood.

All three men looked me up and down, shoes to scalp, then turned back to the road, as if I hadn't said a word.

Because they worked full time in Ramallah and Jericho, Robitaille and Copeland rarely got to places as far afield as Jenin, but they kept abreast of what was going on in more remote regions by meeting with the EUPOL officers who mentored cops all over the West Bank. Every now and then a local PCP chief would inform EUPOL of specialized training that was needed to address emerging crimes, whereupon the Canadians would write up the requests, append suggestions for where they could be packaged into course components and pass them on to Colonel Sabbah and Major Rami at the Jericho academy. When the West Bank's Arab Spring demonstrations erupted in mid-March 2011, the district chiefs began requesting that a component be added to the community policing module to train officers in the skills required for patrolling the West Bank's nineteen refugee camps, home to almost a quarter-million restive and impoverished Palestinians. The need was most urgent in those camps where PCP officers were viewed less as enforcers of Palestinian law than as collaborators with the Israeli occupiers. The camps where the hostility to the Palestinian police was greatest were those such as Jenin, where the PCP passed on information about radicals to the Palestinian Preventive Security Force, who passed it on to the Israelis, who conducted nighttime raids on the homes of those suspected of plotting violent resistance.

Jenin was like all the other refugee camps in that it was populated by the descendants of residents from a specific area of Israel—in Jenin's case, Haifa, forty kilometres west of the camp. The refugees had been resettled nearest to their former homes after the 1948 *nakba*, when the camps were primitive UN tent cities. As in Ramallah, the camps had grown into apartment block neighbourhoods indistinguishable from their urban surroundings. Generation after generation had stayed in the camps because of a promise contained in UN Resolution 194, passed in December 1948: "Refugees wishing to return to their homes and live at peace with their neighbours should be permitted to do so at the earliest practicable date." The refugees in the camps were still waiting for that date. In the meantime, the UN Relief and Works Agency channelled international aid to provide the refugees with housing, electricity, water, education and food subsidies. By continuing to live in the camps the refugees retained their status and the aid, along with the promise made in Resolution 194.

Jenin was at the heart of a paradox of the CivPol mission in Palestine, and Robitaille and Copeland really had no answer to resolving that paradox. PCP community policing did not work in the Jenin camp because most of its population saw the PCP as imposing something they did not want: an accommodation to the occupation, with only a vague promise that if they held their fire long enough, the Israelis around them would leave. In fact, the vast majority of the residents of the Jenin camp did not want to settle for the Israelis leaving the West Bank: they wanted the Israelis to leave Haifa so that they could claim title to their ancestral homes.

Their intractable grievances were stoked by Islamic fundamentalists, but the religious leaders were not the real power brokers in the camp. Most of the residents had clan-based loyalties that outsiders had a hard time comprehending, since the clans were three generations removed from their origins and had evolved into what could more accurately be called gangs. Arafat had been a master at keeping the clan chiefs loyal to him, but now they were loyal to themselves, waiting for their chance to regain the power they had lost after the security sweeps of 2008. "Jenin is our little Gaza here in the West Bank," Major Rami had told me, comparing the camp to the breakaway district on the other side of Israel. "Some of the strongest support for radicals in the West Bank is based in the Jenin camp." Yousef Ozreil, who had been the police chief of Jenin in 2009, echoed that assessment. "Most of what Palestinians feel and hide, the people in the Jenin camp feel and show," he told me. "It is a wounded place. They suffer from post-traumatic stress disorder. They don't back down because they are desperate.

During the intifada the children joined the martyrs' brigades, Islamic Jihad—they were not afraid to die in the fighting."

The only footage of that fighting is contained in Juliano Mer-Khamis's groundbreaking documentary, *Arna's Children*. Born in Haifa, he'd first entered the Jenin refugee camp at age eighteen, in 1976, as an Israeli paratrooper. At the time, he identified with his mother's lineage—Jewish-Israeli—but when he refused an order to frisk an elderly Palestinian, and then struck the officer who gave him the order, he was sentenced to the stockade. When he got out several months later, he enrolled in acting school and discovered he had a lot of talent. A tall man with a baritone voice and looks that were made for the screen, he found success in a number of American and Israeli films, acting opposite Diane Keaton in *The Little Drummer Girl,* a film about Israel's hunt for Palestinian terrorists, and he was eventually nominated for the equivalent of Israel's Academy Award. And yet, in the midst of his upward trajectory as an actor, he demonstrated that such success was not a fully satisfying goal. As he turned thirty, he left Israel for a year of travel and drug use in the Philippines. He returned with a new sense of himself as a political activist and began to perform street theatre in Israeli cities, pouring red paint over his bare torso to protest the occupation, adopting the radical left politics of his mother.

Arna Mer had fought in the War of Independence, but after the 1967 war had begun protesting the occupation. In the late 1980s, during the First Intifada, she founded a school and theatre workshop in the Jenin refugee camp, dedicating herself to helping the children in the camp express their trauma and anger in a non-violent way. In 1993 she invited her son to teach drama therapy at her school. Over the next two years Juliano taught classes and filmed the children and his mother. By the time she died of cancer in 1995, fifteen hundred children were attending her school. Mer-Khamis then left Jenin to resume his acting career but, after the Second Intifada broke out, he learned that two of "Arna's children"—his favourites—had died on a suicide mission in Israel. When the IDF invaded the camp in 2002, he secretly returned to document the lives of his mother's former students amidst the worst of the intifada's fighting. He stayed for seven months, during which time more of his former students died in the fighting. He edited his film into his documentary and used the film's earnings and donations from wealthy American and European supporters to renovate the half-destroyed Turkish warehouse into Freedom Theatre. Mer-Khamis then moved into the camp full time with his Finnish wife. "The Freedom Theatre is a venue to join the Palestinian people in their struggle for liberation, with poetry, music, theatre, cameras," he said in a promotional video in 2008. "The Israelis succeeded in destroying our identity, our social structure—political and economical. Our duty as artists is to reconstruct this destruction. . . . The Freedom Theatre offers the basic elements of life to children, to people, to women, to men—*freedom!*"

The endeavour made Mer-Khamis both famous and infamous in Israel as well as in the West Bank. While locals in Jenin attended his productions in droves, and sent thousands of their children to his school, Jews in Israel and in West Bank settlements saw him as a turncoat, a facilitator of the violent resistance they faced all around them. Meanwhile, the Islamic conservatives in the camp thought he was perverting the morals of the children, particularly after he produced *Alice in Wonderland*. As my taxi driver had informed me as I stood outside the closed theatre, Mer-Khamis's next production was considered by some in the camp to be even more blasphemous than *Alice*. Called *Spring Awakening,* the play was about homosexuality and incest in Wilhelmine Germany.

On the night of April 4, 2011, an Israeli TV station led its evening news broadcast with the report that, at four p.m., a masked assailant had shot Juliano Mer-Khamis five times in the chest as he sat in his car near Freedom Theatre. The station ran footage of Mer-Khamis's red Citroën. The street was pooled with blood beside the open door of his car, which was surrounded by Palestinian onlookers and PCP officers. Three days later, Israel's Channel 10 aired a 2008 interview with the handsome actor. Sitting beside his blond wife, he declared to the interviewer that he had something to announce to an international audience in English. "I'm telling them about how I am going to end my life," he said, looking directly at the camera. "A bullet from a fucked-up

Palestinian who's gonna be very angry that we are in Jenin, with this blond coming to corrupt the youth of Islam. And she's gonna"—here he configured his hand into the shape of an aimed gun—"*Gazhew! Gazhew! Gazhew!*" He threw his head back and mimicked dying. "And she's gonna find me dead on the doorstep," he said, looking at his wife.

In previous cases where Jews had been murdered in the West Bank, such as the Itamar killings, intelligence operatives in Shin Bet and the IDF had moved in to conduct the investigation. But Mer-Khamis had declared himself to be a bi-national resident of the West Bank living full time in the Jenin camp, which put him somewhere between a Jew and a Palestinian. In death, as in life, his case was as confusing as the occupation he fought against, both as a Jew and a Palestinian. Thus, the PCP would be handling the investigation into his murder, under the supervision of the Israeli National Police.

Early on the morning after the murder, I made my way to Jerusalem's Old City, about a kilometre north of the apartment where Robitaille and Copeland lived. Just outside the city wall was an open-air mall, tastefully excavated so that it was almost invisible from the approach to Jaffa Gate. You walked down three levels of stone steps into a narrow arcade that was essentially a trench cut into the hillside, lined with high-end galleries and boutiques. Beside the Body Shop, at a point where the trench opened to spectacular views of the Artists' Colony and the new city below, was an espresso bar called The Aroma. When I entered I saw copies of the morning's *Jerusalem Post* scattered along the countertops facing the view. The headline: "Actor Juliano Mer-Khamis Gunned Down in Jenin. Prominent Israeli filmmaker and peace activist was the son of a Jewish mother and a Christian Arab father from Nazareth."

I was there to meet Chief Superintendent Danny Israel, the INP's head liaison officer to the Palestine Civil Police. I had set up the meeting days before Mer-Khamis's murder, looking for someone who could speak to what it was like for an Israeli cop to work with Palestinians, and to get his views on "the situation" and EUPOL COPPS's training and mentoring. As part of his job, Israel served as the INP's liaison

officer to EUPOL COPPS, attending strategy sessions at EUPOL headquarters that were also attended by Palestinian police.

I spotted him ordering coffee at the bar, dressed casually in jeans and
a long-sleeved polo shirt, striped in blue and white (the colours of the
Israeli flag) and grey (the color of *ha-matzav*). Tall and thin, he was a
gentle-looking man with a friendly expression and brown hair going
grey. We shook hands, carried our coffees to a table by the window
view, and then his phone rang. *"Ken,"* he said into it. He took notes on a
pad for a couple of minutes, concentrating. When he hung up he looked
not at me, but out the window, southeast toward the Abu Tur neighbourhood where Robitaille and Copeland lived. The call had clearly
been about Mer-Khamis's assassination. "For a long time we haven't
had such targeted killings in the camp," he said at last. "It used to happen often when Arafat ran his militias—they behaved like gangsters.
But since 2008 they are disbanded and replaced by the PCP. There has
been relative peace. Now I don't know. This man was well-liked in Jenin
by average Palestinians for his dedication to the children, but also he
was disliked by the old militia types who thought the theatre was un-
Islamic. Just from the preliminary details, he was probably killed for
being a Palestinian peace activist rather than for being a Jewish one."

Israel's phone rang again. "I'm sorry about these calls. I'm afraid
there will be many," he said, answering the phone and putting his pen
to paper again. It turned out he was now coordinating the investigation
into the Mer-Khamis murder. He spoke Arabic fluently and spent as
much time in the West Bank as he did in INP headquarters. Every senior
Palestinian officer I had spoken with had offered the highest praise for
him. In fact, he was the *only* Israeli official I'd heard them praise.

He finished his call and sat back, tapping a finger on the Formica
tabletop, his cop mind working. After a minute, he said, "This is a sad
case. His wife is pregnant with twins—she is due any day. He had his
baby boy in his lap when he was shot. Also the baby sitter was in the
back seat, and she is wounded by shrapnel. The boy is maybe a year old,
so hopefully he will not remember the trauma. Mer-Khamis was very
famous, so it is a big case—they are as interested in Ramallah as here."

An hour after the killing, Prime Minister Salam Fayyad had issued a statement: "We cannot stand silent in the face of this ugly crime. It constitutes a grave violation that goes beyond all principles and human values, and it contravenes the customs and ethics of coexistence." Minutes later, Kadoura Musa, the PA governor of Jenin, told reporters from the *Jerusalem Post* that Mer-Khamis "was a resident of the Jenin refugee camp, and helped build Palestine. He did not deserve to die this way." A team had been set up to investigate the murder, he said. "The person who did this will be caught regardless of his identity."

"Are you the head of the team Musa mentioned?" I asked.

"We call it the coordinator, because the team is equally the INP and the PCP," he said. "So we are working together. I coordinate the Israeli and Palestinian police units. This is my job."

I told him that General Ozreil and Colonel Sabbah had only admiring things to say about the job he was doing.

"Maybe they knew you will be talking to me," he cracked. "You can tell them I praise them too. In fact, we are working toward the same goal and there is no conflict between us as policemen."

He seemed to view his role as different from the IDF's, not as an occupier but as a helpful cop-mentor—the way CivPol viewed itself. I asked him how he came to hold his position, and he said liaison officers of whatever nationality are chosen because they have an ability to get along with people; they represent the accommodating face of one large organization to another. "I do my best in this regard. We relate as one policeman to another. All police face the same problems in terms of criminals, whether they are Israelis or Palestinians. The methodology is the same. On that level we relate very well. On the political level there is an understanding: we are doing a job here so that when your state becomes independent, you can handle the job on your own. They know I support this end. I am very happy in this position—it's a practical one. They are practical, I am practical. When I look back on my career, I can say that in this position I am doing the most good I can for both sides."

———

Danny Israel was born a few months before the outbreak of the Sinai War, in late 1956. He served in the Israeli military from the mid-1970s until the 1982 invasion of Lebanon, when he (and many Israelis who considered the invasion a mistake) underwent a change: he realized Israel was stuck in its own Vietnam and decided to change careers. "For me, to make a better society, law enforcement would be the better path than the military, so I transferred," he recollected. "I was a 1st lieutenant in the army and they gave me that rank in the police. I asked to be put in the Fraud Squad because there were things going on, Israeli politicians taking advantage of their position to exploit Arabs, and I wanted to see it stopped. The situation was complicated enough without making it worse with corrupt Israeli politicians who preyed on Arabs because they thought nobody would care."

In his first year on the job, his Arab informants told him that Rafi Levi, a powerful official responsible for all Ministry of Interior affairs in the municipality of Jerusalem, "was taking anything from everybody." Since the 1967 War, no Jewish official of Levi's stature had been convicted of extorting money from Arabs. Danny Israel investigated and discovered that Levi was, in fact, the go-to man for getting fast-track VIP cards to enter the West Bank from Jordan, as well as for municipal licences and waivers on fines and fees. He was also acting as a major conduit for smuggled goods. For his long menu of favours offered to poorer Arabs, Levi was often paid in *helwayneh* ("children's gifts") or *koussa* ("zucchini"), Arabic euphemisms for non-monetary bribes that included free meals at Arab restaurants and free laundry and home-cleaning services. "We arrested him. There was a long trial in which he used all his contacts to try to get off, but he was eventually convicted and jailed in 1987. That was my first important case and I was very happy."

So were many of the Arabs who'd been Levi's victims, and Israel's reputation as a fair-minded cop not afraid of investigating his own people spread to the other side of the Green Line. In 1996 he moved into the INP/PCP liaison unit, and eventually he became head of the unit.

I asked him if he felt the PCP had progressed in the five years he'd been in charge of the liaison unit.

"Yes, for sure," he said. "Especially because of EUPOL COPPS and their Canadian officers. All together they are training them in all kinds of police activities. The PCP are trying to do a good job. There is also a great deal of Palestinian motivation to prove to the rest of the world that they can be a state in the near future, headed by this progressive prime minister, Salam Fayyad, who is doing his best to modernize the economy and fight corruption. So they are going in the right direction."

"I hear there's a lot of local criticism of the PCP for their collaborating with the Israeli police," I said. "Isn't it undermining their reputation with civilians? They hate the night raids and that the two forces—the Israelis and Palestinians—"

"No, on this point I disagree," he interrupted, leaning forward and placing his palm on the table. "Coordination is not collaboration. The PCP is a civil force; it investigates civil crimes, not terrorist cells. This is not their job, as I see it. As far as I know they are not fighting Hamas—not the PCP. There are other organizations doing it—the Preventive Security Force, the intelligence forces, which I don't really deal with. The PCP are not collaborating in uncovering terrorist cells when they work with the INP. It's not the police who do this. They fight crime, which everyone wants controlled."

I thought about that for a moment. Even if it wasn't the PCP's mandate to head terrorist investigations, wouldn't the force still be required to pass on the kind of information that led to the midnight IDF raids so hated by the population? "This murder might have been done by a radical," I said, moving the conversation from the global to the specific. "So wouldn't the PCP follow leads on that? And if you're coordinating, and they get information on someone with radical views and hand it to you, and you hand it to Shin Bet or the IDF, isn't that collaboration?"

"We are not sure of the background," he said. "It's possible, for example, that there is some other cause of the murder. . . . But if it's Hamas, it will go to the Preventive Security Force, not to the PCP."

I realized the point was important to him. If he thought of the PCP as a strictly civilian force he was training to fight crime in a future independent Palestine, he could separate himself from what the IDF was doing now. Yet, in truth, *all* security forces in the West Bank, both Israeli and Palestinian, were tangled together in the situation caused by the occupation, or, from the Israeli point of view, the situation that necessitated the occupation. Without the help of the Israeli occupiers, the Palestinian Authority had limited effectiveness against cells based in the camps that wanted to strike Israel to end the occupation of the West Bank, or, in some cases, end "the Jewish occupation" of Israel itself. The whole process was circular, perhaps unending—certainly not improving.

From all I had learned, it would be some time before Palestinian forces would have the capabilities of Shin Bet or the IDF, and part of the reason was that they resisted any effort to reduce their numerous competing forces. As a result, they remained ineffective, or worse: more interested in scheming to elbow each other aside for government spoils rather than in doing a professional job. The problems originated at the very top: Prime Minister Fayyad was being stonewalled in his attempts to control corruption and patronage by the PA bosses who appointed the chiefs of the competing forces, who then set the tone of behaviour for those beneath them. The worst sources of Fayyad's frustration came from the old guard around President Abbas, who liked their mansions on city hilltops that the locals of each town referred to as "Thieves' Mountain." The danger, Fayyad foresaw, was that if left unchecked, high levels of corruption could cause whole areas of the West Bank to return to the kind of internecine fighting over spoils and patronage that had been prevalent before the sweeps of 2008. And in the confusion, terrorist cells would thrive, which the IDF would then have to deal with in its usual way. I asked Israel what he had heard about corruption in the PA.

"It's not my job to investigate corruption in the PA," he said. "Of course, I see things. The people who came with Arafat to Palestine in 1994 crossed the Allenby Bridge almost without shoes. Now they all have very nice villas, big luxury cars. Where did it come from? From the salary of the PA? For example, the government of Saudi Arabia gave a lot of money to build a hospital in Qalqilya," he added, referring to a city between Ramallah and Nablus. "I was talking to a woman there, and she said, 'Where is the hospital? Just a small lousy clinic instead of a hospital. My father just died because there is no proper hospital here.' These are the kind of comments I hear from ordinary people. The feeling of the civilians is that there is corruption in the PA. Money comes for hospitals that don't get built. But, again, it's not my job to investigate these allegations. It is the PA's job to launch the bodies that investigate corruption, and my own opinion is that Prime Minister Fayyad, who is very Western-oriented and spent many years in the USA, is dedicated to controlling it. I say again, they are going in the right direction."

His phone rang and this time he spoke in Arabic as he took notes. When he hung up he said, "I am talking with the PCP now. I will be headed to Jenin shortly. I would bring you, but they would not appreciate it."

The search for witnesses was in progress, he said, although so far none aside from the babysitter had been located, which was typical in these kinds of cases in refugee camps. No matter how highly regarded a victim such as Mer-Khamis was in the camp, people would be reluctant to come forward to say what they knew.

I asked Israel if he had ever met Mer-Khamis, and he said he just knew of him from the press reports that covered his controversial career. "In Israel, he was considered highly provocative. He expressed sympathy with the people in the Jenin camp who want to return to Haifa. He actually did not believe in a two-state solution."

Before he could leave, I asked him if he thought there was any hope for that two-state solution. "My nature is to be an optimistic guy," he replied. "All other things like borders and settlements can be dealt with, of this I am sure. The heart of the issues are Jerusalem and refugees. Should they come back to Israel? Millions? It started out as thousands in '48. These millions believe they will return. So they are waiting, with Islamic Brotherhood and Hamas and Iran saying, 'One Palestinian state, with Jews okay, but a Palestinian state with no Israel, by whatever means—Israel is temporary.' This makes Israelis feel they have to stay in the West Bank until there is an agreement. Personally, I don't see Mahmoud Abbas signing a peace agreement because he has to take into consideration the refugees."

"And that's your *optimistic* opinion?"

His phone rang again. "Excuse me."

As I watched him writing in Hebrew on his pad, I considered the position he and all Israelis were stuck with. By responding to the threats of annihilation in 1967 and conquering the West Bank, Israel had pried open a bear trap. The country was still holding it open, unable to let go. Ari Shavit, a prominent Israeli journalist and one-time Peace Now member, would succinctly phrase Israel's dilemma in his book *My Promised Land:* "Here is the catch: if Israel does not retreat from the West Bank, it will be politically and morally doomed. But if it does retreat, it might face an Iranian-backed and Islamic Brotherhood–inspired West Bank regime whose missiles could endanger Israel's security. The need to end occupation is greater than ever, but so are the risks."

Danny Israel said goodbye and set off for Jenin. By the end of the day, the PCP had arrested a Hamas operative, identified by the babysitter out of a lineup, although the suspect was released after the PCP announced that DNA tests had exonerated him. Meanwhile, Mer-Khamis's murder drew large crowds of Arab-Israelis to an Arabic funeral service in Haifa, where his body lay in state in a theatre that had featured him as the star in numerous plays. In Jenin, about a hundred people marched through the city and attended a service in Freedom Theatre, but there was no visible mourning among the population of the camp itself. Two and a half weeks after his death, shortly after I left the Holy Land, a reporter for the *Observer* offered an explanation for what he called the "grim silence." "It has emerged," Conal Urquhart wrote, "that the residents of the camp had serious grievances against the actor-director that may have provided the excuses for an unknown gunman to kill him." Urquhart had discovered that "a fatwa-style leaflet" had been distributed in the camp, setting out a list of charges against Mer-Khamis and attacking him for "his belief in co-existence between Israelis and Palestinians." Specifically, the leaflet stated that Palestinians would never agree to living "with those who stole our land and killed our children." One male resident, standing under a portrait of Saddam Hussein, told Urquhart: "We are Muslims. We have traditions. We looked for our children and found them at the theatre dancing. If he came here to bring jobs that would be good but instead he comes here to corrupt our girls and make women of our boys." The chairman of the camp's governing committee complained that Mer-Khamis's "message was to liberate citizens from the authority of their leaders and children from their parents. Then there was mixing of sexes and dancing. We tried to discuss it with him and persuade him that he was mistaken but to no avail. Public opinion turned against him." The final impetus for Mer-Khamis's murder, Urquhart noted, may have been "his plan to stage a controversial German play that explores teenage sexuality"—the play about homosexuality and incest, *Spring Awakening*. Mer-Khamis was described in the leaflet as "a Jew, a communist and an infidel."

Others were not as sure that Mer-Khamis had been killed as a result of religious outrage. His Palestinian partner in the theatre, the former Al-Aqsa Brigade leader Zakaria Zabeidi, told Israeli Radio that there were power struggles going on in the Jenin camp between rival Palestinian factions, some of whom were profiting from the theatre through jobs and rents, and some of whom felt cut out.

No progress was made in the investigation over the next few months and, as frequently happens in the Holy Land when the civilian police—Israeli or Palestinian—fail to come up with answers to questions that could have a security component, the IDF stepped in, launching a 3:30 a.m. raid on the theatre on July 27, arresting the location manager and the chairman of the board for "acting against the security of the region," according to the IDF. In its usual way, the IDF smashed half the theatre's windows and trashed the place looking for evidence. The theatre employees were held for weeks of questioning without being given access to lawyers, with the IDF probing as much for the

sources of conflict between the rival factions that had possibly precipi-
tated the murder as for the identity of the killer.

Thirteen months after Mer-Khamis's murder, on May 5, 2012, the
home of Kadoura Musa, the governor of Jenin, was surrounded by armed
gunman. When they opened fire, shattering his windows and splinter-
ing his front door, Musa grabbed his own gun and fought back, dying of
a heart attack during the exchange of gunfire. The deputy director of the
PA's Preventive Security Force, Hisham Al-Rakh, based in Jenin, ordered
a large-scale security crackdown in the district, jailing dozens of armed
Fatah militiamen, including Mer-Khamis's partner, Zakaria Zabeidi, in
whose home a gun was found that was alleged to have been fired in the
attack on Musa. (Zabeidi proclaimed his innocence and was eventually
released without being charged). On September 5, Al-Rakh himself was
gunned down while on patrol in the hills above the refugee camp. Jenin
seemed to be returning to its old state of gang-style violence.

By the time I left the Holy Land in April 2011, John Copeland was
devoting his work at EUPOL COPPS almost exclusively to developing
plans for the PCP's forensics laboratory and school in Ramallah. His
timeline was short. The Canadian International Development Agency
had just pledged $10.1-million for the launch of a temporary forensics
facility at PCP headquarters, and plans were being made to refurbish
two floors of the main wing by 2014. Meanwhile, Serge Robitaille continued his feverish work with Major Rami to finish the Jericho police
college's curriculum.

While driving back from my third and last trip to Jericho, Robitaille
and I speculated on the prospects for a peace settlement after he and
Copeland ended their mission in the fall. I mentioned that recent polls
showed a majority of Israelis and Palestinians would be willing to make
concessions for a two-state solution.

"I think more and more people are feeling that way," Robitaille said.
"That's why I sometimes let myself think that the future is promising.
I just don't know how far away that future is."

It would not arrive during the two CivPol cops' remaining time in the West Bank. The Israeli and Palestinian officials following the Road Map to Peace remained stuck where they were in 2003, with no forward movement on any of the issues that separated them and with all the old roadblocks still in place, figuratively and literally. Finally, on September 23, 2011, the day after Robitaille and Copeland had returned to Canada, President Mahmoud Abbas went before the UN General Assembly to ask for Palestine's full membership as an independent state, albeit one without settled borders or a capital and still under Israeli occupation and still demanding a "right of return" to the nation of the occupiers. In Ramallah, delirious crowds filled al-Manarah Square, watching Abbas's declaration on Jumbotron screens. It was, in the end, a symbolic gesture, since the United States threatened to veto the request in the Security Council. "Peace will not come through statements and resolutions at the UN," President Barack Obama announced at the General Assembly. "If it were that easy, it would have been accomplished by now."

President Abbas did not force a vote, settling for observer status and membership in UNESCO. Meanwhile, the U.S. secretary of state, John Kerry, pledged to get the two sides together to work toward a final peace settlement, or, at the very least, "a Framework for Peace"—a Road Map by another name.

Three days after Abbas's speech at the United Nations, I arrived in Ottawa to observe the training of CivPol's latest Haiti contingent, then flew to the stricken land to cover CivPol's longest and most deadly deployment.

Serge Robitaille (left) and John Copeland in Ramallah, West Bank.

The Canadian officers lived in East Jerusalem, overlooking the Dome of the Rock and the Wailing Wall, the cosmic centre of "the situation."

The entrance to the Al-Am'ary Camp in Ramallah, where 8,000 "refugees" have been living since 1950.

The Israeli settlement of P'sagot, which blocks Ramallah's expansion into the West Bank.

EUPOL COPPS headquarters.

General Yousef Ozreil, former police chief of Nablus, Ramallah and Jenin.

Major Rami (centre), head of the training programme for Palestinian officers, had to overcome huge obstacles to pursue his ideal of policing.

Lt. Col. Zahir Sabbah, Palestinian commander of the Police College.

Robitaille.

Jenin theatre director, Juliano Mer-Khamis.

The car in which Mer-Khamis was killed.

Chief Superintendent Danny Israel, the INP's head liaison officer to the PCP.
He coordinated the investigation of Mer-Khamis's murder.

PART THREE

HAITI

Canada Bombaguy

8

BETWEEN CRISIS AND NON-EXISTENCE

THE HAITIAN NATIONAL POLICE ACADEMY occupies about fifty hectares on a plateau in eastern Port-au-Prince, its treed campus nestled between the hilltop neighbourhoods of Pétionville to the south and Vivy Mitchell to the north. Every morning on his way to the administration building, Jean Maximé, the commander of the police academy, looked past the terraced mansions of the wealthy suburbs to where the impoverished city of a million stretched out flat and green to the sea. To the northwest was the dilapidated Toussaint Louverture International Airport, named after the black general who was the architect of the slave revolt that liberated Haiti from France in 1804. West of the airport was Cité Soleil, the vast, gang-ridden slum built on a tidal marsh around the bay. Just south of this violent neighbourhood was Jean-Marie Vincent, a tent city occupied by sixty thousand people made homeless by the January 2010 earthquake. Farther south was the ruined downtown, its collapsed Presidential Palace surrounded by makeshift camps pitched on the Champ-de-Mars, Haiti's equivalent of the National Mall.

In the fall of 2011, there were about nine hundred tent camps of varying sizes around the city, containing about 600,000 internally displaced people. Maximé started each day burdened by the knowledge that the Haitian National Police (HNP) refused to patrol Jean-Marie Vincent, the largest of the camps, despite the fact that the women and young girls inside were being raped by infiltrating gang members from Cité Soleil. For protection the inhabitants of the camp relied on United Nations Police (UNPOL) under the command of the Canadian CivPol mission. The Montreal officer in charge of security for all the camps,

Inspector Jean-Pierre Synnett, had repeatedly tried to persuade HNP officers to enter Jean-Marie Vincent, only to be told: "If you want to give UNPOL officers high pay to patrol in there, then do it." To Maximé, the motivating logic of his men was clear. The tent dwellers had nothing with which to bribe the HNP to make it worth their while to share for even one day the filth and danger that the camp's residents had been enduring for almost twenty-two months. Every time Maximé thought of the mothers and daughters of Jean-Marie Vincent, he felt shame for his force.

Maximé's mission at the academy—his *aspiration suprême*—was to graduate a thousand police officers a year who would willingly patrol the camps, protect their fellow citizens and not give a thought to bribes. Toward that end he was working with an RCMP inspector named Ruth Roy, the CivPol officer in charge of helping him develop a new basic-training curriculum for the sixteen-year-old force, although in most respects Roy, a veteran officer of twenty-nine years, considered Maximé her teacher. He was a scholar and a lawyer who'd written three of the school's textbooks, all of which dealt with the practicalities of offering honest, day-to-day, law enforcement in a collapsed state that was near the bottom of Transparency International's corruption index. The titles of his last two books, published after the earthquake, announced their subjects in terms that were aspirational (*Guide to the Ethics and Ideals of Being a Haitian Police Officer*) and ominous (*Values in Haitian Society: Between Crisis and Non-existence*). "Mr. Maximé is the reason I have hope for the HNP," Roy told me as she led me up the cracked stone stairs of the administration building to meet the academy chief.

At forty-nine, Roy had lustrous auburn hair and a sunburned face that most of the time was lit up by a warm smile. During the two weeks we'd been bouncing around on Haiti's roads, I'd learned that for the eleven months she'd been on mission she'd cultivated that smile (and the hope behind it) even as her mission had run downhill and she'd had to trudge to the bottom to push it back up again. Since she'd arrived in Port-au-Prince, seventy HNP had come under investigation by the

United Nations for their alleged extrajudicial killing of twenty civilians in the capital. In the last few months, reports filed by international police trainers across the country had complained that the HNP were engaging in shakedowns at checkpoints or in narcotics trafficking. Some Haitian officers were even believed to have taken their skills and entered the Port-au-Prince underworld as gang leaders. In May 2011, a pair of suspected ex-HNP officers had invaded the home of three RCMP CivPol cops, hog-tied and tormented them, then led their gang on a home-invasion spree, killing a Rwandan UNPOL officer, a Haitian banker and a security guard. Roy and her two CivPol roommates, who lived in the same neighbourhood as the ambushed Mounties, now took turns wearing their Glock service pistol around the house, in the same way they took turns doing the chores.

Maximé's secretary showed us into an unairconditioned board-room whose Canadian office furniture contrasted with walls bubbled by moisture where they met chipped floor tiles. On all four walls Maximé had proudly hung group portraits commemorating President Michel Martelly's attendance at the academy's graduation ceremonies in May, ten days after his inauguration. The ascension of Martelly, the country's most famous pop singer, to the presidency had marked the first time in Haiti's history that there'd been a peaceful transition of power after a democratic election. His five months in office had not soiled his reputation as "the people's president." Indeed, in honour of his shaven head, even the illiterate kids in the camps for the internally dis-placed called their soccer balls "Martellys." In the boardroom photos, Martelly wore a sash with Haiti's national colours which symbolized the union of the country's two founding racial groups—blue for the majority blacks and red for the minority mulattoes. The most promi-nent photo in the room showed the mulatto Martelly standing between the black HNP police chief, Mario Andresol, and the black Jean Maximé.

I heard two cops outside shout *"Attention!"* and then Maximé strode into the boardroom. He was six feet tall, lean and handsome, with a thin moustache that gave him a dashing air. In his blue pinstripe suit he looked a decade younger than his fifty years, although the impression of youthfulness didn't last long. Five minutes into our interview, I asked him about the widespread corruption in the HNP and he became instantly transformed into an aged headmaster weighed down by his students' poor performance. He put on silver-rimmed spectacles and hunched over the table to read me the opening passage to his book on values, which he said explained "the origin and perpetuation" of his officers' malfeasance. "In Haiti today, moral degradation and anti-social behaviour are a commonplace lifestyle," he read aloud in French. "Antivalues have embedded themselves in our society to such an extent that they have become our predominant values."

He closed the book and slapped its cover, as if driving home its message. Below the title was a map of Haiti with five shattered versions of the word *valeurs* overlaying the country's two peninsulas, which embrace the Gulf of Gonâve, and its serrated border with the Dominican Republic. "The people we are taking into this academy have been raised to cheat and steal, with no discipline, no sense of delaying their need for gratification," he said. "These young people do not have criminal records—we vet them. But they share the destroyed values of our population. This is why we alone in the Western Hemisphere need the UN to protect us—from ourselves."

The United Nations Stabilization Mission in Haiti, known by its French acronym MINUSTAH,* had been using its combined force of eight thousand soldiers and half as many UN police and specialized anti-riot cops to keep order in the country since 2004, and for a decade before that in smaller numbers and under seven other acronyms. Now MINUSTAH was pushing Maximé to recruit and train enough HNP officers to bring the national force from its current strength of nine thousand to fourteen thousand by 2015, the year by which it hoped the HNP would be functional. Maximé was not optimistic about the time frame. The funding allotted to the academy only gave him seven months to train each incoming class. "We need the *time* to undo all the bad that has been done to these young men and women," Maximé said

---

* Mission des Nations Unies pour la Stabilisation en Haïti

to me, his voice rising as if there were a crowd of people listening in. "When we have a country like ours that doesn't function, where we do not have proper schools and good teachers, where family relations are in disarray and where the first lesson children learn from their teachers and parents is how to pay bribes to buy grades, well then it is impossible for the Academy to undo all that negative conditioning in just seven months. I need a year with them, or they will leave here and be influenced by those who take the bad money."

"I try to see another side to the story," Ruth Roy said to me. "Mr. Maximé's forty instructors are very well trained and very competent. And that's the beginning of a turnaround, if there is to be one."

"*Thank* you, *madame*! Thank you!" Maximé said.

As if seized by the hope in Roy's remark, he leaned forward and pointed to the blue and red flag furled in the corner. "You see our colours?" he asked me. "Two fabrics, sewn together. On it is our national motto: 'There is strength in unity.'" After triumphing over Napoleon's troops, he said, Jean-Jacques Dessalines, the first president of Haiti, had ripped the white from the French *tricolore*—the engram of servitude— and offered the new bi-colour to his freed people. Maximé opened his hands to the ceiling, as if acknowledging a miracle. "We are the first black republic, the first country created from a slave revolution! To be a policeman in Haiti, you have a duty to remember this. You must *love* your country above yourself. You must *impart* that love to the people. It is *this* value we teach at the academy. Everyone here must understand the meaning of *La Dessalinienne*, and sing it with Creole pride."

And at that, he broke into the national anthem, his face transformed into an expression of unbounded expectation.

> *For Haiti, for the Country's Ancestors*
> *We must walk hand in hand*
> *There must be no traitors among us*
> *We must be our own masters.*
> *Let us walk hand in hand*
> *For Haiti can be more beautiful!*

"Pou Ayiti ka vin pi bèl!" he repeated in Creole. "Haiti can be *more* beautiful. I was *raised* with this consciousness by my parents. Despite all our troubles, I have always believed that Haiti can be *more* beautiful."

Jean Miguelite Maximé was born in 1960 in rural poverty in Croix-des-Bouquets, east of the capital, and spent his grade school years under the murderous police-state of François "Papa Doc" Duvalier (1957–1971). He entered high school in the equally murderous reign of Papa's over-weight playboy son, Jean-Claude "Baby Doc" Duvalier (1971–1986). His parents were religious Catholics who'd wanted to imbue young Jean with a morality opposed to the rapaciousness of the Duvalier regimes, yet at the same time prepare him for a career that would not get him killed by the Tontons Macoutes—the 300,000 sadistic paramilitaries both Duvaliers used to annihilate dissenters. The Maximés therefore invested their meagre savings in sending young Jean to a high school that would enable him to study abroad. He was a child prodigy, and between the ages of thirteen and eighteen he read the entire classical canon in Latin, including Aristotle's *Ethics,* Plato's *Republic, The Meditations* of Marcus Aurelius, and the Bible. He kept a "philosophical diary" during this period, copying out passages that he felt comple-mented one another on their approach to ethical living, adding his own aphorisms, such as: "Self-discipline is the most important discipline of all" and "When you talk, people do not hear; but when you act, they see." From Corinthians I in the Bible he'd derived the personal code he would live by for the rest of his life, and which he felt summed up two thousand years of humanist wisdom: "But I would have you know that the head of every man is Christ."

He explained to me his interpretation of the passage, which he taught every morning in his values classes at the academy: "The light of purity is in every being and in every nation," he said. "Just as a very bad man has it within him to attain his highest purpose in life, so Haiti can undo its bad behaviour and create a good society. This is God's promise to us."

During the 1980s Maximé had gone to the United States and then to

France to earn degrees in international relations, educational science, public administration and law. Instead of remaining abroad like many educated Haitians, however, he returned to his country at the age of twenty-five to participate in the events that led to the ouster of Baby Doc. Afterward, the interim National Government Council set up a city police force of a few hundred officers, and Maximé became one of its first recruits. "Knowledge and idealism have to be practically applied," he said, explaining why, with all his academic qualifications, he'd joined the police. "Safety, security and justice are the foundations of a democratic society. Without an honest civilian police force, you can have none of these."

The tiny force was mostly window dressing to impress the international community, but Maximé took it seriously, and stayed with it through four changes of government engineered by the military, a 1991 coup that overthrew the legally elected president, Jean-Bertrand Aristide, the ouster of the military in 1994 and the arrival of the first UN peacekeepers and a CivPol contingent of Mounties. One of President Aristide's first reforms upon his return to power was to disband the army and establish a national police force in its place. Maximé transferred to the HNP and over the next dozen years he worked his way up through the ranks to his current position.

He'd dedicated *Values in Haitian Society* to his bodyguard, who'd been shot to death in the spring while defending Maximé against an attack by six gangsters in downtown Port-au-Prince in broad daylight. "With an aching heart and an agonized soul," he read aloud, "I dedicate this book to my childhood friend, Jean Wilkens Gervais, who fell under the murderous bullets of bandits on March 22, 2011, the victim of our all-out crisis of values." He took out a handkerchief and wiped tears from his eyes as he stared at the passage. "Jean was with me during the earthquake. He lived another fourteen months to give his life for me." He looked up from his book. "You know, the earthquake is not an excuse for our current state. Haitian history did not begin at 4:53 p.m. on January 12, 2010. We were already in a state between crisis and non-existence."

"Where were you when the earthquake hit?" I asked.

"There is an HNP office building—or there was," he said, pointing west to the downtown. "South of the Champ-de-Mars and the Presidential Palace. I was standing outside."

He'd just come out of a strategy meeting with senior officers. The meeting had not gone well. Too much time had been taken up with the complaints of a couple of his colleagues about MINUSTAH. "It is the common refrain," Maximé said. "The feeling is, 'We are occupied and it hurts our dignity.' MINUSTAH has many failings, but everyone knows if they leave we will have another coup. I said, 'Please, let us get some police business done here.' So: five minutes of business, then these fellows returned to our national pastime of blaming others for our problems. Finally, there was a debriefing. I said: 'I cannot stay for the debriefing, I have to go.'"

Jean Gervais was waiting for him beside his government car. Gervais noticed Maximé's sour look and asked what was wrong, at which point the ground jumped and a crack split the air, as if the side of the police building behind Maximé had been whacked by a monumental stick. "Earthquake," Maximé said to Gervais. "Be cool." The ground rolled up, then down, vibrated in the trough, then rolled yet higher and even lower, the amplified waves compressed into a continuous violent shaking that seemed to ripple southwest to northeast. Maximé fell against the hood of his car and twisted himself around to see the police building rocking back and forth. Then it collapsed, sending forth a block-wide whoosh of white dust that covered the street. He flattened himself against the hood, looking up through the chalk-collared miasma toward the Champ-de-Mars a few blocks to the north. Beyond the ghostly palms whipping back and forth was the Presidential Palace. "Jesus, Lord Jesus!" Maximé cried as he heard the tremendous noise of the ornate cupolas falling. The heaving of the ground lasted, in total, thirty-five seconds. Then there was quiet. Moments later, the screams began.

On the afternoon of the earthquake there were roughly a hundred Canadian CivPol officers working in Haiti, about two-thirds of them scattered around the Port-au-Prince area. They were serving on a mission that had been running almost continuously for seventeen years, beefed up during the frequent periods of political turmoil or when the criminal chaos that reigned in Cité Soleil grew into a city-wide plague of murder and kidnapping. For the previous seven months, their ultimate commander was RCMP Chief Superintendent Doug Coates, a veteran of three Haiti missions since 1994. Coates, the United Nations' Police Commissioner in charge of seventeen hundred UNPOL officers, was in MINUSTAH headquarters, the Hotel Christopher, three kilometres east of the Presidential Palace, attending a function for a delegation that was visiting from China. Hosting the function with him was Luiz Carlos da Costa, the special representative of UN Secretary General Ban Ki-moon. About the time Jean Maximé was leaving police headquarters, one of the members of the Chinese delegation asked if he could take a group picture of the assembly. The seven-storey hotel was a hundred metres above the city, just off the road that led up to the mountain suburb of Pétionville. Everyone lined up against the top-floor view window. The delegate took the photo: the last recorded image of the ten people in the boardroom.

A moment later, the quake hit and the fifty-year-year old hotel, like most concrete slab buildings in Port-au-Prince, came apart at the seams, falling sideways. When Coates was discovered two and a half days later, he was found draped over Carlos da Costa. "His body was positioned in such a way that it appeared he was protecting his supervisor," said Supt. Jean-Michel Blais, the Mountie who had dug through the last layer of debris to find Coates. "I knew Doug for fifteen years. He would have taken charge of the situation and done what came naturally to him, which was protecting people."

Just before the earthquake, on the other side of a ravine from the hotel, RCMP Sgt. Mark Gallagher, fifty, had been dropped off at his six-storey apartment house on Rue Reimbold, having just flown in after being on leave at his home in New Brunswick. His job was to mentor the HNP but he'd taken on the added responsibility of teaching nights and weekends at the Sacred Jesus Catholic Orphanage in one of the city's slums. Though he was tired, he told the CivPol officer who'd driven him from the airport that he would head to the orphanage that night. Gallagher's body was found a day later, buried under six storeys of rubble.

One by one across the city, CivPol officers got to their feet in the dusty fog and assessed the destruction around them as screams came from every direction. Sgt. Claude Cuillerier of the Montreal Police found a car jack, inserted it in the space between two toppled slabs and crawled inside, pulling on the hands of the trapped, guiding them out one by one. Sgt. Denis Roy of the Montreal Police survived the toppling of a two-storey restaurant, then found his way to a nearby collapsed hospital and dug out a buried child. He performed first aid on other injured patients and spent the rest of the night digging among the broken concrete for survivors in danger of being crushed during the strong aftershocks. Cst. Bertrand Fraser of the Saguenay Police and Cpl. Louis-Philippe Leblanc of the Ottawa Police heard the crying of an infant beneath the debris and dug her out, then crawled into the tiny space and rescued her mother. And so it went throughout the city. Thirteen Canadian CivPol officers from five federal, municipal and provincial police departments would eventually receive RCMP bravery medals for putting their own lives directly at risk to save others. In all, 101 MINUSTAH employees from thirty-three countries lost their lives that day.

The swath of destruction stretched for eighty kilometres along the Caribbean coast and forty kilometres inland. The Haitian government would put the death toll at over 200,000. In addition to the police building Maximé had been in, five HNP stations had collapsed in the capital, killing 79 HNP. Four thousand criminals escaped from the National Penitentiary just west of the Presidential Palace, and another two thousand escaped from the prison annex to the south, heading for their old gang haunts in the slums of Cité Soleil. A million people were left with no shelter in greater Port-au-Prince, and in the surrounding districts another half a million were forced to sleep on the open ground. In all, from Grand Goâve in the west to Croix-des-Bouquets in the east, 300,000 buildings had collapsed or been severely damaged.

———

Ten months after the quake, Ruth Roy arrived in Port-au-Prince, a city in turmoil on several fronts. It was early November 2010 and the capital's residents were fearful of Hurricane Tomas approaching from the south, terrified of a cholera epidemic that was creeping closer from the north, enraged that their president, René Préval, was impotent at helping them recover from the quake, and exasperated at the blatant corruption of Préval's cronies in the House of Deputies and the Senate. As Roy's contingent was driven from the airport to a walled compound for orientation, tens of thousands of young people were rioting in the streets, blocking intersections, throwing rocks and burning tires.

Haiti was Ruth Roy's first CivPol mission, her first experience of widespread disorder, but from the start of her career, she'd always sought assignments that took her into unfamiliar terrain. She was the first woman to qualify for the RCMP's elite Underwater Recovery Team, then led a drive to expand police services for victims of sexual abuse on Native reserves and, long before it became fashionable, was an advocate of "cultural change" within the male-dominated RCMP. She had worked with Mark Gallagher in the Maritimes and, when he was on leave, had listened to his tales of CivPol in Haiti. "It was very moving for me," she recollected. "He didn't want to change the country, but to help individuals one at a time, particularly through his volunteer work at the orphanage. He believed in compassion but not pity." When the earthquake struck, she was working in the Strategic Planning Unit at Mountie headquarters in Ottawa. Like many other French-speaking Canadian cops, she applied for the Haiti mission, hoping that her experience in policing might be of use to the country. "I didn't predict what Haiti needed from me beforehand," she told me. "From what I'd read about Haitians and foreigners, that was one of the problems between them. Aid workers arrived expecting they had the answers before they asked Haitians the questions."

The demonstrations she witnessed on her first day were sparked by fierce competition for an upcoming November 28 presidential election being contested by nineteen candidates. Some had called out their supporters to protest suspected government shenanigans in the placement of polling stations; others were backers of the now-exiled president Jean-Bertrand Aristide, whose party, Fanmi Lavalas, had been blocked from running candidates because of its history of assassinating adversaries; still others were gang members from the slums hired by one party or another to challenge the demonstrations of their opponents.

The front-runner of the campaign was Michel "Sweet Micky" Martelly. Although he had no political experience, his candidacy was bolstered by the fact that most of his musical hits in the last fifteen years were sung in Creole, the language of the poor black majority, and that he was not tied in any obvious way to the ubiquitous corruption of the French-speaking mulatto elite. "We have no love for each other anymore," he'd proclaimed at a recent rally. "The state doesn't serve—it's not about serving the population; it's about getting rich when people get into power."

For two hundred years before the earthquake, Haiti had suffered under people who'd seized power for no other reason than to get rich, leading to one political and economic emergency after another. Each reign of corruption was ended by the next set of people who wanted their own share of the spoils, the cycle adding another layer of instability to the state, which eventually contributed to the high death toll and misery of the quake. On the morning of January 12, 2010, Haiti was the poorest nation in the Western Hemisphere and one of the most dysfunctional countries on the planet. Over four-fifths of Haitians lived in dire poverty. The roads within and between cities were disintegrating into dirt tracks. Frayed power lines looped from spindly poles and the electricity they conveyed was totally unreliable, forcing millions without generators to live by candlelight. Sewers were stinking open ditches. Public structures collapsed on their own because building codes either didn't exist or were unenforced. Most streets overflowed with garbage that just kept piling higher because municipal managers were more interested in skimming the cheques of city workers than in making sure they did their jobs.

To these problems could be added the enormous economic divide between the less than 5 percent of Haitians who were mulatto caste—the descendants of unions between plantation owners and their African slaves—and the over 95 percent who were of undiluted African heritage. It was a racial conflict that had riven the country since independence. In Port-au-Prince, the mulattoes lived high above the city in the mansions of Pétionville and Vivy Mitchell, spoke French, ate at four-star restaurants and drove luxury cars, while the vast majority of blacks lived in squalor down below, spoke Creole, and usually never received more than a few years of primary education. Half of Haiti's ten million people were completely illiterate, and many were so poor that they gave their children away to rich mulatto families to work as domestic servants. In return, the rich families were supposed to feed and school the children, but in practice they beat them, sexually abused them and made them work as long as eighteen hours a day. The tradition of *restavec*—from the Creole word that derives from the French *reste avec*, "stays with"—was among the most disturbing features of the racial and economic divide in Haiti, a legal form of child slavery. Haiti may be the first country created from a successful slave revolution, but the descendants of the blacks who had won their freedom felt constantly betrayed by people who saw governing not as a duty but as a means to maintain control of the state and suck it dry.

The chasm between the races was apparent when I landed at Port-au-Prince's Toussaint Louverture Airport on October 3, 2011. The conveyor was broken and men in jumpsuits had dumped three hundred suitcases onto the linoleum. Bags and boxes flew every which way as the coach passengers on my flight from Montreal fell on the pile. They argued, took sides, joked, laughed, pointed fingers, urged calm, threatened combat and finally shouted in victory when they at last found their overstuffed suitcases in the pile and stumbled off with them. The business-class passengers, on the other hand, hired others to participate in the demeaning melee. They haughtily put a few gourdes of local currency into the hands of the workmen and ordered them to wade into the crowd to grab a chic leather carrier or an aluminum case.

Five hours earlier, in the Montreal departure lounge, the skin colour difference between the two classes had jumped out at me. The dozen people in business class who'd filed onto the plane first were mainly shades of coffee while the 250 in economy were mainly shades of black, representing about the same proportion in wealth and colour-caste as in Haiti at large. In almost any place else but Haiti it's not permissible for a journalist to make note of gradations in skin colour, but I'd been alerted to the significance of the colour line during the week I'd spent in Ottawa covering the training of a contingent of thirty CivPol officers. At the Police College I met a couple of black Haitian Canadian cops taking other courses. "When you go down from the plane," one cracked, "you will see the pilots are foreign *blan*, the rich passengers are Haitian *kafé*, and the steerage are all *authentiques*."

"Welcome to Haiti!" Ruth Roy said, coming up behind me as I watched the chaos. "Don't be afraid to shove your way in. This is Haiti."

RCMP Superintendent Robert Boulet, CivPol's contingent commander in Haiti, had chosen Roy from among the 157 Canadian police-trainers to guide me through the mission because, he wrote me, "her work is central to what we are doing here." He'd pointed out in his e-mail that, in addition to preparing the HNP's training curriculum, Roy was developing a course in gender-based violence, with forty-eight hours of practical training in interviewing female victims of rape, incest and beating—a first for the country's police force. As part of that component she was teaching the HNP how to investigate the abusive treatment of the child *restavecs*. Both of these course components were enthusiastically supported by the head of the Police Academy, Jean Maximé, although Maximé's political and law enforcement superiors were less than enthusiastic about bringing the treatment of *restavecs* under such scrutiny.

After the luggage riot dispersed and I finally got my bag, Roy led me out to the breezeway. "We had a laugh when you e-mailed us you'd take a taxi to your hotel," she said. She pointed to the hundreds of Haitians in threadbare clothes and flip-flops blocking the road and screaming offers to carry luggage. Some of them noticed the Canadian flag patch on Roy's uniform and began chanting, *"Canada bombaguy! Canada bombaguy!"*—good guy Canada. "They mostly like Canadians but they wouldn't know where you were from," she told me. "And after you'd made your way through them, you wouldn't find a taxi because there are none. Bob Boulet said to me, 'Don't let him get kidnapped on his first day.'"

"Welcome to heaven," an Ottawa City constable greeted me wryly at Roy's UN vehicle in the solar furnace of the parking lot. Ray Lamarre, a dead ringer for Robert De Niro, was the spokesperson for the United Nations Police under whose aegis CivPol served in Haiti. As Roy plunged her vehicle into the traffic snarl of overloaded tap-tap buses and creaky trucks spewing black exhaust along Louverture Boulevard, Lamarre remarked from the back seat that when he'd first arrived on mission in March he'd been assigned to the internally displaced persons (IDP) camp that was run by actor Sean Penn's Haitian Relief Organization. A couple of weeks into his mission he'd attended a benefit dinner for Penn's group. Lamarre went up to Penn and said, "It was nice having dinner last year." Penn looked him in the face and said, totally fooled, "Good to see you again, Robert. I appreciate your coming to Port-au-Prince."

Whether or not Lamarre had consciously adopted De Niro's persona, he uttered most of his comments out of the side of his mouth, often with unspokesman-like candour. "See all these shoe salesman on the side of the road? No coincidence we're near the airport. The immigration guys steal 'em from the luggage, give 'em to their relatives to sell. People get to their rooms. 'Now where'd I pack my high heels?'"

Personally, he said, he couldn't blame destitute Haitians for profiting from people who could afford to fly. However, he did blame those thousands of Haitian youths who regularly broke into the IDP camps and stole from people who had nothing. "It's not just the criminal element," he said. "There's a definite breakdown of personal responsibility here, top to bottom. The light-skinned elite who live above the city only care about their mansions and cars and shopping trips to Miami, plus keeping people in power who won't take anything away from them. The poor blacks have retreated to their immediate families, if they're lucky enough to have families, and get by any way they can."

As we passed a potholed road that went up a hillside, he painted a picture of what I could expect after the twenty-minute deluge of rain that exploded like clockwork every evening. "Miles of trash comes down these roads"—mountains of garbage so huge, he said, it plugged the intersections. The citizens of Port-au-Prince—those not living in the exclusive neighbourhoods—had no garbage pickup and made no attempt at dealing with their trash themselves. Instead, they threw it from their windows and trucks and wagons and storefronts right into the street. In the midst of the still extensive rubble from the earthquake, there was more garbage along Louverture Boulevard than I'd seen in any other city, and it smelled like a cesspool. With no sewage system in the city, many Haitians used "flying toilets," relieving themselves in plastic bags and heaving the bags into the gutter. The flying toilets eventually joined the river of garbage that flowed downhill.

Four kilometres on we came to a sudden break in the rubble and refuse—a beige concrete wall set back from a newly paved section of street that was actually swept clean. On the two-metre wall, topped by razor wire, was a brightly coloured logo of a palm tree at sunset, above which were the words CARIBBEAN LODGE—the hotel Robert Boulet had recommended I book to put me in commuting distance of Delta Camp, the UN police headquarters. A security guard pressed a button, the black steel gate across the entrance drew slowly back, and we drove into a bleak compound that looked like an Afghan military base. The "lodge" consisted of 160 cargo canisters refurbished as windowless rooms and stacked in two-storey rows facing a gravel lot where UN vehicles were parked. This was where the CivPol recruits I'd just observed in Ottawa would stay for their first two weeks on mission. They would leave the lodge every day and receive orientation training at Delta Camp two kilometres south and then have the option of moving into rental quarters of their own choosing, either in the capital or, if they were posted to the regions, near the HNP district commissariats in the country's nine other departments.

After I threw my bag in my tiny room, Roy, Lamarre and I sat down for coffee in the thirty-five-degree heat of an open-air restaurant and went over my itinerary. Roy said she'd she show me all aspects of the Port-au-Prince mission and some of the police commissariats in the regions where Canadians were based. Since it was still the rainy season, we'd have to stick to commissariats that fronted on passable roads. Anywhere off those roads and it could take ten hours to drive a hundred kilometres. One commissariat was in Kenscoff, two hours south into the mountains from Port-au-Prince; another, in Grand Goâve, was two hours west along the coast, just twenty kilometres from the epicentre of the earthquake.

"I'll be coming along on most of your trips," Lamarre said, "not so much to give you the UN propaganda but because of the security issues."

"We usually travel in twos when we drive from point to point," Roy explained. Though ordinary Haitian civilians held a very positive view of Canadians (hence, Canada *bombaguy*), on the roads they could not distinguish between the vehicles of UN peacekeepers and Canadian CivPol trainers—which dangerously complicated life for mission members. Before the earthquake there had been numerous scandals involving Third World UN peacekeepers sexually exploiting local Haitian women and minors. As a member of the Conduct and Disciplinary Unit when she'd first arrived, Roy had investigated many of the incidents. More recent scandals involved the cholera epidemic, which had been started by Nepalese UN peacekeepers. And just before I landed, a video had been leaked to the press showing Uruguayan peacekeepers raping an eighteen-year-old boy in their custody. All of this had enraged the country to the point where a road accident involving a UN vehicle could turn into a rock-throwing, tire-burning riot in an instant.

"A lot of it has to do with this historical feeling that foreigners have never forgiven Haiti for overthrowing their slave masters and are always scheming to come back in," said Lamarre, who at forty-eight was studying for a master's degree in history. "When the country collapsed in anarchy in 1915 the U.S. did come in, occupied the place with racist Marines for twenty years. They appointed the lightest skin people to run things and forced the farmers into work gangs to build roads. That seemed a lot like slavery to the Haitians. Then when the country collapsed again in 1994, the UN came in. As much as they need the UN's help, they still see it as an occupying army."

"Another problem is that MINUSTAH is composed of fifty-two different countries," Roy said. "It's UN policy that there has to be a sampling of countries. But they all have different ideas of policing, different competencies, different work ethics and notions of honesty."

"Tell you a story about that," Lamarre said. "Ivory Coast has the largest contingent here, after Canada. So an HNP said to me: 'If the UN is in the Ivory Coast training an incompetent police force, why are the incompetent Ivory Coast officers here training us? The UN must think we're buffoons.'"

9

A RIVER FINDS ITS PATH

THE CHICKENS WERE STILL SLEEPING when HNP Officer Anique Aubristin left the cinderblock home he shared with his wife and six children in Croix-des-Bouquets. He walked a kilometre along a dirt road to the Route Nationale, then stood in line behind a hundred commuters until he boarded a tap-tap bus for the two-hour journey to his police station in the mountain town of Kenscoff. A tap-tap is a pickup with a roof welded to its frame that sits ten but usually carries another twenty people crammed in the aisle and clinging to its back. When riders want to get off they tap the truck's metal sides with a coin. The constant tapping and the truck's lurching acceleration after each stop kept Aubristin from adding even a brief doze to his nightly allotment of five hours' sleep.

His route took him west over the Rivière Grise into the Port-au-Prince district of Delmas. At a dusty intersection a block from my hotel he changed tap-taps for one that took him south past the United Nations' Delta Camp and the Police Academy, then west and south to begin the long climb through the neighbourhoods of Péguy Ville, Bois Moquette and Pétionville—each district higher, cooler and richer than the one before. A few kilometres beyond Pétionville he passed into rural Haiti, the transition marked by deforested mountains covered to their peaks by a patchwork of vegetable plots, perched precariously between the scars of landslides that had taken chunks of the mountains to the canyon below. Aubristin, who was forty-seven, knew it was only a matter of time before all these slopes slipped into the Rivière Froide. The slopes needed trees but the farmers needed charcoal and so were cutting the trees even in the gullies. They had been raised on the proverb *"Ayiti se tè glise"*—Haiti is a slippery land—so they actually expected to lose their plots to gravity. Only 2 percent of Haiti's original forest cover remained, but the Ministry of Agriculture, Natural Resources and Rural Development was too wrapped up in the political turmoil in the capital to coordinate any real attempt at reforestation.

The sun was an hour into the sky by the time Aubristin reached Kenscoff, 1,500 metres above the Caribbean. Here the peaks were covered by a canopy of pine trees, but not because of government intervention. The wealthy from the capital had built dozens of vacation chalets in the area, which were cantilevered off mountains patrolled by private security firms. Guarding the trees was a full-time job. Many of Kenscoff's four thousand citizens lived in pole-and-tin houses and needed charcoal even more than the farmers down below.

Swinging off the tap-tap in his short sleeves, Aubristin felt chilled by the morning's humidity, rising from the slopes and condensing into a fog that would thread through the pines for most of the day. The road was already crowded with locals standing ankle-deep in refuse, selling flatbread, sneakers, belts, lipstick—anything that would earn them a few gourdes. On a knoll beside the road stood the two-storey police commissariat, its rock foundation painted blue and its walls white—the sky-and-cloud colours of all HNP stations. Kenscoff's cops might protect the capital's vacationing rich but the rich paid no taxes, and so the commissariat was as dilapidated as a servants' quarters. The white walls were stained with long trails of black mould, big chunks of plaster were missing and the window slats to the interview rooms had been blown away by hurricanes.

As Aubristin crossed the road, he stopped to ask the street-sellers if they had any new information about a five-year-old girl who'd been kidnapped last week from her home in the nearby town of Fort Jacques. The street-sellers told him they did not believe a human had taken the girl. They were convinced a *loup-garou*—a werewolf—had infiltrated the surrounding forest and that it would be impossible for the police to find the victim without the spiritual help of a *houngan*, or voodoo priest.

Aubristin tried to counter the superstitious gossip. He told the excited crowd that soon gathered around him that the crime was committed by a deviant human, probably a local pedophile who had acted on his criminal desires. If the street-sellers heard any news they should tell someone at the station.

Aubristin began his twelve-hour shift by writing a report about the street-sellers' superstitious reaction to the crime. He was as saddened by his countrymen's belief in werewolves as by their fatalistic assumption that Haiti was built on quicksand. Since they felt the nation was irrational, they also felt they were powerless to affect its future, whereas he had been raised to believe that living a life devoted to order, family and personal discipline would be rewarded. *"Sonje denmen!"* was the credo his parents had instilled in him: *Remember tomorrow!* They were poor farmers in Pion, near Cap Haïtien in the north of the country. From the time he was six they had urged him to finish high school and then join the army. "You will have a job for life, be able to marry and support your family," his father had told him. He'd enlisted at eighteen, served as a private guarding a barracks in Croix-des-Bouquets, married a local girl and been able to rent a house with a good roof. Then, in 1995, just after the birth of Aubristin's third child, President Aristide had disbanded the army and the young soldier was out of work. He'd tried to run a storefront business in Delmas, but the gang situation was terrible. In ten years he'd been held up four times. In 2005, driven by his need for financial security and his desire to bring order to his country, he'd joined the police. After graduating from the academy, he was posted to Kenscoff. Since then he'd sometimes thought about applying for a transfer to a commissariat in the capital, closer to home, but with only six years' service he was still an A1, or constable, and men of his junior rank in Port-au-Prince were assigned to Cité Soleil or the *bidonville* shantytowns clinging to the hills. Twenty-seven HNP had been murdered in the city so far this year, and Aubristin knew his wife and kids would starve if they lost his $312-a-month salary. And so he stayed put, making the long commute to Kenscoff and its own set of problems.

Half an hour into his shift, two Montreal police officers and an officer with the Sûreté du Québec rolled into town to mentor Aubristin and the forty-four other HNP stationed in Kenscoff and in more remote mountain villages. Alain Alarie was the head of the Canadian CivPol mission for the district. He was a red-headed staff sergeant in his late forties who had spent most of his twenty-seven years as a cop in action postings, including the Gang Squad, the Joint Task Force antiterrorism unit and the arson unit. Like Ruth Roy, he'd applied for the Haiti CivPol mission right after the earthquake. He'd been mentoring in Kenscoff for nine months, working seven days a week patrolling the mountain trails with the HNP.

Alarie and his colleagues were talking with Aubristin on the veranda outside the chief's second-floor office when Roy, Ray Lamarre and I pulled up opposite the station. We mounted the two flights of steps and Roy introduced me to the group. Aubristin told us he had arrested two young men yesterday: one had stolen a sack of potatoes and the other had been caught with a homemade gun. Aubristin, his colleagues and the Canadians had walked four hours on trails into the mountains to make the arrests. They had found the men waiting for them, with the incriminating evidence in the hut of their *kazee,* or chief. The *kazee* had sent word to the HNP to take custody of the boys in his *lakou*—a complex Creole word that means, among other things, a walled village.

"They just waited for you to arrest them?" I asked Aubristin. "Why didn't they run away?"

"Sometimes they even come down on their own to turn themselves in," he said. "They don't want to be ostracized from the *lakou,* so they usually follow the *kazee*'s orders."

"He has just told you what law enforcement in rural Haiti is about," Alarie said to me.

"Actually, he's just told you what Haiti is about," Lamarre added. "Even in Cité Soleil. It took the UN fifteen years to understand the *lakou* system."

A *lakou* (from the French *la cour,* meaning "courtyard") is a self-sufficient compound whose half-dozen huts and surrounding agricultural land are privately owned by individuals in an extended family—the most fundamental unit of rural Haitian society. Urban Haitians may be physically separated from their home *lakous*, but most of them are still connected to the model of life that was born there. *Lakous* date from the mid-nineteenth century, when the rural population learned that the government in Port-au-Prince was mainly concerned with stealing from them or drafting them to work like slaves on huge sugar plantations. To survive, each extended family physically and economically walled itself off from the state, forming bonds of loyalty to each other, to their *kazee* and to the land. Until well into the twentieth century, the vast majority of black Haitians lived in *lakous*. When rural people began migrating to the city in the 1950s, they tried to maintain the spirit of the *lakou*, viewing themselves as primarily connected to their immediate neighbours and disconnected from the government.

Some historians think the *lakou* heritage was one of the forces that made Haiti ungovernable, since it inclined most people to ignore laws and work outside the official economy, treating taxes as theft. Others argue that the *lakou* system was the only way Haitians had survived successive governments of organized gangsterism—though the *lakou* tradition sometimes gave birth to organized gangsterism. In 2006, when a Canadian-led UNPOL force launched a campaign to establish law and order in Port-au-Prince's gang-run neighbourhoods, the cops discovered that the arrested gang members considered themselves members of a *lakou*, with the gang boss their *kazee*.

Today, in the countryside around Kenscoff, the *kazees* were still the arbiters of affairs in their *lakous*, but in the last half-dozen years they had changed their attitude to the local police, if not to the government. In 2004 the gangs in the capital had begun recruiting members in the hills above Pétionville and the *kazees* had seen the benefit of collaborating with the HNP. Now, if a *kazee* had trouble with a *lakou* member, he sent word to Kenscoff for HNP assistance, then ordered the offenders to stay put until the cops arrived. Aubristin said the boys who had waited for the HNP knew the importance of their *lakou*. Without that affiliation, they would have to fend for themselves and might not survive. The two boys were in the station's small downstairs jail, awaiting the attention of the division's commandant, Julbert Conseillant, who would decide whether they should be handed over to one of Kenscoff's three investigating magistrates or have their cases dealt with less formally.

While Aubristin prepared breakfast for the prisoners and Ruth Roy chatted with the Canadian officers, Alarie led Lamarre and me into the commandant's office. Conseillant was a stocky man in his mid-forties who sat at a desk with a cell phone to his right and an unholstered gun to his left. He shook my hand without smiling, then looked down at a paper, as if he'd prepared for the interview. He told me Kenscoff had a large contingent of thirteen UNPOL to assist him. "Three Canadians, and then one each from Germany, Rwanda, Jordan, Chile, Romania, Ivory Coast, Guinea, Burkina Faso, Benin and a new one from Spain." He looked at Lamarre, who was translating.

"Perhaps he'd be interested in why Kenscoff needs so many UNPOL," Lamarre suggested to Conseillant. The commandant took the cue.

"The reason is the political dimension here," he explained. "The president's mother lives here. The ex-president, Baby Doc, returned in March and has a house here. Many important persons have their second homes here, so this is a very political area and security is vital."

I asked him what would happen if UNPOL left him on his own.

"You can look around and see we lack the equipment to provide security," he said. "We have no computers, no landlines, the radio doesn't work because it's too old, we have one truck, a jail that only holds two, and the commissariat itself is rundown. I have asked for a remedy to all these deficiencies, but will I ever get it?" He left the question dangling in the air a moment, then added: "There are no roads here. My men must patrol twelve hours a day on trails between villages. I am so close to the capital, but I might as well be at the tip of the Tiburon."

Conseillant was referring to Haiti's two-hundred-kilometre southern peninsula, whose headland was a three-day drive from Port-au-Prince this time of year. He was born in Port-Salut, near the western tip of the Tiburon, in 1964. He had moved to Port-au-Prince in 1981 to finish high school and then attended university, graduating with a degree in civil engineering. The year was 1986. Baby Doc had just fled to Paris and the interim government was in chaos, utterly corrupt and run at the whim of the army's numerous generals. Engineering jobs were based on connections, which he did not have. He lived on the tiny fees he earned drafting plans for state projects whose contractors stole government money and never built a single building or road. Conseillant said his reason for joining the police in 1995 was very simple: "I saw the depredations of the business people, the government and the generals. The people at the top were all together in a group, stealing everything. I knew that with all its political problems, Haiti needed the rule of law to be continuous. I decided to put myself at the service of my country and its laws to help solve the problems caused by people who cared only about themselves." He'd enlisted as an A1 and rose through the ranks until, in 2007, he became head of the drug unit, then of the riot unit. Two weeks after the earthquake, he was promoted to commander of the Kenscoff commissariat. "So that is why I am here now," he said. "A river finds its path."

I asked if he was married and he said he was. I asked if he had children and he said no. Then he looked down at his notes. I thought he might have felt that I was improperly prying into his personal life, so I explained, "I'm doing a portrait of Canadian police and the Haitians they work with, so that is why I ask about your family."

He was still looking down when two tears splashed onto the pages in front of him. "Hold on," Lamarre said. "Something's going on here."

Conseillant looked up and the tears began running down his cheeks. "I lost my children in the earthquake," he said. He took out a handkerchief and began weeping into it. He wept for two minutes, his body shaking. We waited, listening to the chaotic shouts and horns and Haitian *rah-rah* music coming up from the street below. "It was a difficult day for me," Conseillant said finally. "My boys were eighteen and thirteen years old. They were in school and the school collapsed. My wife was buried under our home. She has many injuries. I have to take care of her. She was in a hospital for a long time. Still, two weeks after the quake, they asked me to take over here because the commander was badly injured in the quake, so I came."

"You put duty to your country ahead of your personal tragedies," Alarie said.

"I suppose so. When things are very difficult I ask myself: why did I agree to this transfer? The commute is long and my grieving wife needs me. But the assignment was not something I doubted I should take."

"I was telling you about issues with the HNP," Lamarre said to me, "but that's only part of the story. What's truly amazing about these guys is that they almost all lost family members in the quake but they got back to work right away. In Canada if there's a death in the family, you get stress leave. Here there's no such thing. So you can't tell me that these guys are not utterly dedicated. In my twenty-five years of policing I've never met people so dedicated, who solve problems with so little. They have a strength of courage that I very seldom see. With such suffering this man still does his job. He's got nothing here and he still does his job."

Conseillant put his handkerchief away and reached over to shake Alarie's hand. "You must write that this Canadian Alarie is very good," Conseillant said to me. "He and his Canadian colleagues are always on the move with my men. It is not an easy job walking these mountains for sometimes twelve hours. And when the rain comes down, they are out there exposed. Yet they are always very respectful to our people. Their expertise is second to none. Sometimes they come across people who have died or are extremely sick and there is a risk of infection. But they arrive every morning on time to begin the long patrols."

"I sleep well at night," Alarie told me, smiling. "Our job is to coach and mentor the HNP, and to do that we must be by their sides. After each patrol, we have a debriefing and give some counselling according to our professional standards. We do this every day. For me it is one of the most rewarding experiences of my policing career."

Anique Aubristin entered the open doorway and saluted. He told his chief that the prisoners were ready for the magistrate. Conseillant asked him to order the potato stealer to carry the evidence—his twenty-kilo sack of contraband—back to his *lakou* and return it to its owner with an apology. "Tell him to never steal potatoes again," he said. He ordered the gunmaker, however, to be brought before the magistrate. *"Oui, commandant!"* Aubristin said.

From the veranda we watched Aubristin lead the two young men in handcuffs out of the jail. He undid the cuffs of the potato stealer and told him to hoist the sack. Then he put the gunmaker in the back of the commissariat's pickup. Another officer got in beside him and the truck drove away. Aubristin gave a stern, finger-pointing lecture to the potato stealer, after which the boy balanced the sack on his head and set off on the four-hour hike back to his *lakou*.

"In Canada we'd file the property as an exhibit, then complete hours of paperwork and reports," Roy said to me. "Here they haul his ass out of jail, give him the sack of potatoes, tell him to take it back to the owner, not to do it again, and that's it."

That evening, on the return trip through Port-au-Prince, Ruth Roy pointed to the hills of Vivy Mitchell, where she and two colleagues rented a house. Port-au-Prince may have been a dangerous city for UNPOL cops, but the overburdened United Nations left it up to individual officers to find their own accommodation. It was one of the risks of being on mission that was considered acceptable, Roy said. During orientation, most cops teamed up with three or four others and hired a local agent to find them a house that met UN-recommended security standards. A house was considered "secure" if it was surrounded by a two-metre wall topped by barbed wire. If the house did not meet this standard, the United Nations would hire a contractor to come out and raise a wall and string the wire. To be completely safe at night, some American and European cops spent their entire tour in the Caribbean Lodge, but Roy, like most CivPol cops, hated the thought of being cut off from her Haitian neighbours. She'd teamed up with Jean-Pierre Synnett, the Montreal officer in charge of security for the IDP camps, and his IDP security partner, a Montreal officer named Claude Mercier. Their agent steered them to Vivy Mitchell, where dozens of CivPol cops had settled, because it was close to the Police Academy and Delta Camp, and the neighbourhood was safer than others lower down in the city. "Or so we thought," Roy said.

Five months earlier, on the night of May 14, 2011, three Mounties were sitting on their patio deck at 7 Vivy Mitchell Rd., a couple of blocks downhill from Roy's house. They called themselves the "Oreo Team," since two were Haitian-Canadian and one was white. The white officer, Cpl. Bruno Arseneau, was a fifty-two-year-old francophone from New Brunswick who mentored the HNP's investigations unit. Corporal Rudy Étienne, forty-four, lived in Vancouver and mentored the HNP's kidnap unit. Constable Gilbert Saillant, forty, from Manitoba, mentored the HNP's drug squad. For Étienne and Saillant, the mission was an opportunity to return something to the country they'd left as boys. For Arseneau, it was an opportunity to help reduce the level of fear he knew Haitians lived with every day. Each morning they met up with their students and patrolled with them through the city's most crime-plagued neighbourhoods. Mentoring inexperienced police amid the city's violent emergencies, the three Mounties had never felt so needed.

They'd arrived on mission in late March and, after their orientation, had teamed up on April 13 to rent this two-storey house, at the time the only home their agent could find in Vivy Mitchell that was not a mansion. That night in May, they sat on the patio shirtless and in shorts, waiting for eight o'clock, when they would retire to their upstairs bedrooms to Skype their families. In the half light from the living room they had been discussing the wall to the compound: it was only 1.5 metres high, with no barbed wire. Before closing the rental deal, Étienne had contacted the United Nations and was assured that a construction crew would come out in no time to raise the wall to the two-metre standard and string the razor wire. Despite the Mounties' weekly reminders, no one had shown up to do the work. A Mountie veteran of several Haiti missions had told them that the United Nations was required to hire local contractors and the few honest contractors in the city were booked on other projects for months in advance. "You're totally on your own," the officer had said. The three Mounties had decided to stay in the house, since there were fourteen Mounties living in other houses on their block. In addition, the UN police commissioner, Marc Tardif, and a U.S. consular official lived up the street, and Bill Clinton had a house nearby that he used on visits to the country to spotlight the projects his private foundation supported. "We decided that even if we moved, there was no guarantee we could find a house that met specs," Arseneau, the New Brunswicker, told me later in Delta Camp. "And if we went somewhere else, would it be safer than where we were, surrounded by police officers? Probably not. We decided to wait for the UN to do its job."

Only Étienne and Arseneau sat opposite me in the portable trailer at headquarters as they related this. Gilbert Saillant was now working in the Child Protection Unit and did not want to relive the night's torment in an interview. None of them had ever spoken to a journalist about that May night, but Roy had persuaded Étienne and Arseneau it was important for the public to know what CivPol members faced in Haiti, and why the three of them had decided to complete the mission.

Étienne recalled that at five minutes to eight he was in the midst of telling his roommates that his parents in Canada had been totally against his decision to join the mission when two figures dropped down from the wall into the dark yard. Arseneau at first thought a couple of their Mountie neighbours had hopped the wall for a visit. Then he realized that the figures were wearing balaclavas and were holding guns on them. The intruders came forward in a crouch, fluttering their palms downward, almost patting the ground. One whispered in French. "No talking. Lay face down, quick, or we will kill you."

The three Mounties moved from their chairs and did as they were told, just as they advised civilians to do under similar circumstances. The one who had ordered them to the ground put a gun against the back of Arseneau's head and asked, "Do you want to die, *blan*?" He jammed the barrel hard against his shaved skull, twisting the muzzle into his flesh. "Do not fucking move because I will kill you. Answer me: do you want to die?"

"I have kids," Arseneau said.

"You have not answered me. Do you want to die?"

"No."

"Where are your valuables?"

"The bedroom."

It was apparent that the one speaking was in charge. He sounded middle-aged, while his partner sounded younger. The older one took a step back and kept his gun moving between the three prostrate cops as he directed his partner to tie up Arseneau first. His partner answered, *"Oui, commandant."* The title meant something to the Mounties: in the HNP, junior officers called their superiors commandant.

The underling pulled nylon cord from his pocket and his commandant instructed him to tie Arseneau's hands behind his back, his hands to his feet, and then the vector of the cord to the bars of the fence around the patio. He was then instructed to hogtie Étienne without tying him to the bars and to tie Saillant's hands behind his back.

"They had a plan when they came over that wall," Arseneau told me. "They were most afraid that I, the white guy, would resist, so they tied me up tightest and to the bars."

"They didn't tie Gilbert's legs because they wanted to take him up to the bedroom first," Étienne said. "I was going to be second."

The commandant dragged Saillant to his feet and pressed the gun hard into his spine, jerking his arms upward so the Mountie was forced to lean forward—a police move that immobilizes a suspect. The man steered Saillant across the living room and started up the stairs that led to the officers' bedrooms, then stopped and called back to his partner: "They are trained cops. Kill them both if they try anything, the *blan* first."

Étienne, attempting to bridge the gap between Haitian Mountie and Haitian robber, called to the commandant in Creole, "We will do whatever you want. Everything is insured. You can take everything. But just remember, we all have children."

"That doesn't matter to me," the commandant said.

The Mounties kept most of their valuables in CivPol-issued heavy plastic barracks boxes, which they stored under their beds. The boxes had a three-feature lock mechanism—the key had to be inserted a third of the way in, turned partway, inserted another third of the way in, turned again, and then inserted the last third and turned a third time. That made the key difficult to duplicate and the lock impossible to pick, but also an ordeal to open when you were under duress. Sprawled on the bedroom floor, his hands tied behind his back, Saillant tried to instruct the commandant in the delicate art of opening his barracks box. The man soon became frustrated and pointed his gun at the lock, ready to shoot it off. "Please don't do that," Saillant said. "If your partner downstairs hears the shot he will panic and shoot my buddies. Let me open it. I'll get it open."

"Get the fuck up and do it," the commandant ordered.

Standing with his back to the box, the muzzle of the commandant's gun aimed at his forehead, Saillant miraculously got the lock to spring. Fifteen minutes after they'd entered the bedroom they came down the stairs, the commandant digging the gun into Saillant's spine with his right hand, his left arm holding a backpack filled with Saillant's laptop, wallet, camera and a utility belt heavy with a holstered Glock pistol and magazines.

By now the tight nylon cord had cut the circulation to Arseneau's hands and feet and Étienne noticed he was shivering uncontrollably in the thirty-five-degree heat. "My partner is going into shock," Étienne said to the commandant.

The man knelt beside Arseneau and placed the gun against the side of his head. "Do you want to die?"

"No," Arseneau said.

"Then stop shivering."

The commandant ordered the underling to untie Étienne's feet next and steered him upstairs, where the procedure with the barracks box was repeated. As Étienne was opening his lock, the commandant took out the keys he had taken from Arseneau's pocket. Étienne became worried that the man would ask him to open Arseneau's box, and then order the underling to shoot the blan, whom he obviously feared and hated. Playing for time, Étienne told the commandant that the locks were all different and that he couldn't open Arseneau's locker.

The ploy seemed to work because the commandant marched Étienne down the stairs and went back to Arseneau, only to discover that Saillant had persuaded the younger robber to slightly loosen the cord on the blan's hands and feet, arguing that if Arseneau went into shock and lost consciousness, he wouldn't be able to open his barracks box. The commandant was furious at this insubordination and immediately let Arseneau know who was in charge. He put his gun to Arseneau's head, twisted the muzzle into his scalp again, then moved it between his eyes. "Do you want to die, *blan?*"

"No," Arseneau repeated.

"Then do not try anything when we untie you. Do you want to die?"

"If he said it once, he said it a hundred times," Arseneau told me. "Every step of the process, he asked me, 'Do you want to die?' Up the stairs, into my room, getting me to open the barracks box, putting me face down on the floor, digging the gun into my head and saying, 'Do you want to die? Do you want to die?'—just to torture me. After he emptied my box he began tugging at my wedding ring. I had put that ring on thirty years ago and had never taken it off, and now with my hands swollen from having been tied up, it wouldn't come. He put a foot on my back and pulled until I thought my finger would dislocate, then he cursed me in Creole and stepped off me. He began looking in my desk. I was sure that if he found my knife he would take it and cut my finger off. I said, 'Look, look here!' I straightened my finger as much as possible, and he stood on my back again and, thank God, the ring came off."

Starting down the stairs, Arseneau had to make a decision. The commandant was on the banister side of the stairway, which only came up to his waist. All of Arseneau's valuables were in the commandant's left arm hanging over the banister and he was descending the stairs turned slightly to the Mountie, with his right hand pressing the gun in his side. Then he leaned over the banister to check what was going on below, making him vulnerable to one quick shove that would pitch him over the rail to fall twenty feet to the tile floor. "I don't care how you land— you're landing to stay," Arseneau recalled thinking. "Nervous as the guy was downstairs, there was a chance he would have run like hell, especially after being told the white guy was the most dangerous one to watch. Then he sees his boss fly over the railing? But there was that other chance that he starts shooting. Were they going to kill us or let us live? There was an opportunity but I didn't take it. A minute later I went through heavy regret when they tried to get our guns out of our holsters."

Like the barracks boxes, the holsters had a three-point feature—in this case, to prevent someone from coming up behind an officer and grabbing his weapon. You could not simply undo the latch and slip the gun out. You had to undo the latch, tilt the gun forward, move it to a release position, pull it farther out, then tip it forward and draw. The commandant and his partner were trying in vain to extract the guns while standing over their Mountie captives.

"And they're loaded," Étienne told me. "So I said, 'Please, you could have an accidental discharge. Go do it on the lawn.' But the commandant and his buddy kept trying to remove them while standing over us. They didn't care if the guns went off. We all agree that this is the point we thought we were going to be murdered."

"We were thinking, 'They don't want to dirty their own guns to finish the job,'" Arseneau said. "Why else would they want to take our guns out of the holster right there?"

"I had a flash about my son," Étienne said, "a flash about my family; what are they going to think when our bodies are found, what are people going to say? Like we are bad cops, we were not ready—the guy that teaches the kidnap squad got kidnapped. All kinds of humiliating things like that went through my head." Étienne began to weep as he related this. "My family—my son! I *felt* him. I didn't want him to think ill of me for dying like this. If I had to die that night, I wanted him to know I had died having done the right thing by coming on mission—that it was not just because of a stupid incident."

Arseneau also began to weep, the experience so close, so raw. "I said my peace, said goodbye to my wife and children. I tried to accept, I came on mission for a reason. I knew the amount of risk I would face was higher than back home. I thought the good I could do made it worth the risk. I didn't know if what I had done in seven weeks had changed much in Haiti, but I said to myself, 'Okay, you did your best as a Mountie and a mentor.' I wasn't going to beg for my life."

As the robbers stood over them, still trying to release the guns from the holsters, Étienne attempted a last-ditch negotiating tactic. "Listen, my friend," he told the commandant. "I appreciate your situation, what you are facing now. There are police all around us. If you shoot us, they will hear. They are all sitting downstairs in their yards, and they will come pouring out at you."

"Fifteen or twenty cops," Saillant said. "You will not get far. Somewhere up this block you will be intercepted."

The commandant seemed to weigh this logic for a moment, his hand on the loaded Glock in its holster, the Mounties' lives hanging in the balance.

"Just take everything, the belts, everything, and go," Saillant said. "You will get away."

Arseneau saw the commandant look at him with contempt, his pistol in his right hand, the holstered gun in his left. Then the commandant jerked his chin at his underling and the two ran across the grass and leapt the wall.

"I gotta tell you, Rudy and Gilbert are my heroes," Arseneau said, reliving that moment of unbounded relief. "I was still shaking from shock, but they stayed calm and spoke in Creole to the commandant. They took a situation of probable murder and turned it."

Saillant had a Leatherman knife in his back pocket, which the robbers had not discovered. He manoeuvred it out of his pocket, cut Étienne's binding, and in a few moments they were all free. The robbers had taken their cell phones, so to alert the authorities they had to run across the street to their Mountie neighbours. A Code 3 went out and UN pickups arrived with shotgun-wielding Formed Police Units—UN anti-riot cops. A dozen FPUs guarded the vulnerable house until, a week later, a construction crew showed up and raised the wall to two metres and strung the razor wire.

As it turned out, high walls and razor wire did not protect others in the neighbourhood. As soon as the FPUs left, the nearby home of a Haitian banker was invaded by an unknown number of gangsters. The banker shouted for help and was shot dead. Three weeks later, gangsters invaded the home of the U.S. consular official. The official was away but his security guard interrupted the robbery and was shot dead. A month before my trip to Haiti, in early September, the home of a Rwandan UNPOL who lived next door to the three Mounties was invaded. The Rwandan ran for the door and was shot dead. Arseneau, Étienne and Saillant heard the shot and grabbed their guns, but by the time they got to the street the invaders were gone.

Three murders close by, I thought, all of them after the Mounties had looked death in the eye themselves. "But you decided to stay," I said. "Why?"

"Because this is a *mission*," Arseneau pronounced, as if there were no other answer. "We knew what we were getting into. The people of Port-au-Prince live their whole lives in fear of this kind of violence. Our mission is to help train the HNP to protect them. When you're on a mission like this, you don't abandon the people you came to help. You stick it out."

"For myself, what led me here was the same thing that made me stay," said Étienne. "I left Haiti when I was seven and came back for my grandmother's funeral in 2008. I could not believe how bad the situation was. They had no functioning police force to deal with emergencies. I said to myself, 'For ten million people something bad happens here every day, and the HNP need training to help the country.' So that was my motivation to apply for the mission. I was not called until after the earthquake, but always in my mind was what I saw in 2008. Then, after I arrived here, I could not leave just because something bad happened to poor little me."

On November 7, 2008, around the time of Étienne's visit to Haiti, a three-storey school in Pétionville collapsed on its own, burying several hundred children in the rubble. In Haiti, the HNP is responsible for all emergency services, including rescue, ambulance and firefighting. Dozens of Haitian police converged on the scene, with no first-aid supplies or rescue equipment. They joined the neighbours in digging with their bare hands for survivors. When severely injured children were pulled from the rubble, the police carried them to the back of a car and drove them to the hospital without first stabilizing their broken limbs or necks, or treating their bleeding wounds. In total, ninety-three children died, at least some from the trauma of being carried from the scene by panicked police. Five days later, another school collapsed in the Canapé Vert section of Port-au-Prince. Most of the hundred students were playing in the yard when the building came down, but nine were injured by falling debris. Their treatment by the HNP was as chaotic as their response in the Pétionville school disaster.

The HNP's rescue performance was repeated on a regional scale in the aftermath of the 2010 earthquake. Volunteers from St. John Ambulance Canada, working as part of the CivPol contingent after the quake, realized that the HNP desperately needed to be trained in first aid and emergency preparedness. In August 2010, CivPol and St. John Ambulance collaborated in founding First Aid Instructor Training in Haiti (FAITH), a train-the-trainer program based at the Police Academy. It was designed as a "cascade program"—a CivPol term that refers to the multiplying effect of training a core group of police instructor-trainers who train approximately ten times their number of police instructors, who in turn train ten times their number of ordinary police officers. The two-year goal was to graduate fifty instructor-trainers, who would train four hundred instructors, who would go out into the country and train all nine thousand police officers.

In February 2011, Montreal Police Constable Alain Nadeau began overseeing FAITH's teaching program at the Police Academy. When I arrived in Haiti, Ruth Roy told me that for the past seven months Nadeau had been mentoring an HNP officer named Joseph Tardee, who coordinated all Haitian instructor-trainers. Tardee was only an A4, or staff sergeant, but, given the number of people his work affected nationwide, she said, Nadeau considered him among the most important Haitian cops at the academy. She introduced me to Nadeau, who led me to Tardee's office. "Just his work alone here is helping to change the country," Nadeau told me.

Tardee was a slightly built, unassuming forty-three-year-old who was so soft-spoken I could hardly hear his voice above the hum of the air conditioner in his trailer. He said that before he would begin the interview, he wanted me to see a class taking place in the neighbouring portable. "Do you have children?" he asked me as we crossed the narrow alley. I told him I had a grown daughter. "I ask you to remember when she was a baby."

In the classroom a couple of dozen A3s, or sergeants, were observing an HNP instructor-trainer as he cradled an infant doll along his extended forearm. On the greenboard behind him, the officer had written: "PREVENTING THE ASPHYXIATION OF A BABY." On a table beside him were half a dozen other dolls for the students to practise on.

"The momma doesn't know what the baby has swallowed," the instructor said. "But if the baby is coughing hard or crying, *wait!* Why do we wait?"

"The baby can cough up the object on its own," an officer answered.

"Correct," the instructor said. "But if no crying, observe the danger signs. Ribs and chest heaving in. High-pitched sounds as the baby pulls for air. Unconsciousness. Blue skin."

The instructor sat down in a chair and turned the infant doll face down on his forearm. "In your hand, hold the baby's chest, your fingers on the jaw. Point the baby's head down so it is lower than the body. With your other hand, like this,with your palm, five quick hits between baby's shoulder blades . . ."

Ten minutes later, walking out of the class, Tardee said to me: "Canada has a lot to be proud of for this program. It's a direct way of serving the people of Haiti. Until a year ago, if officers came on a choking baby, they would not know what to do. Now we have twenty-five instructor-trainers and two hundred instructors, and so far three thousand HNP have been trained in basic first aid."

We went back into his office, where I asked him how he had started down the path that had led him to his current position. He thought on that in silence for at least thirty seconds. "How long do we have?" he finally asked, smiling. I told him there was no time limit. "All right, I will tell you from the very beginning. It started with the *restavecs*, Haiti's child slaves, when I was just a child myself."

Joseph Tardee was born in 1968, in the Artibonite Valley, an agricultural region that cuts across central Haiti. The valley's rice plantations were worked by sharecroppers, the fields owned by absentee landlords who lived in mansions in Gonaïves, the department's capital. The sharecroppers were so poor that many of them gave one or two of their children to the landowners as house servants, believing the usual promise that the children would be treated well and offered an education in return for their labour. Tardee's father was a miller, and his mother baked bread. When Tardee was nine, his mother asked him to deliver a palette of bread to a landowner's home. As he entered the home he saw a *restavec* girl being beaten with sticks by both the mistress of the household and her teenage son. "The girl was on the floor. She was my age and screaming pitifully," he told me. "The son continued to beat her, even as the woman came and took my bread. When I saw that, I tried to talk to them, to tell them it was not right. But they dismissed me. The next time I delivered bread, I saw the same thing. I tried to tell them about God's will, because I was taught that in a child's eyes you can see God—but nothing worked. I saw many cases like that growing up, and I began to say to myself: 'It is important for me to have some power to stop that, an ability to use power to stop it. We need the rule of law to help God's children.' It was always in my mind—maybe I can help God's children by applying the law."

Tardee was raised as a devout Seventh Day Adventist, believing it was his weekly duty to personally experience the presence of God through Bible reading in church, garnering advice on how to deal with life's problems. As a boy, he always received the same advice during his overwhelming experiences of God: he was reminded to give himself up to the commandment of Jesus Christ that he serve others and that he begin each day with a determination to help at least one individual. "When I was in high school, it came to me during prayer that if the *restavec* owners would not stop beating the children at my request, a way to help the *restavecs* was to study the law and perhaps find a way to get the owners to stop beating the children by legal action."

Tardee entered the University of Haiti in 1986, the year Baby Doc fled to Paris, and, in the midst of the succession of military coups that followed, studied for degrees in law and theology. In his senior year, Jean-Bertrand Aristide was elected president, promising economic reforms that would benefit the poor. Tardee then drew up a brief which argued that the abusive treatment of Haiti's hundreds of thousands of *restavecs* was illegal both under both Haiti's laws against assault and under the Lord's Golden Rule. He filed his brief with members of Aristide's Fanmi Lavalas party in the Senate and House of Deputies, who seemed to take the young man's petition seriously. Six months later, Aristide was overthrown in a military coup and fled to the United States. It suddenly became dangerous in Port-au-Prince to argue against the elite's treatment of *restavecs* and Tardee moved to Cabaret, northeast of the capital, where he worked as a law clerk and lay minister. After Aristide was reinstalled as president and founded the HNP in 1995, Tardee joined the force.

"I joined the police for three reasons," he told me. "It is a direct way of helping an individual every day; it is a direct way of bringing the rule of law to my country, helping the population of Haiti by applying the law; and being an officer would enable me to help the *restavecs*. I thought, Perhaps I cannot change the servant system, which is legal, but I can stop the beatings, which are illegal."

He was assigned to a commissariat in Carrefour, just west of the capital, but his attempts to bring individuals before magistrates on charges of beating their *restavecs* proved fruitless. In order to lay charges, he needed to persuade his commanding officer that a crime had been committed. But each time he reported a beating to his commandant, the commandant would meet with the *restavec* owners, after which Tardee would be informed there was no reason for a magistrate to investigate the incident. "Some in our police force take money from people who do bad things," he said. "If you are hungry and steal a chicken, you will probably go to jail. But if you beat *restavec* children, even if you break their bones or burn them with boiling water, nothing happens."

In 1998 he founded an organization called the Haitian League for the Defence of the Children, enlisting nine fellow Adventists in Carrefour. He then established satellite chapters in Adventist churches in Cabaret, Port-au-Prince, Gonaïves and Cap Haïtien. "My goal of keeping the children from being beaten was continually thwarted by our unequal system, so I then decided I must at least try to give the beaten children medical attention. Their wounds went untended and sometimes would become infected and I did not know what to do to help them." He married a woman in Cabaret, and, after the birth of their first child at the local hospital, he asked the nurses if he could observe them as they went about their jobs. Over the next two years he volunteered at hospitals in Cabaret and Carrefour, and acquired enough knowledge and experience to enable him to take a test in the capital offered by USAID and become certified as a first-responder. "I used my salary to buy bandages, splints and antiseptic creams," he said. "When I encountered a beaten *restavec*, I would ask the owner's permission to treat the child. They did not stop me, because they wanted the child to return to work."

From 2002 until the earthquake, Tardee taught first aid to members of the Haitian League for the Defence of the Children in Carrefour and Cabaret, and travelled at his own expense to other satellite chapters to teach basic first aid to chapter presidents, who would then teach it to the chapter members, who would in turn teach members of their Adventist congregations. When CivPol's FAITH program started after the earthquake, Tardee was already practising FAITH's train-the-trainer "cascade" method, which he had come up with completely on his own. He joined the FAITH program and was shortly promoted to coordinate the instructor-trainers.

"Where were you when the earthquake happened?" I asked.

"I was in Cabaret with my wife and two boys," he said. "My house suffered only slight damage, but the homes of two of my sisters were totally destroyed. I stayed in the city as a first-aid worker and my sisters moved into an IDP camp. I saw the conditions in the camp so when I came to the academy to join FAITH, I went on the weekends to the camps in the city to administer first aid. Have you been to any of them?" he asked.

I told him I would see one of the internally displaced persons camps the next day, accompanied by Jean-Pierre Synnett. "Yes, I know him," Tardee said. "He is in the camps every single day, protecting the children. Once I thanked him for his work, for leaving his wife and family in Canada to help us, and he told me: 'We live on one planet. We have to help each other.'"

"The main thing for me is that they can sleep safe during the night," Jean-Pierre Synnett said, pointing to an image on his computer that highlighted Port-au-Prince's seven largest IDP camps. "We have about 400,000 people living in these camps and it is easy to rape the ladies. And they have kids with them. So the criminals rape the ladies and rape their kids."

We were in the intelligence nerve centre that Synnett had set up to keep track of all crimes committed in the camps. When he'd first arrived in the capital seven months earlier, policing in the IDP camps had been merely reactive. The UN Police who patrolled the camps had rushed to the scene of a crime and dealt with its aftermath, then gone on to the next. Synnett had converted this crime-chasing model to a system that used community-based and intelligence-led policing to build a data bank that helped him to anticipate and prevent crime. He had deputized a hundred camp residents as block-watch officers and trained the three hundred UNPOL officers he commanded to interview the deputized civilians after each crime, then to immediately phone in reports to his intel centre in Delta Camp. Each morning, Synnett assessed the data to determine his crime-prevention strategies. "Let me show you how it works," he said.

He moved to a computer monitored by a Turkish officer named Fatmah, who was assigned to enter information about crimes in the camps as it was being phoned in. On Fatmah's screen was a Google image of Camp Jean-Marie Vincent, the largest and most dangerous of all the IDP camps. Superimposed on the camp were small, colour-coded squares showing the locations and types of crimes committed in the last few months, including murders, rapes, thefts, bombings and shootouts between gang members. The latest squares—red and green—were from early that morning.

"I look for patterns of crimes in a certain area of the camp and possible environmental causes," Synnett said. "Can I do something about the environment to prevent a recurrence of the crime?" He clicked on the red square. "Here is a rape at four in the morning." A pop-up window gave him details of the crime that Fatmah had entered. "The rape happened near portable toilets that were installed only yesterday, so there is no street light yet by the toilets." He clicked on the adjacent green square, signifying an armed robbery. "The robbery happened ten minutes after the rape. What I see is that both crimes were committed by the wall that separates Cité Soleil from the camp. And this report in the information window says the suspects in both crimes left the camp through a drainage ditch under the wall. This is according to what my block watchers told UNPOL. So right away, I knew what I had to do: put a street light by the new toilets and have the UN put bars where the perpetrators probably entered the camp." He moved the cursor and clicked on a cluster of black squares on the other side of the 1.5-square-kilometre camp. "Likewise, here there are reports of fights between young men in one location, over two days. Probably two rival gang cells have moved into the camp. If I do nothing, these guys will soon be raping and killing. My solution is to discover who doesn't belong in that location and eject them."

"It's a continual moving target," I said.

"It is always a moving target, exactly as at home," he replied. "In Canada we are proactive, we do intelligence-led policing based on community policing. But my three hundred UNPOL are from fifty countries. In Benin, Ivory Coast, Pakistan, Nigeria, they don't do that. They are reactive. So it was something I changed as soon as I arrived."

Synnett was a salt-and-pepper-haired man in his fifties who had spent eight years as a paramedic before joining Montreal's police force in 1984. Haiti was his second CivPol mission; during his first, in Ivory Coast in 2004, he had travelled into the northern jungle to help broker a truce between a violent rebel faction and the central government. The rebel faction had agreed to the surrender terms. After returning to Montreal he had worked as head of his force's internal affairs section and then as head of its public corruption unit. In the fall of 2010 he had heard about the rampant crime in the IDP camps and applied for the CivPol mission to Haiti. Shortly after he arrived in February 2011, he was put in charge of security for the camps, and by the spring had revamped UNPOL's policing tactics. His approach had reduced the per capita crime rate in each of the big camps to approximately what it was in their surrounding neighbourhoods. The rate was still astronomical by Canadian standards, but at least now it was not more dangerous to live in a tent beside Cité Soleil than it was to live in Cité Soleil itself.

After Synnett had studied that morning's crime reports and had analyzed the clusters, he took me along on a morning tour of three very different camps in order to give me an idea of the crime-prevention strategies he had worked out. The first camp was close to Delta Camp and often visited by foreign dignitaries on their short visits to Haiti. We drove south for a kilometre on Boulevard du 15 Octobre and then turned west on Route de Cazeau. After two kilometres bouncing on pot-holed pavement and half a kilometre climbing steeply up a gravel road we came to Camp Caradeux, surrounded by a four-metre cinderblock wall. It was probably the safest of the camps on Synnett's daily patrol, although he said it had to be continually monitored because there was material worth stealing inside the walls. The Brazilian government had donated thousands of sheets of plywood and the fifty thousand camp residents had built sturdy one-room huts with fibreglass roofs. "It looks fine; it's the showpiece for the foreigners," he said, "but everything you're looking at is open to being stolen. And not by everyday thieves."

Synnett knocked on the plywood door to a hut where a deputized woman named Staisy lived. She opened her door, holding the hand of a little boy. *"Banjo Madam! Ki jan ou ye?"* Synnett asked in Creole. She said she was fine, but on questioning her further Synnett discovered a problem. Some women in the camp had ordered her to tell representatives of the United Nations that she wanted a new governing committee of camp residents to replace the current committee that was responsible for her sector. Synnett made a note on his pad and said he would look into it.

The problem in this camp, Synnett said as we strolled the lanes, was not the usual run of violence in other camps, but organized crime. The governing committee for each sector made representations to UN reps on the needs of camp members, but there were illegal committees in the camp who charged people for the materials that had been donated and allocated, or else stole and sold the materials on the street, where a sheet of Brazilian plywood could fetch thirty dollars. "These professional gangsters don't belong in here," he told me. "They come in with false papers they bought from a Haitian ministry official, and then pay them kickbacks on their illegal business. So what we've implemented in the camps is a list of who's entitled to supervise materials and who is not. It would be easy to just close our eyes and say it's the law of the jungle and whoever gets the materials, that's okay. But it's important for me and my team to know who legitimately belongs here—otherwise we'll get a mafia king in here and he'll soon be the boss of the camp. I don't tolerate corruption in these camps. Even from those who turn a blind eye. I don't tolerate them."

"Who's turning a blind eye?" I asked.

"As I told you, I have UNPOL from fifty countries," he said. "It is UN policy to have a sampling of all these different countries in different units. So, as they do their policing in Ivory Coast or Benin or Nigeria, so they do it here. There's a lot of UNPOL corruption from these countries. They take bribes from these people who run the illegal committees."

"And you report them?"

"To start with I reported them to the UN. There was an investigation, but then the terms of these UNPOLs were up and they went home. Their replacements came and did the same thing. So now I have personal talks with them. What I say in those talks I cannot tell you, but when I hear what they are doing, then I have my talk with them." He looked down the gravel lane at two blue-helmeted UNPOL engaged in an animated conversation, casting nervous glances his way. He gave them a wave, which they did not return. "Those two have stopped their bad behaviour," he said, smiling.

We left Caradeux and headed west to his next stop, IDP Camp Accra. There were main roads through Delmas that led to Accra, but most of the streets were so clogged with traffic that Synnett took off cross-country on dirt tracks through neighbourhoods that looked like tropical villages. Stands of bamboo ten metres high lined lanes filled with chickens, goats, naked children and barefoot women on their way to market with palettes of eggs stacked a dozen-high on their heads. "The people are very poor here but they are better off than up there," Synnett said, pointing across a canyon to a *bidonville* clinging to a nearly vertical hillside. *Bidonville* means "town of cans," an apt description of the many shanties whose roofs and walls were made from scrap metal. The canyon wall was littered with the detritus of shacks that had tumbled off the hill during the quake. He said that some people called the semi-rural district we were driving through the "real" Port-au-Prince. "I come here often because they are wonderful people; they take care of each other. When the earthquake happened, they crossed the ravine and did most of the rescue work the first night."

Twenty bone-jarring minutes later we climbed a hill to Accra, its ten thousand tents crammed together on the baked grounds of an old iron foundry. During the nightly tropical downpours, water rushed down from the surrounding hills in torrents. As soon as the rain stopped, the ground dried, but in the alleys of the camp the rain left behind a metre-deep layer of garbage from the townships above. Every morning the residents pushed the garbage into a steep ravine on the west side of the camp, which now was filled several metres deep with tires, cans, paper, coconut husks, fruit peel and thousands upon thousands of Haiti's "flying toilets." The ammonia stench rising from the ravine burned my nostrils as I looked down its length. Synnett pointed to the other side of the ravine, ten metres higher than the camp, where several hundred squatters outside the camp boundary had pitched all manner of rickety tarp structures. During one rainstorm, the edge of the hillside had given way and some families had wound up in the rat-filled ravine of garbage below.

"Accra is a high-risk camp," Alix Bellegarde, the United Nations' camp manager, told me as we stood by his plywood headquarters, which was defended by a dozen UNPOL in full riot gear. "The people do not like the conditions here and there is unrest. There was a protest fire a few days ago and seventy-five tents burned. It was arson with a candle. They are also afraid they are going to be evicted and are angry at everybody."

Accra, like many of the camps in Port-au-Prince, stood on private land, and the owner of the foundry had filed an eviction notice against the United Nations' International Organization for Migration, which ran the camps. The deed-owner wanted his land back to restart his foundry. Bellegarde had tried to negotiate with the owner, but the owner was pursuing his eviction notice through the Haitian courts, known for being open to influence.

"The problem is," Synnett said, "most of these camps were set up on any spare ground in the emergency days after the earthquake. Nobody had time to plan. The people congregated and the UN came and distributed tents. Suddenly there were 1.5 million IDPs, a lot of them on private land. Because the owner wants these people off his land, we must transfer them to houses. But first we must have those houses and we don't have them. It's a major camp; we can't just evict them. The IOM is doing the best it can, but look around. It's a hell here, and yet people are using Accra to make money for themselves."

"Who's making money off Accra?" I asked.

"The NGOs!" he said, so angrily that I was taken aback. Synnett was outraged that the staff of some non-governmental organizations were using his crime statistics to convince their sponsors that they were needed in IDP camps, and then never showing their faces in an actual camp. Instead, they were living the high life in Port-au-Prince, directing money that should have gone to the camps to their own "capacity building." They resided in modern hotels or rented air-conditioned houses, drove late-model SUVs and ate in four-star restaurants. He contended that very little of the money donated to a number of the NGOs that were using his statistics actually got to Haitians.

"What do they do with all their money?" Synnett asked. "Can you see the result of any investment here? I go to a meeting every week with these people. About 95 percent of them have never even been to an IDP camp! I beg them, 'Please, come with me to an IDP camp. Just give me one hour a week and you will see what they need. All the UN needs to clean up the garbage in Accra is a front-end loader and a dump truck. It's so basic!' But—never! They spend the money they raise on their drivers and cars and offices and restaurant meals. It's corruption! Job corruption by Western and European NGOs! It's a real scandal."

Synnett translated some of what he'd said to me for Bellegarde's Haitian assistant, who told me: "Most of their time is spent raising money for the next year. Haiti is a rich place for some NGOs. It's a vacation for them."

Synnett and I walked through the lanes, accompanied front and back by an armed guard of Bangladeshi UNPOL. We stopped at a tent and called to the family within. A man who looked sixty stepped out in a T-shirt and shorts. "Nicolas, this is my friend Terry from Canada," Synnett said in Creole. "I am showing him where I work."

Nicolas shook my hand and invited us in. We took off our shoes and entered a tent of about nine square metres, with a pristine white sheet on the floor, two stacked cardboard boxes, two pairs of sneakers hanging from the pole, a plastic jug of water on a tray table, and a cot with a woman sitting on it, an infant on her knee. The woman was Nicolas's daughter. She had lost her husband and two children in the earthquake and Nicolas had lost his wife. He offered us water from his jug, which Synnett politely refused. Synnett asked him about the protest fire, and Nicolas, who was one of Synnett's block-watch officers, confirmed it was a political action, although burning the tents of your neighbours to protest their poor living conditions made no sense to him. He gave

Synnett the names of the ringleaders and Synnett said he would pass them on to Bellegarde. Nicolas thanked Synnett for coming by every day. "*Moun pa se dra,*" he said, which Synnett translated for me as, "A protector is like a cloak."

When we left the tent a few minutes later, Synnett said: "Right here is the ravine, but in Nicolas's home it is clean. Not a spot of dirt on their clothes or on the floor. I deeply respect them, more than I can say. This is the most gratifying work I have ever done in my life." He had a short conversation with Bellegarde outside the UN hut, then called to me. "Come, my friend, we will now follow la Rive Flaveur to Jean-Marie Vincent."

In the car I looked for the river on my MINUSTAH map. A blue line squiggled from the mountains of Pétionville, snaked northwest through Delmas, passed below Accra, and finally, five kilometres west of us, spread into a tidal marsh called La Saline, atop which Cité Soleil had been built. The river was not named on my map. It turned out that Synnett had christened it *Flaveur* because it was choked with aromatic garbage for its entire length.

Water from the ravine that bordered the Accra camp emptied into the river, and the stink stayed with us on the Route de Delmas all the way to an abandoned military airport, built on La Saline and surrounded on the north and west by Cité Soleil. The airport's several square kilometres of flat concrete sat baking in the heat, with two camps sprawling over the runways, separated by a dirt road. Synnett pulled over and pointed to the gate to the right, beyond which a crowd of a dozen young girls, all missing legs, stood on crutches as they waited to fill buckets with water. When each bucket was full, they balanced themselves on their crutches, hoisted the bucket to their heads, and, like gymnasts on a beam, smoothly made their way back to their tents without spilling any water. "This is a small camp of only eight hundred," Synnett said. "It is part of Jean-Marie Vincent but we separate it because all the people in this camp lost limbs in the earthquake. Across the street, there are sixty thousand people, so it is better for them here."

He turned the wheel and entered the gate. Ahead of us was a main street of sorts that stretched for a kilometre, lined on either side by heavy canvas tents. For two kilometres along the west and north borders of the camp, he said, the tents bordered the streets of Cité Soleil, protected by a one-metre cinderblock wall, topped by spear-pointed metal bars. Synnett parked his car and walked straight to the scene of the rape that had been reported that morning. Between the new portable toilets and the wall was a rock-lined drainage ditch that emptied into Cité Soleil through an ungrated stone culvert. While half a dozen shotgun-wielding Nigerians stood guard, Synnett called the United Nations Logistics Base at Louverture Airport. He got through to a French general and requested that a crew be sent over right away to put a barred grate over the culvert. "To tell the truth, I don't know how long it will take them to fix this," he said, after he hung up. "I will have to post one of these UNPOL here at night until it gets fixed. It is a lot of man hours for one spot. It should be an HNP who does that job, but they won't come in here. I have tried many times."

Claude Mercier, Synnett's CivPol colleague in charge of the camp's security, came up to us. "How do you like the environment?" he asked me.

I told him that I didn't think I could take a year's posting here.

"You would be surprised," he said. "This is a city unto itself, with all the excitement." We walked back to Main Street and he pointed to a flea market. "We have markets, the kids play soccer in the lanes, lots of music and dancing and festivals—life goes on here."

I asked how people could afford to shop in the market and he said the camp had its own economy, based on barter. Just like anywhere else, people bought cheap and sold dear. "Someone buys three blocks of ice on credit, sells it for five door hinges, pays the ice seller two hinges, gets a haircut for one hinge. The barber buys a melon or CDs with his hinges or whatever else he gets. There is trade, there is an economy."

CivPol itself contributed to the needs of the camp through a charity organization run by Synnett's wife, a Dominican woman named Ivelisse Valdez, who worked as a civilian employee of the Montreal police. She headed two volunteer organizations in the department of six thousand:

One Employee, One Book and One Employee, Two Shoes. Most Montreal cops exceeded her requests for donations by a factor of five. She shipped the books and shoes to Synnett and Mercier for distribution to the children in the camps. "It is why you see the children have nice runners," Mercier said. "In their tents they have French textbooks that they use in the school. Sometimes they try to trade the books or shoes for CDs, but we discourage that."

"The bigger problem is that they have something to be stolen," Synnett said, as we walked down Main Street. Indeed, the armed robbers last night had stolen a family's shoes from their tent before fleeing the camp. Nevertheless, he said, the camp was safer now than a couple of months ago, and much safer, both for IDPs and CivPol officers, than when he and Mercier had first arrived. Six months earlier, a constable named Patrick Sestier had been standing on this very corner when a gun battle broke out between gang members. When Sestier got up from his crouch, he saw the shape of his body outlined in holes in the aluminum sheet behind him.

"We used to have two murders a day in this camp," Synnett said. "Two months ago I arrived at eight in the morning and two people were shot dead right in front of me."

"Look there," Mercier said, pointing down a side street to a wrecked commuter plane with a tent around its door, the family playing cards outside. Beyond it was the fuselage of a Sikorsky helicopter, its blades and half its nose gone.

"It always reminds me of a Mad Max movie here," Synnett said. "When we had the earthquake a lot of prisoners escaped the jail, and when CivPol caught them in Cité Soleil, they used that helicopter as a temporary jail. Now three families live in there." He pointed to an upside-down seaplane, its floats in the air. "Two other families live in there. It's considered luxury because they have an aluminum home, even if it's upside down."

We were walking down the lane between planes and helicopters, stepping over amputated wings and propellers, when Synnett stopped, in sight of the wall. "This is the worst part of the camp because it's opposite what they call the Boston area of Cité Soleil, where the most powerful gang has its headquarters." He pointed over the wall, to the shacks and shops across the street. "Timun Cycle is the name of the gang. Those fights I showed you on the computer this morning, that's probably Timun Cycle members infiltrating the camp, making competition for another gang. They all have 9-millimetre guns." He looked at the Nigerians standing in a circle around us, each covering a point of the compass, as if we were in a combat zone. "We use the Formed Police Units to confront Timun Cycle. Usually they run home when they see six Nigerians with shotguns."

"Usually, but not always," Mercier said, smiling. "Nevertheless, little by little we are convincing them that this is an occupied zone where they don't belong."

"I'm a happy man working in the IDP camps," Synnett said, as we walked back to his vehicle so he could take me to my hotel. "When I tell the Americans or Europeans that this is my mission, they say: 'How can you stand it? It's so hot, so dirty, so dangerous.' But the *best* work is here in the IDP camps, the most fulfilling for a police officer. We work directly with the population and the help goes directly to them. We try to fulfill all roles because we are from Canada and generalists, whereas a lot of UNPOL from Europe and the States are specialists. They don't want to get their hands dirty with general problems. So they never experience the double blessing that we receive when we work with these people. We get gratification from serving them and we also witness the dignity and self-respect they maintain in the midst of this environment. By example, they teach us how to live our own lives."

10

NO MAN CAN BLOT OUT THE SUN

EVERY TWENTY KILOMETRES OR SO along the seaside road to Grand Goâve, Ray Lamarre leaned forward from the back seat and pointed to an HNP checkpoint. He'd driven the Route Nationale before and had noticed that the checkpoints were always on the shady side. "Anyone running drugs knows the HNP won't stand on the sunny side," he told Ruth Roy, who burst into laughter behind the wheel. When we got to the Grand Goâve police station, the two CivPol cops based there told us the checkpoints were run by the HNP's Traffic and Highway Directorate, which used them as little more than toll booths. Cars above the level of a jalopy were stopped at one or another checkpoint and had to offer a contribution to the livelihood of the police guarding the road. Part of the take was passed along to their commanders.

Though she'd never made the drive to Grand Goâve, the checkpoint racket was not news to Ruth Roy; nor would it have been news to any CivPol cop working in Haiti for more than a month. Haitian civilians talked openly about police extortion on the roads, but few would come forward with a complaint. Either they were frightened of police retribution or they were so accustomed to payoffs that they expected a magistrate to demand a bribe in order to charge a cop for the same offence. In any case, the cop could then pay the magistrate a bigger bribe to end the matter. The CivPol officers in Grand Goâve, Constable Handy Hilaire, a Haitian-Canadian Mountie, and Robert Grégoire, a Montreal staff sergeant, had informed the UN command about the suspected shenanigans at the checkpoints. UNPOL had passed the information on to the Haitian Ministry of Justice, which oversaw the HNP. The Ministry of Justice gave the information to a magistrate for investigation. No results were discernible. And so the racket continued.

"Every government department in Haiti is rife with corruption," Robert Boulet, CivPol's contingent commander, told Roy and me over lunch a couple of days after we got back from Grand Goâve. "Particularly the Ministry of Justice."

Roy concurred. "You could probably take everything that's wrong with this country back to corruption. At the root of it, somebody is corrupt and taking money off somebody else." That was why, she added, Canadian cops in Haiti did their jobs with the sinking feeling that their work with honest HNP officers was being constantly undermined by the unchecked behaviour of corrupt officers.

The roadside toll booths were the mildest manifestation of the systemic police corruption that plagued the country. Drug trafficking, armed robbery, kidnapping and extorting sex from women were also favoured sidelines of some Haitian officers, according to almost every Canadian cop I talked to. Jean-Pierre Synnett had explained to me that when a crime was committed in a tough neighbourhood, the police who showed up considered anyone as fair game for arrest, closing the case with a minimum of effort. In the event the HNP arrested the right person, the criminal would merely pay off a magistrate and be back in the neighbourhood in a few days. That was why Haitians were more likely to practise mob justice and lynch a suspect than to call the police.

"There *is* a solution to all this," I was told by an RCMP superintendent named John White. "Get rid of all the criminals within the HNP and all the police who shouldn't be police. But that's not feasible. Why? Because to take such sweeping action, the UN would have to turn Haiti into a colony and there's no way the Haitian government would allow that. They're in charge of their national police." Unfortunately, the corrupt politicians in charge of the HNP had little motivation to clean up the force. "One good president can't turn this country around," White said. "Michel Martelly is an optimistic guy, but he's surrounded by people with entrenched interests."

I'd been directed to White by just about every officer I'd spoken with about HNP corruption because of his wide-angle view on the problem. White had an office in Delta Camp, where he supervised CivPol's operations in all commissariats and IDP camps in the West Department, which included Port-au-Prince and Grand Goâve. A few months earlier he had been stationed at a UN base in Cité Soleil, overseeing the HNP's thirteen commissariats in Port-au-Prince. White was considered the best-connected Canadian cop in Haiti, particularly in Cité Soleil, the crime capital of the country and also the capital of HNP criminality. Seventy percent of Haiti's crimes were committed in Port-au-Prince, and a large percentage of the city's mayhem emanated from its worst slum. A week after our first meeting he took me on a ride-along to show me his methods and qualified successes.

In age, rugged looks and jaded realism, White reminded me of Tommy Lee Jones in the film *No Country for Old Men*. He was a sixty-year-old Nova Scotian who'd been with CivPol continuously for a decade, the last three years as part of its retired officer program. He'd been on six missions in four countries, including forty-two months on three deployments in Haiti, and about a year each in Kosovo, East Timor and Afghanistan. He was the cop who'd replaced Joe McAllister as mentor to Kandahar's chief of police, Matiullah Qati Khan, arriving at Camp Nathan Smith three days before Matiullah was murdered by his own men. White had lost three friends on the Haiti mission: Doug Coates, Mark Gallagher and Mark Bourke, the latter a retired Mountie who'd been shot by gang members in Cité Soleil in 2005, when the district had been almost as dangerous as Kandahar.

Taking me to meet one of the commandants he mentored, White drove by the wall of IDP Camp Jean-Marie Vincent and into Cité Soleil. We passed a ramshackle market and then a T-intersection, with the street to the right blocked by a thousand people sifting through the market's refuse. Like wolves trailing a herd, a predatory crew of Timun Cycle gangsters observed the crowd from the curb. They wore a uniform of sorts: black baseball caps, mirrored sunglasses and necklaces that hung like breastplates on their bare chests. The youngest of them hexed me with finger horns but the older ones impassively watched White's UN Nissan roll by.

"Gang shootouts can happen anywhere here," White said. "We find dead bodies all the time. When I was based here in May, we were getting thirty kidnappings a month. Legitimate businessmen were the targets, trying to get their products to the port." He pointed west out his driver's-side window to a line of rusted warehouses. "Cité Soleil's the main transit point for coke, but the trade is controlled by people who live outside. The exploiters. The powerful people who have impunity. The gangs are just their gofers."

"And the HNP are in with the gangs?" I asked.

"When they're criminals themselves, there's no difference. The honest ones are under threat to play it their way. 'We know where you live.'"

White's cell phone rang and he reported our location to head-quarters, then began discussing with the caller a meeting he had to attend later in the day. Suddenly I smelled a stink of sewage that defied even the SUV's air conditioner. It came from a scum-covered lagoon on our left. Rising from the poisonous pool were half a dozen corrugated iron shacks, the tenants squatting over cooking fires they'd built on duckboard, to which they'd tied a skiff. It looked like a *lakou* village on cinder blocks, the sulphurous lagoon forming a moat that offered protection from the depredations of Cité Soleil's lawbreakers, who operated under the noses of the law enforcers.

After he hung up, White said: "Have I been able to change the systemic corruption in the HNP? No, I have not been able to change the systemic corruption in the HNP. That will take a generation, if not more. Have I seen individual officers enforcing the law according to the values and principles we've taught them? Yes, I have seen that, and it is the beginning of the process of change."

White may have been a realist, but he was not a cynic: he was a practising Catholic who believed corrupt people could reform their lives. In 1972, he'd graduated from St. Mary's University with a Bachelor of Arts degree in political science, emerging from his studies with the view that "the world was neither black nor white, but shades of grey." He'd married after graduation and, because an academic career didn't appeal to him, he'd followed in the footsteps of his stepfather and joined the Mounties. He spent most of the next thirteen years as an investigator in Atlantic Canada, arresting thieves, batterers and murderers, observing how violent and deceitful people could change over time if they were lucky enough to get into a decent rehabilitation program. In January 2001, stuck at a desk job in Ottawa, he signed up for his first CivPol mission. During a year's posting as regional commander of Mitrovica in war-ravaged Kosovo, he'd supervised Canadian officers as they taught the fundamental values and universal principles of good policing to Kosovar cops who had never known the concepts before. He became sold on CivPol's mission, and stayed with the organization, serving as its director between 2006 and 2007. Today, at the core of his long-term approach to HNP corruption, was a provocative thesis: whereas in Canada you have honest cops who go corrupt, in Haiti you have corrupt cops who go honest. He was endeavouring to encourage that transformation by working directly with the commanders of the largest commissariats of the West Department. We were on the way to meet Cité Soleil's commandant, Aristide Rosemond, a cop who'd been under CivPol's mentorship for the last four years.

White made a slow turn through a traffic jam of pushcarts and wheelbarrows and drove for half a kilometre until we came to a sun-drenched open area with a newly painted blue and white building in the middle. Written across its front were the words: *Commissariat de Police de Cité Soleil.* The district's police station was ground zero in the HNP's fight against crime—even as some of its officers worked for the enemy.

White opened his door and was greeted by two teens in shorts and flip-flops, who said they would watch his SUV—a friendly form of extortion in the capital, where you always paid for protection when you parked on the street, even in front of a police commissariat. White gave them a few gourdes so they wouldn't key his car.

"J.P. Synnett told me Aristide Rosemond has two faces," I said as I climbed out into the heat.

White stopped and squinted at the ground, scratching his full head of greying hair. "I'll give you an example of where that comes from," he said. "Several months ago one of our new officers came into the main entrance here and saw two HNP beating a fourteen-year-old female. He went over and stopped them. There was a female HNP observing this and she came over to speak to him. He thought she was going to thank him. But she said, 'You're not in Canada now!'—she was upset that he'd stopped the beating. So he reported them all to Rosemond, who had to tell him, 'You haven't been here that long, you have no idea of the kind of people I have to work with.'"

He explained that even if Rosemond had attempted to punish the officers involved, he had no guarantee his efforts would have prodded them to obey his orders: insubordination was a huge issue in the HNP. "Another example," he said. "Rosemond can tell his cops to patrol Synnett's camp. They say they will and then don't. I wish officer discipline had progressed a little further by now, but the way they're brought up, it hasn't. The Americans just painted this place," he added, waving at the front of the station, "but the HNP needs more than a paint job."

We walked into the lobby, the floors so polished you could see the ceiling lights mirrored on the tiles. Opposite the entrance was a mural of Haiti's coat of arms and the shield of the HNP. In metre-high blue letters beside the shield was a reminder to every cop who entered the building: "Honour. Respect. Discipline."

"Rosemond put those words up there," White said.

We mounted the stairs to the commandant's office. Divisional Inspector Rosemond was a trim, mustachioed fellow of forty-eight, who seemed extremely nervous about meeting me. On an Internet search of his name I found him quoted in only two articles. In one, published in March 2011 in the far-left expatriate weekly *Haïti Liberté*, based in New York, he denied allegations of brutality against a resident of the Boston area of Cité Soleil. "I do not know anything about this incident," he told the paper. "I do not know who that man is." The other article was published in the British newspaper *The Telegraph* a week after the earthquake, when criminals from the capital's collapsed prisons had overwhelmed his district. "Even as we are digging bodies out of buildings, they are trying to attack our officers," he told the *Telegraph* reporter as they stood together on the street, surrounded by HNP cops holding automatic weapons.

Rosemond shook my hand limply and pointed to a chair across the desk from him. On the edge of the desk, facing me so I could read its title, was a thick book: *Lessons from the Bible*. There was a chair beside me, but White remained standing, placing himself at the apex of a triangle between Rosemond and me, the better to translate and perhaps to encourage Rosemond if he was lost for an answer. I recollected what Synnett had told me would happen to Rosemond if he tried to interfere with the criminal component of the HNP in Cité Soleil. "John will get the call, Rosemond is dead. Two bullets. Shot by his own people." Rosemond had never been interviewed at length by a foreign journalist, and looked as if he dreaded what was coming.

"I want to thank you for your service to your country," I told him.

"*Merci, merci!*" he replied, then extended both his hands and asked for my notebook. He wrote his full name, full title, rank, cell phone numbers and e-mail address. He read the words over carefully, checking for errors, and handed me back the notebook. I was touched. Police commanders in Haiti didn't have business cards and I hadn't interviewed one who'd taken it upon himself to give me all his information without being asked.

"We thought we had an opportunity to arrest one of the heads of Timun Cycle here yesterday," Rosemond volunteered. "We encircled Médecins Sans Frontières, where a gang leader was being treated for gunshot wounds, but it wasn't him."

"I was telling you the kidnap rate in May," White said to me. "He's lowered that considerably in the last four months."

I asked Rosemond how he'd accomplished such a feat, and he said that under CivPol's guidance he'd beefed up the anti-kidnap unit that patrolled the roads to the port that were used by businessmen targeted by the gangs.

"Are you in danger personally?" I asked.

"I definitely am a target of the bandits because of what I am trying to do here," he replied. "There are HNP shot in Haiti on a daily basis. Personally, I am not afraid. They would kill me if they could, but I am willing to accept the risk because I am a professional police officer."

"He's had a number of close calls," White said to me. "By the way, he's wearing the same Mountie cargo pants I gave him when we first met in 2007."

I realized that White was implying that in the capital's most lucrative posting for corrupt cops, only an honest commander would wear the same pants for four years. I was curious how Rosemond had out-competed other officers for an appointment to Cité Soleil, so I asked him to take me through the various stages of his career.

Aristide Rosemond was born in Gonaïves in 1963, and joined the army in 1982, under the reign of Baby Doc. He served as a commissioned officer for the next thirteen years, which included the decade of army-backed coups in the late eighties and early nineties. When the army was finally disbanded in 1995, Rosemond had joined the police and moved up to become the commandant of the Les Cayes commissariat, on the southern Tiburon Peninsula. At the time, the Tiburon coast was a major landing point for smuggled contraband from South America, which would then be transported overland to Cité Soleil's port. From Les Cayes, Rosemond was promoted to President René Préval's elite palace guard, a position that required influential allies. In August 2007, Préval appointed him commandant of the Cité Soleil commissariat, where he had come under the mentorship of John White, who was then working as CivPol's contingent commander in Haiti.

"Effectively, the Canadians are the best trainers," Rosemond told me. "They give us both practical lessons and also moral lessons. They are serious about the work they do. Their words remind me of the teachings in the Bible: to do good, to serve, to protect, to practise self-discipline. In the environment of Cité Soleil, it is easy to become discouraged. I've known John for over four years. He has taught me not to be discouraged, to pursue the law in the name of the light because no man can blot out the sun."

"You're a religious man," I said, placing my hand on *Lessons from the Bible*. "I notice you study scripture."

"Yes, I respect the writings in the Bible. I respect the many poor civilians that I work with—they are vulnerable, and it's written in the Bible that we have to assist those who are vulnerable. I've never done anything bad to good people. I want to bring bad people to justice. My objective is to establish a respectable level of security for the people living in Cité Soleil. Not only Cité Soleil, but Port-au-Prince and the entire country. That is the goal of the HNP. I have a dream where I will one day see a Haiti where we don't have rapes, murders or kidnappings."

"But there are rapes and murders in Jean-Marie Vincent," I said. "The HNP don't patrol the camps."

"If my people don't go in the camp, they are being disobedient," he said. "Their reports to me state they go in the camp to keep order when called."

He lowered his eyes to *Lessons from the Bible*. Still looking at the book, he lifted his hands and dropped them on the table. "What else can I do?" he said. "I am not in Canada."

I asked if he was in line for a promotion, and he said the next step up for him was director of the West Department, the province White was overseeing.

"Will you have the power to fire corrupt commissariat commanders in the West Department?" I asked.

He listened to the translation, looking at me blankly, then moved his eyes to my pen, which was poised to transcribe his response. Synnett had told me that the wife of the director of the West Department had been shot dead last year as a warning to the director, Jean Brize, after he'd tried to discipline a commissariat commander. Rosemond spoke quietly with White, who said to me: "He says his objectives are as he stated. To establish a respectable level of security in Haiti."

As always in my interviews with commanders, I wanted to understand at least a little about Rosemond's personal life, so I asked him if he was married. Three times, he said, to women who'd borne him twenty children. I was picturing that, and thinking about my next question, when Rosemond told us that the Queen of Spain would be arriving at the port on her yacht shortly. A big ceremony was planned, and he had to get down there to supervise an honour guard.

"Can I take a picture of you?" I asked.

With obvious relief that the interview was over, Rosemond shot to his feet, positioning his arms stiffly at his sides and throwing his head back. He remained at attention until White moved beside him, at which point the two cops smiled and put their arms around one another.

As White walked me back to his car he said, "Ol' Rosemond. Twenty kids!"

After we climbed in, I mentioned Phil George's experience in Afghanistan. "A whole year Phil had worked with the intelligence chief in Kabul. The guy was honest, then took a bribe and Phil's mission was shot." I asked if White ever worried he might be disappointed by Rosemond.

He started the car, but then just sat there, looking at the newly painted police station.

"The people we work with anywhere in the world, we always ask ourselves: Is the person in front of me corrupt?" he said at last. "If the whole organization is systemically corrupt, why would this person not be? But I did bring you here because I believe Rosemond is working toward his best instincts." Rosemond was probably no saint, White added, and coming from the army, he probably had "a background." But he'd proven himself receptive to CivPol's mentoring.

"I think he's been influenced by us and he's trying to influence others. That's the way I view the mission—influence several commandants, who begin influencing others. Slow progress is the best we can hope for in Haiti. That's the nature of the business. I've seen private security firms come in here, they have an encounter with the HNP, they tell us, 'It's a lost cause!' Well, these are people who are living in a failed state. They have nowhere to go. They asked for our help. Police officers don't refuse a call for help."

"Please explain something to the Canadian trainers who will read your book," Jean Miguelite Maximé said in the boardroom of the police academy, drawing himself up in his seat at the end of our interview. "Right now we have crooked children who become crooked police. The people in the academy are intelligent, so they see the way we want them to act, and they act that way, but when they are out of our sight, they go back to their old ways. They pretend. In the academy it is 'Yes sir!' but as soon as they leave, it all changes. We need a reorganized society, we need to retrain the Haitian mentality because it is wrong now—it is not noble. If we train the children in honesty, then we will have good police recruits. The lessons they need to learn are not in the academy but in school!"

"You want me to tell Canadian officers that it will be twenty years before you get a class of honest recruits in here?" I asked Maximé.

He held his hands out to the furled Haitian flag in the corner. "Twenty years is only 10 percent of our history. Let us plant the tree now and watch it grow. The officers in the academy will see it growing from the ground. They will be affected by the sight. They will look at Canadian officers and say, 'The children of Haiti are learning the same lessons in school I am learning from these Canadians. It is a higher lesson for me too.' And so, little by little, one officer at a time, we will have a new country."

The next day, as Ruth Roy drove me to the airport, I mentioned that in Afghanistan and Palestine, and now in Haiti, I'd heard the same sentiment expressed by CivPol officers. "They say things are changing slowly, one officer at a time. Do you ever think it sounds like false optimism?"

She stopped the car in front of the air terminal breezeway, which was mobbed by the expectant luggage carriers who had greeted me on my arrival. She was only a couple of weeks from the end of her mission, entering that period of self-assessment when all CivPol officers ask themselves what they have accomplished. In a few days she and her contingent would be replaced by the officers I had observed being trained in Ottawa. Before she left the country, she would help in their orientation at Delta Camp.

"I think you do have to have a sense of optimism," she said, "but my optimism is measured. When CivPol arrives in a country, it's because the country is flat on its back. The odds are basically against the mission. You have to have faith that you'll do something that will move the country a tiny bit in the right direction. Have I done that by developing the training curriculum and the gender program? Maybe the graduates won't turn out to be good investigators of gender-based violence or all the crimes Haiti has to offer, but at least they will have it in their minds that protecting people is the goal they should be working toward. I've observed some of the officers we've mentored when they don't know I'm watching. Instead of hurting Haitians, they help them."

The Haitian National Police Academy in eastern Port-au-Prince.

Jean Maximé, the commander of the academy. His ambition was to graduate a thousand officers a year willing to protect their fellow citizens.

Ottawa Police constable Ray Lamarre, UNPOL's spokesperson in Haiti, with RCMP inspector Ruth Roy, who was working on the academy's basic training curriculum with Maximé.

Port-au-Prince.

The Kenscoff area police headquarters, where officers confront a dizzying disparity between protecting the rich in their vacation homes and serving the rural poor.

Kenscoff's commandant, Julbert Conseillant, who joined the Haitian police in 1995 because "I decided to put myself at the service of my country and its laws to help solve the problems caused by people who cared only about themselves." He lost his children in the earthquake.

HNP officer Anique Aubristin with Alain Alarie, the head of the Canadian CivPol mission for the district.

Aubristin dealing with the potato thief.

Kenscoff's main street.

RCMP corporals Rudy Étienne and Bruno Arseneau, who were the targets of a brutal home invasion in the Vivy Mitchell district of Port-au-Prince, where many Canadian CivPol members live.

Inspector Jean-Pierre Synnett, the Montreal officer who was in charge of security for all the internally displaced persons' camps in the fall of 2011.

Camp Jean-Marie Vincent, established on the site of an abandoned airport—a place the HNP refuse to patrol.

Synnett inspects the fence and unguarded culvert where assailants from Cité Soleil infiltrated Camp Jean-Marie Vincent and sexually assaulted a woman.

Synnett and Roy.

Cité Soleil, the crime capital of the country.

RCMP superintendent John White, considered by his colleagues to be the most knowledgeable Canadian cop on all things Haitian, with Cité Soleil's commandant, Aristide Rosemond.

The newly painted HNP headquarters in Cité Soleil.

The corner where CivPol Mountie Mark Bourke was killed by gang members in 2005.

CivPol's contingent commander, Robert Boulet, and Roy visit the place where their colleague, Mark Gallagher, died during the earthquake. Gallagher was the one who inspired Roy to volunteer to serve in Haiti.

The UN headquarters at Hotel Christopher, destroyed in the quake. RCMP Chief Superintendent Doug Coates, then the commissioner of the 1,700-member UN police training mission to Haiti, lost his life when the building collapsed.

CONCLUSION

THE CANADIAN CODE

THERE'S A NIGHTMARISH SCENE in Jerzy Kosiński's *The Painted Bird* in which a drunken miller gouges out the eyes of his servant plough-boy. The attack is witnessed by the seven-year-old protagonist of the novel, who is hiding from the Nazis. Early the next morning, as the child flees the miller's property, he is startled to see the ploughboy exactly where the miller threw him. The hero of the novel realizes that, unlike himself, the boy cannot flee. He is stuck where he has been so grievously mutilated.

Whole nations are like that ploughboy—stuck where they have been mutilated. In this book I have attempted to tell the story of a band of Canadian police officers who answered their call for help. CivPol is probably the least known of Canada's foreign aid programs, yet in the last quarter-century thousands of Canadian officers have served overseas wearing CivPol's patch. They landed amid devastation and gunfire on a mission to train a police force to protect civilians and provide the security necessary for national recovery.

The officers in this book were well prepared to carry forward that mission, partly by training but also because they left home with a special Canadian quality: humility. It is one of the better angels of our national nature, and it has allowed our officers to effectively mentor police in lands very different from our own. When Canadian police trainers arrive in a foreign country, the first thing they do is ask questions; the second thing they do is listen to the answers. They know they do not have the solutions to a country's problems. What they do have is a framework for ethical behaviour and a philosophy of community policing that connects a police force to its citizens. Local police can then use the framework and philosophy to fashion an institution that protects the innocent, pursues the guilty and enforces the law equally and honestly. These principles of law enforcement apply to all cultures, but they are implemented differently within cultures—a fact considered self-evident by Canadian cops who have been raised to appreciate the need to protect cultural rights side by side with the need to protect human rights. It is a subtle understanding that permeates our national consciousness and is embedded in our Charter of Rights. And it puts Canadian cops in a good position to convey the message that human rights *must* trump cultural rights when a culture oppresses women and minorities. Canadian police trainers get their point across without proselytizing about the exceptionalism of their own society. They teach collaboratively and by example—a methodology far superior to shouting and lecturing. Dave Critchley, CivPol's Afghanistan commander when I was covering that mission in 2010, was none-too-subtle in separating the Canadian approach from the one practised by his American allies. "We begin by asking our trainees, 'How can we help you foster democratic law enforcement?' whereas the Americans tell them, 'We're gonna free the shit out of you.'" Long before I went to Afghanistan, in my first conversations with Joe McAllister, he emphasized that his goal was to teach police the lawful means to keep bad people from hurting good people "within their cultures."

The question is: Has CivPol succeeded in its missions?

Joe McAllister served in Afghanistan one more time after his deployments that spanned the years 2007 to 2011. He returned in September 2012 as a senior police advisor in Kabul, and left in June 2013. Based partly on my assessment of what he left behind, I titled the Afghan section of this book, "A Lost War but Not a Lost Cause." Canada withdrew from Kandahar in July 2011 and from all of Afghanistan in March 2014. Our military and police departed at a time when the Taliban were still in control of large swaths of the terrain the Canadians had sought to expel them from—a lost war by military definition. Yet the *cause* for which Canada fought is not lost. On April 5, 2014, the Afghans held the first round of a presidential election and resoundingly said no to the Taliban, voting in overwhelming numbers for two candidates who were the most highly educated and politically moderate of the eleven on the ballot: Abdullah Abdullah, a physician and former minister of foreign affairs, received 45 percent of the vote; Ashraf Ghani Ahmadzai, the former chancellor of Kabul University, received 31.6 percent. Both ran on a platform that advocated universal education, women's rights and constitutional democracy. Unfortunately, the June 14 run-off election between the two candidates was marred by allegations that Ashraf Ghani's backers had skewed the results through ballot-stuffing, and in July the two sides came under intense international pressure to agree to a fair audit of the ballots. As I write, the outcome of the election is uncertain, the political climate is tense, and (as always in Afghanistan) violent resentments may supplant high-minded rhetoric. What is beyond dispute is that there was less violence than expected at polling stations during the first and second election rounds, in part because the Afghan National Police protected those stations, willing to risk their lives for the right of Afghans to freely choose a president. Thousands of those Afghan cops had been trained by our Canadian CivPol officers.

Despite the betrayals by its political leaders, the ANP of today helps more people than it harms, and the Afghan public has taken notice. By the end of 2013, according to a national survey conducted by the Asia Foundation, 85 percent of the population thought the ANP was "fair with the Afghan people"; 86 percent thought the ANP "improves security"; and 80 percent thought the ANP was "efficient at arresting criminals." There was considerable regional variation within those numbers, however; in Kandahar and other southeastern provinces, from 25 percent to 65 percent of the people voiced approval for the ANP, the lowest figures occurring in the Taliban-dominated rural areas.

Given the ethnic, tribal and religious fault lines in Afghanistan, no one can predict whether the country will succeed or fail. But if it avoids a civil war within its own security forces, and holds its own against the insurgency, it could endure in a fashion that approximates that of its troubled neighbour, Pakistan. If that turns out to be the case, Afghanistan will at least have moved from its mutilated state when Canada first arrived, and possibly will eventually progress down a path that may lead to national recovery. McAllister, now working out of Ottawa overseeing the RCMP's emergency response teams, watches the news anxiously every day, wondering how the cause for which he gave so many years of his life will fare.

John Copeland and Serge Robitaille returned to Canada from Palestine at the end of September 2011. Copeland retired from the Ottawa City Police and Robitaille resumed his job in Ottawa as manager of specialized training for the RCMP. The Road Map to Peace in Palestine was defunct by then and its successor, the Framework for Peace, collapsed at the end of April 2014, when Palestinian Authority president Mahmoud Abbas announced that he had reached a deal on forming a "unity government" with Hamas. In protest, the Israelis abandoned the peace talks, saying they would not negotiate with a terrorist organization. The unity government met for the first time in early June, staffed by politically unaffiliated lawyers, businessmen and academics appointed by the PLO and Hamas. In a communiqué, the new cabinet renounced violence and recognized Israel's right to exist. However, they did not address the fact that Hamas still proclaimed its right to pursue its violent struggle to remove Israel from the map. The first Palestinian elections since 2006 are scheduled for December 2014, and Hamas is planning to run candidates in both the West Bank and Gaza.

Throughout the ups and downs of the negotiations, Canada has maintained its CivPol mission in Ramallah, working to bolster a Palestinian Civil Police force that can keep the peace in an independent nation. Results have been mixed. In April 2013, Abbas's reformist prime minister, Salam Fayyad, resigned over his inability to wrest control of the economy from the PLO's corrupt old guard. "Old patronage networks ultimately proved stronger than the technocrats," Kimberly Marten, author of *Warlords: Strong-Arm Brokers in Weak States*, wrote in *The New York Times* at the end of June 2013. "Fayyad never managed to control the rat's nest of overlapping Palestinian security agencies, whose constant infighting was encouraged by struggles within President Mahmoud Abbas's Fatah party." The infighting has led to the resurgence of radical groups in certain sectors of the West Bank, just as Fayyad had predicted. In January 2014, the PCP withdrew from full-time policing of the Jenin refugee camp, outgunned by the armed militias that had achieved their old place of dominance in the camp. Today, the Israeli army enters the camp periodically to kill or capture men they consider to be ticking time bombs—usually members of the militant Islamic Hamas Party and Islamic Jihad.

The Palestinian Civil Police, though ill-served by its political leaders, has nevertheless pushed forward on its plan for developing a professional force, an effort met with favour by the population. On May 11, 2012, EUPOL COPPS chief Henrik Malmquist announced the results of two independent surveys on Palestinian attitudes toward their police. One found that 78 percent of Palestinians in the West Bank held a positive view of the PCP, higher than for any of the other security services; the other found that over 91 percent of Palestinians said they would choose to call the PCP when they felt endangered.

Two months later, on July 8, 2012, the Palestine College for Police Sciences opened in Jericho. Today, each semester, five hundred men and women complete a Canadian-developed curriculum in Canadian-built classrooms. They maintain their physical fitness in the Canadian-built gymnasium. And they undergo scenario-based training in Canadian-built facilities.

No one can say where the Israel-Palestine conflict is headed, but both the Palestinian Authority and the Israelis have requested that CivPol continue its mission, viewing a professional PCP as crucial to the conflict's eventual resolution. The intercession of a non-denominational

God would probably help the peace process along. On June 8, 2014, the Pope hosted Israeli president Shimon Peres and Palestinian president Abbas for a multi-faith prayer service in the Vatican garden behind St. Peter's Basilica. They all prayed for an enduring peace between two states living side by side. A month later, Israel and Gaza were at war.

When Ruth Roy returned from Haiti in November 2011, she'd hoped to hire on with CivPol at its Ottawa headquarters. No position was available in the organization, which was about to enter the first stages of domestic and international contraction. Instead, she signed on as a member of the Prime Minister Protection Detail as an operations officer. When the PM travels overseas, Roy accompanies him, supervising his team of bodyguards and drivers.

Haiti and Canada's CivPol's mission there have never been far from her mind. On the streets of the country, crime went up in the months after Roy left Haiti, and confidence in the HNP went down, according to a survey conducted by the Brazilian think tank Instituto Igarapé, published in March 2012. "For the first time since 2007, overall support for the Haitian National Police is on the decline, with residents expressing concerns that police are unable or unwilling to protect them from crime," the survey report stated. "Since November 2011, there has been a marked deterioration in public support for the police." Only 40 percent of Haitians felt "the HNP is doing a good job"; 22 percent felt "the HNP is unable to protect me from crime"; and, most sadly, 17.5 percent felt "the HNP is unwilling to protect me."

Nevertheless, the training of cops is proceeding according to the United Nations' timetable. The ranks of the HNP have increased, from 9,000 when Roy left, to 11,228 in May 2014, including almost a thousand women, many of whom staff the gender-based violence unit that Roy established. MINUSTAH now hopes that fifteen thousand officers will be trained by 2016, the year the stabilization mission, along with CivPol's role in it, is scheduled to end.

As usual, Haiti's political situation is in turmoil, but while there have recently been large anti-government demonstrations, none of them (as yet) have been violent. The government is currently fractured by a dispute over who will oversee elections scheduled for the fall of 2014. On March 19, President Michel Martelly signed an agreement with his supporters in the Senate to hold parliamentary and municipal elections in October, to be overseen by a board composed largely of his backers. His main opponents, supporters of the ousted Jean-Bertrand Aristide, rejected the accord and took to the streets to call for Martelly's resignation. At the very least, they demanded, Martelly should agree to an "umpire board" in which Aristide's backers were fairly represented. At the heart of the dispute is a belief that whoever umpires the election will throw it the way of the candidates they back. "If elections are not held this year, this would mean that . . . the Parliament would be dysfunctional," Sandra Honoré, the head of MINUSTAH, warned in May. Despite the HNP's poor reputation among the public in the spring of 2012, Honoré's current assessment of the force is that it is "on a definite path of improvement in its performance [and] the manner it acquits itself of its security responsibilities."

The test of the HNP will come later this year if demonstrations over the October elections become violent. A coup is unlikely while MINUSTAH is present, but the manner in which the unrest is contained by the HNP will be remembered by the Haitian people. Until the withdrawal of MINUSTAH, Canadian cops will be there, mentoring the HNP in the killing heat and the deadly streets of Haiti's cities.

In the introduction to this book I mentioned a 2010 visit I made to the RCMP training academy in Saskatchewan, and the respect I noticed the force pays to its fallen. At the time, the head of the academy was Assistant Commissioner Roger Brown. In April 2013, Brown took command of the New Brunswick division of the Mounties. Fourteen months later, he became a consistent presence on the news.

On June 5, 2014, three Mounties were shot dead in Moncton, allegedly by an angry gun fanatic who specifically targeted them for being Mounties, wounding two other Mounties in his rampage. A few days later a regimental funeral was held in Moncton, attended by police officers and an overflow crowd of civilians. Journalists covering the service noted that the memorial was the second to be held in the wake of a mass murder of Mounties in less than a decade. On March 3, 2005, four Mounties had been gunned down in a Quonset shed on a farm outside of Mayerthorpe, Alberta. They were staking out a stolen car parts operation when the owner, a man with a history of violent offences, emerged from hiding with a hunting rifle and ambushed them.

Both funerals were televised live on the CBC, as the whole nation mourned the murdered members of its national police force. There was a profound reason for the heart-stricken emotions expressed by the public in the wake of these killings that went beyond the deaths of the individuals involved, and even beyond the public's patriotic attachment to the red serge as a symbol of our nation. I believe that at the core of Canada's grief for its dead Mounties was a poignant awareness of the humanist code that our cops had died for. Cops don't ask us to love our neighbours as we love ourselves. Nor do cops ask us to do unto others what we would have others do unto us. That is too much for a cop or a state or the law to request of individuals in a democracy. Rather, cops want us to refrain from harming each other. They hope that at every juncture of our lives—whether we are encountering crises at work, in our families or in our neighbourhoods—we will pause and say, I will not do to this person in front of me what I do not want this person to do to me. I will, first of all, do no harm.

Every action a cop takes, from writing the most routine traffic ticket to the most dramatic emergency response team takedown, is designed to prevent us from wilfully committing a selfish act that could, in some way, harm someone else. Each officer, while fallible, wakes up every morning knowing that he or she is the embodiment and enforcer of this code, which is the foundation of civilization itself. They believe it is a code worth dying for.

The Canadian public knows its police officers attempt to honour this code. When cops lose their lives in the course of their work, we know they have died to protect the innocent from being harmed.

The CivPol officers I have described in this book, as well as the thousands of other CivPol veterans, have taken this code overseas and tried to share it with recruits who have grown up under warlords, dictators and death-worshipping fanatics. Our cops have taught the code in military compounds and academy classrooms, in city squares whose surrounding buildings were pocked by machine gun fire and at checkpoints where the next driver could very well have been a suicide bomber. They have taught it in the deserts and jungles and ruined cities of over two dozen failing states, and at great risk to themselves.

Canadian police arrive on mission with no sense of certainty that the Canadian way is *the* way. But they live by the code of not harming others, and of protecting the innocent from being harmed. They feel that code is universal, shared by all societies. It is CivPol's mission to teach that code to overseas police forces in countries where it is so routinely violated that citizens live in a constant state of fear. Sometimes CivPol succeeds in a measured way, and the local police go on to teach the code to recruits long after a CivPol mission has ended. Some of those states, like East Timor, Sierra Leone and Kosovo, have recovered from their trauma and, though not free of problems, are functioning. Sometimes CivPol fails. Somalia, the Democratic Republic of the Congo and South Sudan have all returned to violence and lawlessness that, at this writing, is unchecked by the police whom CivPol trained.

With this book I have endeavoured to show Canadians what members of their police have been doing for the world beyond our borders for twenty-five years, largely unnoticed by the media and unheralded by our politicians. At home, they are sworn to serve and protect, facing the possible consequences of that domestic mission every day. On missions abroad, they teach local police to serve and protect in red zones where the possibilities of injury and death are far greater than they are in Canada. Yet they continue to sign up. The number of CivPol missions and CivPol officers may now be reduced from the Golden Year I covered in this book, but the spirit and cause of the RCMP's International Peace Operations Branch remains intact. That organization is ready to be called upon to dispatch officers to any failing state in need of an honest, professional police force—one that will live by the code of not doing harm and protecting others from harm.

I honour here all the officers who have been part of those missions. They are the embodiment of who we are as Canadians: brave but humble, living by right principles but not imposing the way we live on others. The actions of CivPol officers demonstrate their ideals, and we could give no greater gift to the failing states that ask for our help.

ACKNOWLEDGEMENTS

WORDS CANNOT EXPRESS MY GRATITUDE to the more than 120 men and women who granted me in-person interviews so that I could tell the story of Canada's police training missions in failing states. The people I interviewed include: Canadian police officers deployed overseas and the local police they mentored; RCMP officers and civilians who oversaw the foreign missions from Ottawa; officers being trained in Ottawa for overseas missions; and police trainers from other nations who worked side by side with our Canadian police trainers. In addition, I talked with numerous civilians in Afghanistan, Palestine, Israel and Haiti to solicit their views on both Canadian police trainers and their own national police forces.

CivPol officers allowed me to accompany them as they did their work overseas in often tense and dangerous environments, and then took hours from their rest time to tell me their biographies. I wish I could have written a book twice as long and included all of their stories, but I had to choose individual officers who were representative of basic sectors of the training missions in order to offer a comprehensive portrait for a general reader. I am just as grateful to those whose stories I had to leave out of the book as I am to those whose stories I included. I could not have written this book without the time each of them spent explaining their ideals, their lives and their work to me. I thank all the men and women connected to overseas police training who, during the four years of my research and writing, helped advance my knowledge of the missions to which they were dedicated.

All the Canadian CivPol officers interviewed for this book worked under the aegis of the RCMP's International Peace Operations Branch (which in 2013 changed its name to International Policing Development). I would like to express my thanks to the RCMP for giving me unfettered access to CivPol officers and for granting me permission to accompany them on their missions. I arranged and paid for my own travel, accommodation and meals, and scheduled interviews with CivPol officers according to my own research needs. At the outset of the project, the RCMP agreed that this book would be an independent journalist's assessment of the CivPol training missions and its officers. The RCMP graciously cooperated in my research, but this book is not a collaboration. I was allowed to do my reporting free of RCMP supervision.

When Canadian officers sign up for a CivPol mission, they take a leave from their home police service. In these acknowledgements, I have included the names of the officers' home police services and the rank they held at the time I interviewed them. CivPol assigns city or provincial officers a rank that is closest to the one they would hold if they were in the RCMP.

Below I have listed the officers, officials and civilians who aided my research in important ways through in-person interviews. Certain officers have requested that I not name them, either because of the classified nature of their work or because they felt they were not authorized to speak on subjects that we discussed.

I would like to thank RCMP Deputy Commissioner Gary Bass, commanding officer of the Pacific Region and British Columbia's "E" Division. Bass invited me to deliver the keynote address on the first morning of the RCMP Pacific Region's Leadership Conference, held in May 2009 at the force's training centre in Chilliwack, B.C. On the second day of the conference, Superintendent Joe McAllister, who had just returned from Kandahar, gave a talk on the RCMP's role in police training in Afghanistan. The talk was classified, but Bass arranged for me to interview McAllister after the conference. He spent many hours explaining to me the role of the International Peace Operations Branch around the world.

If I had not met McAllister, I doubt I would have been drawn to write this book. His experiences on police training missions in Kosovo, East Timor and Kandahar, and the knowledge he had gained of the worldwide mission from having worked at CivPol headquarters beside his friend, Supt. Doug Coates, opened my eyes to an aspect of Canadian foreign aid that I had not known existed. After the Haiti earthquake, McAllister and Bass paved the way for me to get in touch with CivPol headquarters. By the time McAllister left for his next Afghan training mission in June 2010, I was already well into planning my trip to join him there in November.

I am deeply grateful for the assistance of Yoan St-Onge, the civilian communications strategist at the International Peace Operations Branch who helped me map out my research itinerary over the next eighteen months for Afghanistan, Palestine and Haiti. Each phase of my research required months of preparation and unending forms that had to be filled out for the various domestic and international agencies that had to approve my joining CivPol officers on their missions. St-Onge took me through the various stages and, where necessary, Gary Bass and Joe McAllister wrote letters of recommendation backing my project. I was greatly helped in all this paperwork by Bass's executive officer, Inspector Jodie Boudreau, who spent many hours contributing to my efforts to report on the overseas missions. When St-Onge left CivPol in 2011, his replacement, Martine Courage, worked just as hard on the Haiti phase of my research. She also paved the way for my trip to CivPol headquarters before I left for Haiti.

Before I set out on the first phase of my research in Afghanistan, I was hosted at Depot, the RCMP training academy in Saskatchewan, by its commander, RCMP Assistant Commissioner Roger Brown. I was given a tour of the facilities by RCMP Cpl. Karen Hamelin, a CivPol veteran of Ivory Coast. Hamelin left shortly thereafter for a CivPol deployment in southern Sudan in the tense time before the region became independent of Sudan. I thank her for her insightful reflections on her Ivory Coast mission and her thoughts about her upcoming mission.

My preparation for traveling to Afghanistan, both journalistic and moral, was greatly supported by the knowledge and kindness of two journalists with vast experience in the country: Arthur Kent here in Canada and Murray Brewster, the Canadian Press's premier war correspondent who was based in Kandahar. Kent put me in touch with Peter Juvenal, the owner of the Gandamack Lodge in Kabul, and Brewster spent hours arranging to get me body armour for my time in Kandahar. I would like to express my gratitude to Juvenal, an award-winning war photographer, for his perspectives on the Afghan police, and to his wife, Hassina Syed, president of the Syed Group of Companies, for her perspectives on dealing with the Afghan government. Fayez Hamdard, the manager of the Gandamack, was also very helpful to me during my stay at the lodge. Special thanks to Obai, McAllister's driver in Kabul.

I am grateful to Emma Welford, head of public diplomacy and communications at the Canadian Embassy in Kabul, and to her assistant, Kristine Racicot, for their views on Canada's mission in Afghanistan during my time in the country. They took me on a day's tour of Kabul, for which I am grateful.

The following Canadian and Afghan National Police officers gave freely of their time in interviews with me in Kabul: RCMP Assistant Commissioner Dave Critchley, commander of the CivPol mission in Afghanistan, interviewed at the embassy (and in Camp Nathan Smith, Kandahar); Superintendent Joe McAllister, deputy commander of the CivPol mission in Afghanistan; OPP Inspector Phil George, CivPol mentor at the Major Crime Task Force; Col. Yousef Mohammad Ahmadzai, ANP Intelligence Chief, Major Crime Task Force; Balees, Ahmadzai's translator; RCMP Supt. John Brewer, mentor of the Afghan Border Police; OPP Sgt. Russell "Rusty" Watson, mentor of the Afghan Border Police; Master Sgt. Christopher Benke, U.S. Marine MP, who served as Brewer's and Watson's driver and protection; Lt.-Gen. Mohammad Yonus Noorzai, Chief of the Afghan

Border Police; Major Abdul Ahmad, who was in charge of security for the Border Police compound; Sgt.-Mjr. Matiullah Jabberi, Afghan Border Police; Col. Wajie Maihanyan, Afghan Border Police, who shared with me her experiences as a woman on the force; and Lt.-Gen. Abdul Rahman, Afghan Deputy Minister of Security.

I am grateful to the following people for the time they gave me in interviews and help on my project at Kandahar Airfield: Lt.-Gen. Marc Lessard, Commander of the Canadian Expeditionary Forces; Murray Brewster, Canadian Press (who I mention again because I owe him a debt of gratitude for finding me a bunk in a tent during the chaotic period of "the surge"); Mathew Fisher, Postmedia journalist; Toronto Police Sgt. Jeff Alderdice, who gave me insights into emergency-response-team training of the ANP; Dr. Howard G. Coombs, special advisor to the commander of Task Force Kandahar; Captain Annie Djiotsa, Canadian Forces Public Affairs Officer; Navy Lieutenant Jordan Holder, Media Operations; Katherine Heath-Eves, Civilian Public Affairs Officer; U.S. Army Stf.-Sgt. Jason Stadel, Media Support Center; and U.S. Navy Petty Officer First Class Donald Peachey, Media Embed Office.

Special thanks to Toronto Police Sgt. Steve Moore, who, on his way to his posting in Dand, was a companion to me on my flight from KAF to Camp Nathan Smith.

At Camp Nathan Smith, my journalistic needs were looked after by Adam Sweet, DFAIT's public affairs officer. I am grateful to the following officers for granting me hours of interviews: RCMP Supt. Vic Park, the contingent commander in Kandahar; RCMP Insp. Pierre Landry, Deputy Contingent Commander; RCMP Cpl. Karen Holowaychuk and her female ANP students, Magulla, Ziagula, Murican, Gulsherin and Gulab; RCMP Cpl. Candice McMackin and RCMP Cst. Lorant Hegedus, who, in tandem, taught the Criminal Investigation course; ANP Col. Rahim, chief of the Criminal Investigation Department in Kandahar, and his Criminal Investigation class of three dozen ANP. I would like to particularly thank the following students in that class: 3rd Sgt. Gran Mohammad, 3rd Sgt. S. Mohammad, 3rd Sgt. Noor Mohammad and

3rd Sgt. Janan. I would also like to thank three ANP members in the six-month officer training course, all 3rd sergeants: Atal, Janan and Mirzal. Although the Ottawa City undercover constable I call "Sandy" asked that her name not be used in this book, others know and honour her for her service, as do I. Thank you to Toronto Police Cst. Phil Sinclair for allowing me to sit in on his class on interviewing sources and witnesses. Special thanks to Zaman Raofi, head of the Canadian-funded Kandahar Human Rights Organization, and instructor of the human rights and rule of law classes at CNS. I would like to thank Agha La Lai, the deputy chief of Kandahar's Provincial Council, for his thoughts on the situation in Afghanistan and for introducing me to other members of the Provincial Council, who also contributed their ideas to this book. Canadian Forces Combat Photographer Master Corporal Pierre Thériault offered me valuable insights into what our soldiers faced under fire.

When it came to interviewing Afghans at CNS I would have been mute and deaf were it not for the interpreting skills of "Junior," "Lucky," "Behroz" and "Patman." Junior, who lost his legs to a Taliban rocket in 2006, sat down with me for two hours to tell me his life story and offer his reflections on ethics, religion and his feelings about Afghanistan's problems. He too lives by the code of not harming others, and I thank him for his time.

I would like to thank Corrections Officer/Trainer Robert James Cater, for his insights into the 2008 Sarposa prison breakout. I interviewed Cater in Vancouver in July 2011, at Joe McAllister's much-delayed celebration of his wedding to Canadian diplomat Jennie Chen. I am grateful to Chen for sharing her reflections on serving as a political advisor to generals in Kandahar from 2008 to 2009.

In March 2011, I set out to cover the CivPol mission in Palestine. I would like to thank numerous people for their invaluable insights and the aid they contributed to my reporting, particularly RCMP Stf. Sgt. Serge Robitaille, contingent commander of the Palestine CivPol mission, and Ottawa City Police Inspector John Copeland, training advisor to the

Palestinian Civil Police (PCP). Both men invested a lot of their time in order to give me an understanding of their mission, their lives and their ideals.

For aiding my research and granting me interviews in Ramallah, I would also like to thank Henrik Malmquist, head of mission for EUPOL COPPS; Julio De La Guardia, public information officer, EUPOL COPPS; Czech National Police 1st Lt. Ondrej Lyer, EUPOL COPPS; Finland National Police Officer Satu Koivu, EUPOL COPPS; PCP Brig. Gen. Yousef Ozreil, chief of the PCP's Media Relations Department; and PCP Mjr. Sufian Omeryah, Public Information Officer.

For aiding my research and granting me interviews in Jericho's Palestine College for Police Sciences, I would like to thank PCP Mjr. Omar Bari Munir, deputy commander of the college; PCP Lt. Col. Zahir Sabbah, commanding officer of the college; PCP Mjr. Rami Ahmad Mahmoud Hussein, in charge of the training programme at the college; PCP Capt. Khalid Arar Shawabke, who served as translator for the college; Brendan Keiman, project manager, UN Office for Project Services, who explained the logistics of the construction project to me; Gerry McCool, UN Operations job foreman at the college, who took me on a tour of the building project; and Wendy Taeuber, a project management specialist at the college on contract with the UN and the Canadian Department of Justice.

On the tense day after the murder of Juliano Mer-Khamis in the Jenin refugee camp, I received invaluable help for my research into the relationship between the Israeli National Police (INP) and the PCP from INP Supt. Daniel Israel, liaison officer with PCP and EUPOL COPPS.

A list of the Palestinian and Israeli civilians I interviewed about the conflict would go on for pages. I thank them all, and particularly Burhan Bani Odeh, manager of the City Inn Palace Hotel in Ramallah, and Chira Dorfman, who lived in Tsfat, Israel, and from whom I received important insights into the Orthodox Jewish perspective on "the situation."

At the end of September 2011, I travelled to Ottawa to research the manner in which CivPol missions were planned and directed from the headquarters of the International Peace Operations Branch (IPOB); the way officers were prepared for a mission at Ottawa's Canadian Police College; the way they were kitted out at the Department of Defence Building; and how PTSD and injuries that officers suffered on mission were handled. I am grateful to the following people who gave generously of their time: Martine Courage, communications advisor, IPOB; RCMP Supt. Mike McDonald, director of IPOB; RCMP Insp. Kevin Miller, officer in charge of Operations; Dr. Sylvie Bourgeois, civilian officer in charge of Health Services; RCMP Stf. Sgt. Mike Tessier, Branch Support Service; RCMP Stf. Sgt. Ken Hobbs, program manager, Americas; RCMP Sgt. David B. Muirhead, Project Coordinator for Afghanistan and Asia; RCMP Sgt. Demetrios Stefanopoulos, mission staffing coordinator; RCMP Stf. Sgt. Gilles Déziel, Logistics; RCMP Stf. Sgt. Julie Faucher, program manager for Africa, Mideast and Europe; Stephanie Coté, civilian analyst for Haiti and the Americas; and RCMP Cst. Gilles Dery, chief instructor for CivPol at the Police Training College, who allowed me to sit in on his training classes for Haiti and Ivory Coast and in addition gave me a minute-by-minute account of his experiences in Port-au-Prince during the earthquake. I would also like to thank Montreal Police Investigation Agent Sébastien Boerr, a CivPol officer-in-training who granted me an extensive interview about his motivations for going on mission to Haiti and his expectations for that mission. I spoke with several other officers during their training for Haiti and Ivory Coast, but they preferred not to have their names used in this book.

I would like to express my gratitude to the CivPol officers and members of the Haitian National Police (HNP) who gave freely of their time in interviews in Haiti. First and foremost, I would like to thank RCMP Inspector Ruth Roy, in charge of working with the HNP to develop a training curriculum for the Police Academy, as well as a gender-based violence programme that was later adopted by the United Nations for training police officers internationally. Roy was my tireless mentor and companion during my time in Haiti. She went on to win the 2013 Woman Law Enforcement Executive of the Year Award, sponsored by the National Association of Woman Law Enforcement Executives and Motorola Solutions.

For aiding my research and granting me interviews in Port-au-Prince, I would also like to thank: Ottawa City Police Cst. Ray Lamarre, spokesperson for the UN Police (UNPOL) in Haiti; Inspector General Jean Miguelite Maximé, commander of the HNP Academy; deputy commander of the HNP Academy Bernard Ellé; RCMP Sgt. Ron Rose, senior planning and performance analyst for UNPOL personnel; RCMP Cpl. Bruno Arseneau, who mentored the HNP's Judicial Police, the equivalent in Canada of an investigations unit; RCMP Cpl. Rudy Étienne, who mentored the HNP's Kidnap Unit; HNP Commander Harrington Rigaud, who worked with UNPOL to build new HNP barracks; HNP A4 Joseph Tardee, the HNP Police Academy's coordinator of First Aid Instructor Training in Haiti (FAITH); Montreal City Police Cst. Alain Nadeau, Tardee's mentor at FAITH; William Black, civilian Project Manager of FAITH; Marie Stéphanie Jean, Haitian administration officer of FAITH; Montreal City Police Commander Jean-Pierre Synnett (inspector rank in CivPol), in charge of security for all internally displaced persons camps; Fatmah, from the Turkish National Police, Synnett's assistant who coordinated computer crime-mapping of the IDP camps; Staisy, a resident of IDP Camp Caradeux; Alix Bellegarde, the UN International Organization for Migration's camp manager at Accra IDP Camp; Nicolas and his daughter in Camp Accra; Montreal City Police Commander Claude Mercier, in charge of security for IDP Camp Jean-Marie Vincent; RCMP Supt. John White, supervisor of CivPol's operations in all commissariats and IDP camps in the West Department; HNP Divisional Inspector Aristide Rosemond, commander of Cité Soleil commissariat; Securité de Quebec Lt. Bernard Lebland (CivPol rank inspector) and RCMP Sgt. Denis Chiasson, developers of an intelligence-led policing plan for the HNP; RCMP Supt. Douglas Redmond, chief of Development and Capacity

Building for UNPOL and the HNP; RCMP Superintendent Robert Boulet, Haiti contingent commander; and RCMP Assistant Commissioner Marc Tardif, MINUSTAH police commissioner.

For aiding my research and granting me interviews in Kenscoff, I would like to thank Montreal Police Stf. Sgt. Alain Alarie, police advisor in Kenscoff; HNP Divisional Inspector Julbert Conseillant, commander of Kenscoff commissariat; and HNP A1 Officer Anique Aubristin.

For aiding my research and granting me interviews in Grand Goâve, I would like to thank Montreal Police Stf. Sgt. Robert Grégoire and RCMP Cst. Handy Hilaire, HNP police mentors. Both officers were caught in the middle of two anti-government mobs in the area and barely escaped with their lives. During his mission posting, Grégoire developed a program for HNP officer training in the use of weapons, and advocated for the upgrading of HNP guns, which most often were rusted and useless. I regret that I could not go into their posting to Haiti in greater depth. They are two brave officers who had progressive ideas on reforming the HNP. I would like to thank them for arranging interviews with two of the HNP officers they mentored, HNP A4 Ata Gracie and HNP A4 Elie Cezaire, who gave me important insights into policing in the district that was near the epicentre of the earthquake. I am also grateful to Grégoire and Hilaire for introducing me to Voodoo *Houngan* (Priest) Andreasus, in the Grand Goâve countryside, who gave me much insight into his religion.

An author who takes years to research and write a book better have a publisher and editor who understands the high hurdles of his project. From the outset, Anne Collins, the publisher of Random House Canada and my editor for twenty-two years, understood the challenges that this book presented. I often wonder what I have done to deserve Anne. As she has always done for me, she recognized how this book should be told, and guided it to its present form over a long period of research and writing. If I've had any success writing *Worth Dying For,* I share it with Anne. If I've made any mistakes, they are my own.

Throughout the four years I spent on this project, my wife, Leslie Hoffman Gould, never lost faith that the book was worthy of the time I invested in it. From the moment she met Joe McAllister she understood that Canada's mission to train police in failing states was a story crying to be told. With her deep and profound humanism, Leslie embodies the Canadian Code defined in the book's last chapter. Since the age of twenty, I have done nothing of value independent of Leslie, and so I have dedicated this book to her and to our marriage.

Thanks also to the staff at Random House Canada who have worked long and hard to get this book into print, and in particular: managing editor Deirdre Molina; Brittany Larkin, Carla Kean, and Leah Springate in production; Jane McWhinney, copy editor; and Shona Cook, the book's publicist. Special thanks to Michelle Roper.

I am deeply grateful to the Canada Council for the Arts for awarding me a grant to help me research and write this book.

It is impossible for me to measure or express my thanks to the CivPol officers killed in the line of duty. They are remembered by their CivPol colleagues, who know they gave their lives in a cause worth dying for.

A NOTE ON SOURCES

Extensive source notes can be found at www.PenguinRandomHouse.ca/
worthdyingfor *keyed to the page numbers in this edition.*

INDEX

(with separate sub-sections for Afghanistan, Haiti and Palestine)

TERRY GOULD is a Brooklyn-born investigative journalist who focuses on organized crime and human rights issues. He has won more than fifty awards and other honours for his reporting. His previous book, *Murder without Borders*, the product of four years of dogged travel and investigation, told the life stories of journalists who were assassinated as they reported truths about the powerful in the world's most dangerous places. For that work he won the Canadian Press Freedom Award, the Arthur Ellis Award for Best Crime Non-Fiction, and the Spanish Press Freedom Award and was a finalist for the Writers' Trust of Canada Shaughnessy Cohen Prize for Political Writing. Gould lives in Vancouver.